THE NEW EMPIRE

BROOKS ADAMS
AUTHOR OF "THE LAW OF CIVILIZATION AND DECAY"
"AMERICA'S ECONOMIC SUPREMACY," ETC.

University Press of the Pacific
Honolulu, Hawaii

The New Empire

by
Brooks Adams

ISBN: 1-4102-0810-9

Reprinted from the 1903 edition

University Press of the Pacific
Honolulu, Hawaii
http://www.universitypressofthepacific.com

PREFATORY NOTE

LAST spring I undertook to prepare for publication several essays and addresses which I supposed were connected together closely enough to present a consecutive chain of thought. On attempting an arrangement I found that I was mistaken, and that to be understood I must recast the whole. When I reached this conclusion it was too late to withdraw from the task, and the consequence has been that I have written the following volume much faster than I have ever before done similar work. I fear that the literary form may have suffered, but I apprehend that, in substance, the book is comprehensible.

All my observations lead me to the conclusion that geographical conditions have exercised a great, possibly a preponderating, influence over man's destiny. I am convinced that neither history nor economics can be intelligently studied without a constant reference to the geographical surroundings which have affected different nations. I therefore make no apology for having dwelt upon geography, but I wish to say a word concerning my maps.

To illustrate my text thoroughly I should need to publish an atlas. This being impossible, I have contented myself with presenting a few rough sketches, on a small scale, to accentuate the more salient theories. Should any one be enough interested in

the subject to examine into details, he will have to
resort to special works.   I regret to say this is not
easy, as the collections of maps in American libraries
are surprisingly defective.   My greatest difficulty has
lain here.   In maps dealing with so large an area
upon so small a scale I have not aimed at technical
accuracy.   The Mongol invasions, for example, are
only summarily indicated, so as to show, in a general
way, the limits of the incursions, and the paths followed.   I have even had to abandon at times the
scale.   My effort has been to convey an idea.   I
know not if I have succeeded, for I have had no
precedent to guide me.   Maps ordinarily represent
repose, but I have tried to suggest motion by colored
lines drawn from fixed bases to an ever-changing seat
of empire.   In civilization nothing is at rest, least of
all the circulation, and the arteries through which that
circulation flows vary in direction from generation to
generation.   As they fluctuate, so do the boundaries
of states.

I have marked the southern routes in red, the
northern in green, so that the migration of trade may
be read on each map at a glance.   Had the conditions of publication admitted, it would have been easy
to show by colors how one political organism has
melted into another, as the displacement of the centre
of international exchanges has caused a recentralization of the territory tributary to local markets.

I believe it to be impossible to overestimate the
effect upon civilization of the variations of trade-
routes.   According to the ancient tradition the whole
valley of the Syr-Daria was once so thickly settled
that a nightingale could fly from branch to branch of

the fruit trees, and a cat walk from wall to wall and housetop to housetop, from Kashgar to the Sea of Aral. From the remains he saw, Schuyler judged the legend to be true.[1] Bagdad also was once the most splendid capital of the world. The reason is explained by the description which Marco Polo has left of the ships which, even in his day, sailed from the great port of Hormus, at the mouth of the Persian Gulf. "The vessels built at Hormus are of the worst kind, and dangerous for navigation, exposing the merchants and others who make use of them to great hazards. Their defects proceed from the circumstance of nails not being employed in the construction. . . . The planks are bored . . . and wooden pins . . . being driven into them, they are in this manner fastened (to the stem and stern). After this they are bound, or rather sewed together, with a kind of rope yarn stripped from the husk of the Indian (cocoa) nuts. . . . The vessel has no more than one mast, one helm, and one deck. When she has taken in her lading, it is covered over with hides, and upon these hides they place the horses which they carry to India. They have no iron anchors; . . . the consequence of which is, that in bad weather, (and these seas are very tempestuous,) they are frequently driven on shore and lost."

In such ships men made short voyages, and freight rates were correspondingly high, with a probability of total loss. Powerful vessels, especially steamers, carry cheaply, fast, and directly, consequently intermediate stopping places are abandoned, and the caravan for through travel has ceased to pay. The main trade-

[1] Turkestan, I., 67.

route across Central Asia has thus been displaced, and so it has come to pass that Bagdad has sunk into a mass of hovels, and the valley of the Syr-Daria is a wilderness.

The fate of the empire of Haroun-al-Raschid exemplifies an universal law.

BROOKS ADAMS.

QUINCY, August 27, 1902.

CONTENTS

APPENDIX

LIST OF MAPS

INTRODUCTION

During the last decade the world has traversed one of those periodic crises which attend an alteration in the social equilibrium. The seat of energy has migrated from Europe to America. The phenomenon is not new, as similar perturbations have occurred from the earliest times; its peculiarity lies in its velocity and its proportions. A change of equilibrium has heretofore occupied at least the span of a human lifetime, so that a new generation has gradually become habituated to the novel environment. In this instance the revolution came so suddenly that few realized its presence before it ended. Nevertheless, it has long been in preparation, and it appears to be fundamental, for it is the effect of that alteration in mental processes which we call the advance of science.

American supremacy has been made possible only through applied science. The labors of successive generations of scientific men have established a control over nature which has enabled the United States to construct a new industrial mechanism, with processes surpassingly perfect. Nothing has ever equalled in economy and energy the administration of the great American corporations. These are the offspring of scientific thought. On the other hand, wherever scientific criticism and scientific methods have not penetrated, the old processes prevail, and these show signs of decrepitude. The national government may be taken as an illustration.

When Englishmen first settled upon this continent they came as pioneers, and they developed an extreme individuality. Thinly scattered in widely separated colonies along the coast, little independent communities came into being which had few interests in common. Consolidation began late and took an imperfect form, the conditions then existing generating a peculiar administrative mechanism. The organization reached after the Revolution was rather negative than positive. The people suffered from certain effects of decentralization which interfered with commercial exchanges. These they tried to remedy, but they deprecated corporate energy. They provided against discriminations in trade, violations of contract, bad money, and the like, and they made provision for the common defence, but they manifested jealousy of consolidated power.

Each state feared interference in local concerns more than it craved aid in schemes which transcended its borders, and accordingly the framers of the Constitution intentionally made combined action slow and difficult. They devised three coördinate departments, each of which could stop the other two, and none of which could operate alone. And they did this under the conviction that they had reached certain final truths in government, and in the face of the law that friction bears a ratio to the weight moved.

Even with such concessions to tradition, no little energy was required to overcome the inertia of that primitive society, for on such societies tradition has a

preponderating influence. Patrick Henry well represented conservative Virginia, and Henry denounced
the Constitution day by day "as the most fatal plan
which could possibly be conceived for enslaving a
free people." Henry could not comprehend the
change in the conditions of life about him, because
he had been bred to believe that the institutions he
knew were intrinsically good. He revered them
much as he revered revealed religion; as an end in
themselves, and not as means to an end. Every
considerable political innovation must thus affect a
portion of the population, for men always live to
whom a change in what they have been trained to respect is tantamount to sacrilege. This temper of the
mind is conservatism. It resists change instinctively
and not intelligently, and it is this conservatism which
largely causes those violent explosions of pent-up
energy which we term revolutions. Still, changes,
peaceful or bloody, must come, and it behooves each
generation to take care that such as it shall have to
deal with shall be accepted without shock. Intellectual rigidity is the chief danger, for resistance to
the inevitable is proportionate to intellectual rigidity.

The Romans were rigid, and the massacres which
attended their readjustments are memorable. The
slaughter of the Gracchi, the proscriptions of Marius
and Sulla, and the lists of the Triumvirs are examples.
On the other hand, Cæsar miscarried because of too
high intelligence. He measured circumstances ac-
curately, and because he did so, he misjudged others.
Had he comprehended the stupidity of Brutus, he
would have killed him. With conservative popula-
tions slaughter is nature's remedy. Augustus applied

it. He substantially exterminated the opposition;
then the new organization operated.

Similarly the French, in emergency, have always
resorted to massacre to overcome obstruction, from
the crusades against the Albigenses in the thirteenth
century to the Commune of Paris in the nineteenth.
It was not only Saint Bartholomew, and the persecu-
tions which followed the revocation of the Edict of
Nantes, which brought about the Terror of 1793; it
was rather a thousand nameless butcheries like those
which occurred during the reign of Louis XIV. The
incapacity of the French to ameliorate their fiscal
system generated an unequal taxation which provoked revolt, and revolt caused repression frightful
in ferocity. At Rennes in 1675, as a punishment for
insubordination, the town was given up to pillage,
and la Rue Haute, the main street, was destroyed.
The inhabitants, old men, women, and children, were
driven forth into the fields "without a refuge, without food, and without a place to sleep." They
perished from exposure and want.

Rome and France are extreme examples of conservatism, but they illustrate the better the working
of a law. All administrative systems tend toward
induration; more especially political systems, because
they are most cumbersome. Conversely, nature is in
eternal movement. Therefore the disparity between
any given government and its environment is apt to
be proportionate to the time which has elapsed since
the last period of active change. When a population
is flexible, adjustment is peaceful, as in the case of
the adoption of our Constitution, or the passage of
the first English Reform Bill; when a population is

rigid, a catastrophe occurs, like the civil wars in Rome, or the Terror of 1793 in France.

Measure the United States by this standard. Since the Constitution went into operation in 1789 every civilized nation has undergone reorganization, some, like France and Germany, more than once. And yet nowhere have all the conditions of life altered so fundamentally as in North America.

In 1789 the United States was a wilderness lying upon the outskirts of Christendom; she is now the heart of civilization and the focus of energy. The Union forms a gigantic and growing empire which stretches half round the globe, an empire possessing the greatest mass of accumulated wealth, the most perfect means of transportation, and the most delicate yet powerful industrial system which has ever been developed. By the products of that system she must be brought into competition with rivals at the ends of the earth. The nation, in its corporate capacity, has to deal with problems domestic and foreign, more vast and complicated than were ever before presented for solution. In a word, the conditions of the twentieth century are almost precisely the reverse of those of the eighteenth, and yet the national organization not only remains unaltered, but is prevented from automatic adjustment by the provisions of a written document, which, in practice, cannot be amended.

For the present generation the manner in which change shall come is a matter only of speculative interest, since before the existing structure can crumble, those now in middle life will have passed away. To the rising generation it is of supreme moment, for the forces at work are gigantic, and the velocity extreme.

Man cannot shape his own environment, but he alone of all animals can consciously adapt himself to the demands of nature. He does so by education. This faculty is an incalculable advantage in the struggle for existence, for by education the young can be trained to dexterity in almost any manual or mental process. Intellectual flexibility may be developed as readily as intellectual rigidity. Science has won her triumphs through such training. The scientific schools perform their functions well. Their discipline creates an open mind; scientific methods of thought are now paramount in our industries, and it is to this faculty that America, in a very large measure, owes her industrial success.

It is an axiom that the manufacturer who is least bound by tradition is the man who, other things being equal, will succeed. He who can cast aside the prepossessions of a lifetime, abandon his old equipment, and adopt what is newest, is held to be enlightened. The doctrine is reduced to a rule of conduct. The railway manager reckons that his locomotives are capable of a given amount of work. He extracts that work as fast as possible, because he can replace an old machine by a better. The British manager acts on the opposite principle. He rests his engines, repairs them, cares for them, and boasts that he can exhibit some relic of the time of Stephenson.

Penetrate the recesses of British society, and one chief cause of this conservatism is disclosed. The nation is intellectually inelastic, and it cultivates rigidity by confiding its education to the clergy, who are preëminently a rigid class. The result is that Englishmen fall behind. They own, for example, the South African gold mines, but they do not work them.

In England the old processes of so-called liberal thought still prevail. In America these have been superseded in science, and in those walks of life which are regulated by scientific methods. They still survive in colleges, as distinguished from technical schools, and colleges very largely shape opinion in the United States, not only on political, but on a great variety of other subjects. No better illustration of this tendency can be chosen than the attitude maintained toward history.

History presents a double aspect: First, the commercial and literary; second, the educational and scientific. The man who writes a history either as a social or political speculation, or else for sale, differs from no other adventurer. He writes for a market, as another man manufactures for a market, and most of the best historical work has been done under these conditions. Thucydides, Tacitus, Cæsar, Gibbon, and Macaulay produced their books for private ends or else for sale, and in either case the result was the same. No one bought who did not care to read, and no one read without the inclination. It was a trade in luxuries like the trade in spices.

Modern educational and scientific history stands on a different basis. It is assumed that there are facts in the past which it imports all the world to know, and much money and time are spent in unearthing them. For many years governments, corporations, and individuals have vied with each other in publishing archives and editing documents, while monographs on all sorts of special subjects abound; but no attempt has been made to digest what has been gathered. Meanwhile the mass of material is accumulating rapidly. Libraries are no longer able to buy and catalogue the volumes which appear, and he who would read intelligently must first learn to eliminate. Apparently it is assumed that the accumulation of facts for the facts' sake is an adequate end, and yet nothing serves so little purpose as undigested facts. A fact in itself has no significance; neither have a thousand facts. What gives facts their value is their relation to each other; for when enough have been collected to suggest a sequence of cause and effect, a generalization can be made which scientific men call a "law." The law amounts only to this, that certain phenomena have been found to succeed each other with sufficient regularity to enable us to count with reasonable certainty on their recurrence in a determined order.

Science is constructed from such approximations. History as taught in our colleges ignores the advantage of generalization, and discourages all attempts to generalize. Yet it may be doubted whether advantage accrues to any one from the mere accumulation of historical details. Unless reduced to order, so as to offer a basis of comparison, past facts bear little upon present events. The change of conditions impairs their relevancy. Certainly it is fatuous to burden the memory with them, for a gazetteer is fuller and more accurate than any human memory, and is always at hand.

To such reasoning the teaching profession objects that their specialty differs from all others in that it deals with human actions. These actions either are not regulated by the same laws which pervade the rest of nature, or, if they are, the causes of which they are effects are so complicated as to elude us, unless we gather a very much larger number of observations from which to generalize than we now possess, or are likely to possess in the immediate future. A dilemma is thus presented. Either human experience cannot be formulated; or, at best, it can be only by amassing more facts than the mind can grasp. In either case the same conclusion is reached. Generalization must be abandoned, and the collection of " historical material" must be accepted as the end for which so much money and time are spent. If this be true, it is doubtful whether the sums expended on historical research and on professional salaries might not be made to yield a better return.

Possibly, however, professional historians are mistaken in their estimate of the difficulty of historical generalization; possibly, also, the reasons they allege against making the attempt are not those which influence them most. Still, as these reasons are seriously advanced, they must be seriously examined.

On their face the objections proposed seem inconclusive, for they rest on fallacious premises. They assume, in the first place, that human actions are the effects of peculiarly complicated causes; and in the second, that an imperfect generalization is valueless. Both assumptions are incorrect. The causes which have combined to cast a single grain of sand upon the shore are infinite, and the infinite can neither be surpassed nor understood. We cannot understand what the sand is or how it comes to be where it lies.

and yet we can make geology useful. Also it is a maxim of science that results are obtained by approximation through error, and that the truths of one generation are the errors of the next.

The scientific man accepts his limitations and does not expect to arrive at absolute verity. He observes, and when he has advanced far enough to begin to generalize, he formulates his ideas as an hypothesis to serve as a basis on which to work until some one has suggested something better. There is hardly a general scientific proposition which is not called in question, and it is precisely by such questioning that knowledge is reduced to a serviceable shape.

For example, one of the most cherished postulates of science has been that "a thing cannot act where it is not," a postulate which Newton himself agreed to; and yet that postulate is directly contradicted by gravity. Nobody can guess what gravity is, or how it operates, and yet laws can be formulated which enable us to use it for multifarious purposes.

The atomic theory was at one time generally adopted, and now chemists are discussing whether it is not more of a hindrance than a help. The famous nebular hypothesis of Kant and La Place played a great part in astronomy, but it is conceded that there are fatal objections to receiving it as a solution of the secret of the formation of stars. The work of the astronomer is based on fictions. " In calculating the attraction of a homogeneous sphere upon a material point . . . the astronomer begins with two fictions — the fiction of a 'material point' (which is, in truth, a contradiction in terms), . . . and the fiction of the finite differences representing the molecular constitu-

tion of the sphere." [1]   The theory of the conservation
of energy is expected to " prove the great theoretical
solvent of chemical as well as physical phenomena,"
and yet in regard to the planetary system Lord
Kelvin has formulated his conclusions thus: —

" 1. There is at present in the material world a
universal tendency to the dissipation of mechanical
energy.

" 2. Any restoration of mechanical energy, without
more than an equivalent of dissipation, is impossible
in inanimate material processes, and is probably never
effected by material masses either endowed with
vegetable life, or subjected to the will of an animated
creature.

" 3. Within a finite time past the earth must have
been; and within a finite period of time to come the
earth must again be, unfit for the habitation of man
as at present constituted, unless operations have been,
or are to be, performed which are impossible under
the laws to which the known operations going on at
present in the material world are subject."

The axioms of mathematics are disputed.   A school
of geometers now conceive of space as curved, so that
lines which we have regarded as straight may prove
to be a closed curve, and parallel lines meet.   " A
whole pencil of shortest lines may [thus] be drawn
through the same point."   Moreover, mathematicians
regard space as having various dimensions, so that
the solar system in its march through the universe
may be approaching regions where there will be four
dimensions.[2]

[1] *The Concepts and Theories of Modern Physics*, Stallo, 297.
[2] See *On Some Recent Advances in Physical Science*, P. G. Tait.

The list might be prolonged, but to little purpose, as the principle is undisputed. All scientific men agree to the tentative condition of generalizations, and yet science advances, the proof being the control obtained over natural forces. If satisfactory results can be reached elsewhere by using well-established methods of observation and generalization, there seems no reason, at first sight, why the same methods should not be applied to humanity, especially as Darwin drew his inferences regarding evolution by these processes. On considering more attentively, however, the possibilities which are disclosed by such investigations, the hesitation of the universities appears less inexplicable. Certainly no fundamental religious dogmas are threatened, since neither the attributes of the soul nor of the mind are in question ; but if communities of men are to be studied as though they were communities of ants, learned bodies might be forced into positions which would make untenable their present tacitly accepted platform of principles.

Submission to tradition is one of the strong instincts. In primitive ages it is absolute; life is regulated by ritual. The code of Leviticus instructs men how to eat, and wash, and shave, and reap, and the law was changeless, to be kept by " thy son and thy son's son all the days of thy life."

A religious truth, of course, cannot vary, for truth is immutable and eternal, and no believer in an inspired church could tolerate having her canons examined as we should examine human laws. But it is not only in religion that tradition wields power. It is often preponderant in politics, and a political principle is not seldom preached as a tenet of faith. Not so very long ago the Anglican clergy maintained as orthodox doctrine the divine right of kings, and, to come nearer home, the language of the Declaration of Independence varies little from that of a Catholic council. The Declaration lays down an immutable law, "We hold these truths to be self-evident." The Church enunciates a verity in slightly different terms, but no more dogmatically, "This holy Synod doth now declare." Even in science tradition has not been altogether eradicated. Some years ago, on retiring from the presidency of the American Association for the Advancement of Science, Professor Langley took the occasion to remonstrate against this tendency.

"The final conclusion was irresistible, that the universal statement of this alleged well-known fact, inexplicable as this might seem, in so simple a matter, was directly contradicted by experiment. I had some natural curiosity to find how every one knew this to be a fact ; but search only showed the same statement (that the earth's atmosphere absorbed dark heat like glass) repeated everywhere, with absolutely nowhere any observation or evidence whatever to prove it, but each writer quoting from an earlier one, till I was almost ready to believe it a dogma superior to reason, and resting on the well-known ' *Quod semper, quod ubique, quod ab omnibus, creditum est.*' " [1]

Professor Langley went on to say : "The question of fact here, though important, is, I think, quite secondary to the query it raises as to the possible unsuspected influence of mere tradition in science, when we do not recognize it as such. Now, members of any church are doubtless consistent in believing in

[1] *The History of a Doctrine,* S. P. Langley, 20.

traditions, if they believe that these are presented to them by an infallible guide; but are we, who have no infallible guide, quite safe in believing all we do, from our fond persuasion that in the scientific body mere tradition has no weight?"

Here lies the divergence between the scientific and the liberal training. Professor Langley insists that nothing must be taken as fixed, and that the mind should be held open to proceed to successive generalizations as the range of observation expands. The College proceeds on nearly an opposite principle.

The College assumes certain ethical premises, and the conclusions of study must be made to square with these. This is as it should be from the inductive standpoint, for the College is the offspring of the Church and the daughter of the mediæval convent. Nevertheless such an assumption places liberal in antagonism to scientific methods, and especially between inductive and ethical history the gulf cannot be bridged.

If men are to be observed scientifically, the standard by which customs and institutions must be gauged cannot be abstract moral principles, but success. Those instincts are judged advantageous to animals which help them in their struggle for life, and those prejudicial which hamper them. They are means to an end. So with physical peculiarities. A beast's color is good if it serves to protect; and bad if it make him conspicuous to his enemy. Similarly with men. Institutions are good which lead to success in competition, and are bad when they hinder. No series of institutions are *a priori* to be preferred to others; the criterion is the practical one of success.

The same rule applies to men themselves. They are the best who conform most perfectly to the demands of nature, or who, in other words, succeed best. Nature eliminates those who do not satisfy her requirements, and from Nature's decree there is no appeal.

These generalizations can with difficulty be reconciled with any body of fixed ethical principles. Evidently they form a doctrine of expediency founded on necessity. The theory is that men will arrive at precisely the same end, in either case; only by flexibility will they avoid suffering. In fact, nothing is more sensitive to the exigencies of an environment than a moral law. According to conditions of time and place murder, cruelty, piracy, slaving, polygamy, celibacy, deceit, and their like, have been exalted into virtues; while it is not so very long since the Church declared the healing of the sick by scientific means and the taking of interest for money to be crimes before God. As the environment changes, those men are gradually selected who conform thereto; the rest perish more or less miserably. The scientific education would tend to diminish the agony of adaptation.

Followed to their root, also, the two systems of thought will be found to be as opposed in their practical methods as they are in regard to the temper of mind which they propagate. The one is analytical and administrative, the other idealistic and slack. A few examples will explain the difference between them.

Large public libraries are now admittedly in an unsatisfactory condition. Libraries may indeed speculate in curiosities, or be used for amusement, but here they are considered only as educational institutions or workshops.   Viewed thus, none are complete, for the books printed outrun the means of buying, cataloguing, and housing.   Administration has broken down ; and administration has broken down because it is unscientific.   Men of liberal education have collected libraries who have never been taught to generalize.   These men look on a book as a unit, precisely as in history they look on a fact as a unit.   When a book is supposed to have a certain degree of merit, it is deemed worthy of purchase, almost regardless of its subject.   Thus the whole range of knowledge is thrown open, and the result is bewilderment.

On no principle of generalization can the book, apart from ordinary books of reference, be considered as the unit.   The subject is the unit, and the book has a value only in relation to its subject.   A single book, like a single chapter, word, or fact, needs a context to explain it ; therefore a library collected on the basis of individual books must be incomplete, and an indifferent workshop, because no man can thoroughly finish any task therein.   To find all his tools he must travel elsewhere, and everywhere he is met with the same difficulty, because all general libraries are collected on much the same system, and all duplicate each other.

Supposing, however, that liberal education like science were based on a series of generalizations, a different result would be attained.   The book would not then be regarded as the unit, nor of value as a thing in itself, but only of value in so far as it related to the contents of the collection to which it might be added.   The department of knowledge would thus become the unit; and in growing the library would grow not by volumes but by departments. The next generalization would be uniting several libraries, covering many departments, under one management, so that their books might be mutually accessible and few duplicated. This generalization might be broadened indefinitely so as, at last, by an exchange of books of many libraries, to make an almost perfect collection in all important departments, and that at the lowest cost.

Precisely the same phenomena are disclosed in museums devoted to the fine arts. Like libraries, museums may speculate in bric-a-brac, but the true function of an art museum is conceded to be education. The theory on which they have been formed has been a liberal *a priori* theory. It has been taught that certain objects are in themselves beautiful, because they conform to a conventional æsthetic standard, and that such objects should be purchased for their own intrinsic merit, apart from the contents of the museum. Such a theory conflicts with the inductive method.

If art be viewed as a product of an environment, art is, like language, a form of expression; therefore a heterogeneous mass of pictures, laces, statues, porcelain, and coins has no more significance than would have stray lines taken at random from the poets of a thousand languages and printed side by side. The carvings and glass of the cathedral of Chartres spoke as clearly and more emphatically to the mediæval peasant than any book can speak to us, and we cannot appreciate that masterpiece unless we comprehend the language in which the Church of the twelfth century addressed the people. To the Greek likewise the coin had a meaning. We cannot exhibit a few Greek coins as a model of what coinage should be, for those coins would be unserviceable now. They convey no lesson unless they be read in the light of Greek economic civilization.

Our architecture, when dealing with iron and steel, with matter of fact factories, railway stations, and warehouses, is admirable. When it strives after an æsthetic ideal, it is a failure; and, logically, it could be nothing but a failure, because it is unintelligent.

A body of material produced during certain epochs is arbitrarily selected as worthy, and from this material architects are thought to be justified in borrowing whatever may suit their purpose, or strike their fancy, irrespective of the language which their predecessors spoke, or the ideas which they conveyed. The arms of a pope may be used to adorn the front of a New England library, or the tomb of the Virgin for a booth at an international commercial exhibition.

If men would translate or adapt a poem, they must first soak themselves in the language and the temper of the poet, and artists who would borrow with effect must first be archæologists and students of history. Approached thus, the heterogeneous collection of æsthetic objects can only be a stumbling-block. The value of the museum must be proportionate to the perfection with which it displays the development of the artistic side of any civilization, and the intelligence with which it offers the key to the form of expression which it undertakes to explain. This is generalization.

The same defective administration arising from imperfect generalization appears in the University.

Until within about a generation the American College retained substantially the methods and the curriculum which had been in use when it served as a divinity school. About 1870 an expansion took place, based on the theory of the intrinsic value of the fact, precisely as the expansion of the library has been based on the theory of the intrinsic value of the book. The aim of the new University came to be to teach everything, little attention being given to the coördination of the parts. The result could not be other than wasteful and disjointed. Suppose two foundations each teach one hundred subjects, those subjects being substantially identical; they obviously duplicate each other, while they divide their resources by one hundred. Suppose each, on the contrary, to teach but fifty subjects, the original hundred being distributed between them, they double their teaching power, and still offer to the public precisely the same field as before. They suppress waste and increase efficiency.

The theory on which the modern University system rests is fallacious. The worth of the University lies not in the multitude of units taught, but in the coördination of parts and the intensity of effort. What our civilization demands is the maximum of energy, and that maximum cannot be attained when the money which would bring one department to the standard is divided between two. American universities would have now abundant funds for all necessary work of the highest grade were there no waste. They are poor because of bad administration.

It is true that the worst examples of duplicate foundations are effects of the clerical *a priori* rea-

soning, yet, when all allowances have been made for
sectarian narrowness, the fact remains that colleges
do not attempt to add to their efficiency and stop
their waste by intelligent cooperation among themselves, as manufacturers would coöperate who did
not mean to be ruined. They do not even go so far
as to coordinate their instruction by departments and
by sub-departments, so that every student who receives
tuition shall receive it with that degree of intelligence
which comes from knowing where he stands in regard
to the sum of human knowledge. And yet such a
generalization, at least in regard to departments, would
be easy. Every science is so generalized that each spe-
cialist can know at any moment how his part stands
to the whole. If he need to broaden his sphere of
knowledge by examining other branches, he can
choose those most advantageous with celerity and
certainty. The student at college is launched upon
an unknown sea, like a mariner without chart or
compass. He has little to guide him in ascertain-
ing what departments are really kindred. Even the
courses of history are often arranged according to
the taste of professors, and with no relation to historical sequence.

Take economics as an example. During the
eighteenth century Adam Smith, having carefully
observed the conditions which prevailed in Europe
and especially in Great Britain, wrote a book ad-
mirably suited to his environment, and the book met
with success. Then men undertook to erect the
principles of that book into an universal law, irrespective of environment. Then others theorized on
these commentators, and their successors upon them,

until the most practical of business problems has been lost in a metaphysical fog.

Now men are apt to lecture on political economy as if it were a dogma, much as the nominalists and realists lectured in mediæval schools. But *a priori* theories can avail little in matters which are determined by experiment.

Political economy as a dogma is as absurd as would be a dogma which taught an infallible way to manipulate the stock market. Success in competition comes solely through a comprehension of existing conditions and the capacity to take advantage of opportunities. One community, such as Rome, may do well by robbery; another, like Great Britain, when she enjoyed a monopoly of minerals and of manufactures, may flourish upon free trade; a third, like Germany with her sugar policy, may find her advantage in attacking a rival by export bounties ; while a fourth may thrive by seclusion, as did Japan, as long as circumstances favored. No one can say *a priori* what will succeed ; the criterion is success.

The inference is that if a man would study economics to some purpose, he must study them practically, as he would any other business. He must begin by learning the principles of trade and finance as they are presented by actual daily experience, just as the soldier, the sailor, the lawyer, and the doctor learn their professions. Then if he wish to generalize, he can examine into the experience of other countries, past and present, and observe how they won or lost. In other words, he can read geography, history, archæology, numismatics, and kindred branches, and extend his horizon at his pleasure.

Thus men work who expect to earn their bread in the walks of active life, but colleges do not classify.

History, geography, and economics are related branches which mutually explain each other, and none of which can be well understood alone. They also aid each other, for the sequence of cause and effect sustains the memory; and yet they are never taught together, although to learn the three combined would take little longer, and demand less effort, than to learn any one singly. It is a curious commentary on liberal methods, that geography, which is eminently practical, is only applied in military or possibly technical schools. There is, perhaps, no thorough collection of maps made on scientific principles in any public library in the United States.

Lastly, it remains to consider how the introduction of inductive methods in social matters would affect the community at large by the destruction of its ideals; for ideals would probably suffer.

He who is dominated by tradition exalts the past. In the concrete case of an American he believes more or less implicitly that the contemporaries of Washington and Jefferson arrived at political truths which, at least so far as he is concerned, may be received as final. The man who reasons by induction views the work of Washington and Jefferson otherwise. He views it as the product of the conditions of the eighteenth century, and as having no more necessary relation to the conduct of affairs in the twentieth, than Franklin's methods in electricity would have to the manipulation of a modern dynamo. The United States now occupies a position of extraordinary strength. Favored alike by geographical position, by

deposits of minerals, by climate, and by the character
of her population, she has little to fear, either in peace
or war, from rivals, provided the friction created by
the movement of the masses with which she has to
deal does not neutralize her energy.

Masses accumulate in the United States because
administration by masses is cheaper than administration by detail.   Masses take the form of corporations,
and the men who rise to the control of these corporations rise because they are fittest.   The process is
natural selection.   The life of the community lies
in these masses.   Derange them, and there would immediately follow an equivalent loss of energy.   They
are there because the conditions of our civilization are
such as to make it cheaper that they should be there,
and if our political institutions are ill-adapted to their
propagation and development, then political institutions must be readjusted, or the probability is that the
whole fabric of society will be shattered by the dislo-
cation of the economic system.   America holds its
tenure of prosperity only on condition that she can
undersell her rivals, and she cannot do so if her
administrative machinery generates friction unduly.

Political institutions and political principles are but
a conventional dial on whose face the hands revolve
which mark the movement of the mechanism within.
Most governments and many codes have been adored
as emanating from the deity.   All were ephemeral,
and all which survived their purpose became a jest
or a curse to the children of the worshippers; things
to be cast aside like worn-out garments.

Under any circumstances an organism so gigantic
as the American Union must generate friction.   In

American industry friction will infallibly exist between capital and labor; but that necessary friction may be indefinitely increased by conservatism. History teems with examples of civilizations which have been destroyed through an unreasoning inertia like that of Brutus, or the French privileged classes, or Patrick Henry. A slight increase in the relative cost of production caused by an imperfect mechanical adjustment is usually sufficient to give some rival an advantage, and when a country is undersold, misery sets in. People who cannot earn their daily bread are revolutionary, and disorders bred by violence achieve the series of disasters which began with the diversion of trade. Such was the fate of the great cities of Flanders, of Bruges, of Ghent, and of Ypres.

The alternative presented is plain. Men may cherish ideals and risk substantial benefits to realize them. Such is the emotional instinct. Or they may regard their government dispassionately, as they would any other matter of business.

Americans in former generations led a simple agricultural life. Possibly such a life was happier than ours. Very probably keen competition is not a blessing. We cannot alter our environment. Nature has cast the United States into the vortex of the fiercest struggle which the world has ever known. She has become the heart of the economic system of the age, and she must maintain her supremacy by wit and by force, or share the fate of the discarded. What that fate is the following pages tell.

The liberal education tends to instil a reverence for fixed standards; therefore an adherence to these methods must encourage rigidity and make innovations proportionately difficult, and this in the face of a huge, complex society, moving with unexampled velocity. An extension of scientific training to branches hitherto controlled by conservatism would doubtless alter moral standards, but probably only by anticipating by a few years an inevitable intellectual transformation. The advantage would be that we should facilitate adjustment and distance our rivals by reaching first a predestined goal.

The following essay is an attempt to deal, by inductive methods, with the consolidation and dissolution of those administrative masses which we call empires. The same method might be applied to any phase of civilization, artistic, literary, or military. My observation leads me to surmise that the intellectual stimulus of an environment acts very uniformly, and that where a community is roused to activity in one direction, it will be active in all directions in which it has capacity to succeed, or in which opportunity for success is afforded.

This book is purely tentative and only suggests an hypothesis to serve as a stepping-stone to something better. No man who works by inductive methods can hope either to be complete, or to reach a final result. He cannot do so, because he attempts to deal with infinite sequences of cause and effect, and his mind is finite. Like any other generalization, this will serve its purpose if its method be right and it prove suggestive to others. Its object is to be set aside by those who follow and improve.

From the days of Roger Bacon to those of Darwin scientific methods and scientific theories have not commended themselves to the conservative. They

could hardly do so, since they undermine tradition.
Among many examples which might be cited of resistance to innovation one must suffice.   It is, perhaps, the most memorable.   On June 22, 1633, the
Holy Office enunciated the following decree in the
trial of Galileo for heresy : —

1. That the sun is the centre of the world and immovable is a proposition absurd and false in philosophy, and formally heretical, as being expressly
contrary to Holy Scripture.

2. That the earth is not the centre of the world,
nor immovable, but that it moves even with a diurnal
motion, is in like manner a proposition absurd and
false in philosophy, and, considered in theology, at
least erroneous in faith.

To escape torture Galileo recanted, but still he
murmured, "e pur si muove."

THE NEW EMPIRE

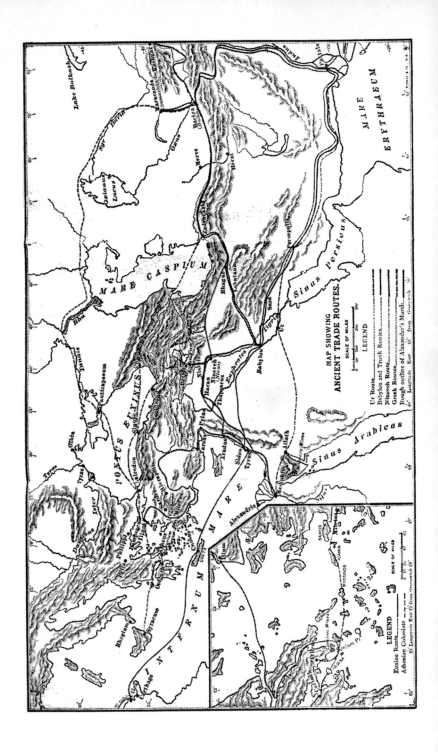

MAP SHOWING
ANCIENT TRADE ROUTES.

SCALE OF MILES

LEGEND

Ur Route
Babylon and Trunk Routes
Nineveh Route
Greek Routes
Rough outline of Alexander's March.

THE NEW EMPIRE

CHAPTER I

Two propositions seem indisputable: First, that self-preservation is the most imperious of instincts; Second, that in his efforts to prolong his life, man has followed the paths of least resistance.

Without food or the means of defence, death is inevitable, and as few communities have succeeded in entirely feeding and arming themselves from their own resources, they have supplied their deficiencies from abroad. No man will knowingly use inferior weapons in war, but the apprehension of want is almost as drastic as the fear of defeat; even savages try to improve their tools. For example, the Stone-Age inhabitants of central Europe imported jade axes from the confines of the desert of Gobi because jade takes a better edge than flint. Yet the cost of conveying jade across the Pamirs from Khotan to Germany would now be excessive, and then must have represented a prodigious sacrifice.

From the beginning, therefore, men have obtained wares from strangers. They have done so both by force and by purchase; but as battle is uncertain they have inclined toward trade, and to trade, buyer and seller must meet. Usually they have met at the junction of the paths leading to the sources of sup-

ply. Here houses have multiplied, a wall to protect
the houses has been built, and within the wall the
neighboring population has gathered on certain days,
or at certain seasons, and thus has germinated the
market or fair. Fairs have always been frequented
in proportion to their consequence, the more noted
having been thronged by foreigners. Nevertheless,
no fair can thrive unless accessible, and none can be
accessible with approaches closed either by defects
or robbers; hence, some system of road-building and
police must precede centralized trade. Nor can business be transacted without a tribunal to decide dis-
putes. Accordingly, an administrative mechanism
must have always existed at market towns, and the
growth of this mechanism at the more important has
created capital cities. Thus, it may be inferred that
the structure we call civil society is an outgrowth of
trade. Finally, as one army and one administrative
corps are cheaper than several, the tendency has
been toward amalgamation; the lesser market sinking into insignificance, and the petty state into a province. Many independent kingdoms once flourished
together in Mesopotamia, but, when consecutive history begins, all had been welded into a single organism with Babylon for a heart.

As communications improve and markets broaden,
roads stretch out across continents and join oceans;
then the empires traversed by such highways cohere
in economic systems, since they have a common interest to resist the diversion of their traffic. Sooner
or later, however, parallel routes between the same
termini are opened, competition between the systems
acquires intensity, and economic competition in its

intensest form is war.   Hence, from the beginning
of history, rival systems have fought with and destroyed each other.   If one system conquer, consolidation may follow, and an equilibrium may be
obtained which may endure indefinitely, as did the
Roman Empire; but if neither can win a decisive
advantage, the war may end by forcing commerce
into other channels, and both combatants may perish.
Such was substantially the fate of the Greek states.

Among the inventions which have stimulated
movement and consequently centralization, none has
equalled the smelting of the metals.   Smiths have
made from metal superior weapons and tools, and
races using these implements have, in the end, en-
slaved or exterminated neighbors adhering to wood
and stone, wherefore a supply of metal early became
essential to existence in the more active quarters of
the globe.   To procure ore men have wandered far
and wide, and thus while the introduction of metal
induced a more rapid concentration at the heart of
the civilized mass, it caused a proportionate expansion at the circumference.   Yet no empire and no
system can expand equally in all directions, for the
resistance to expansion is variable, consequently
growth is irregular; and as the shape of the organism
changes, the arteries connecting its extremities must
alter their course to correspond.   But an alteration
of the course of the circulation presupposes a displacement of the heart, and for this reason society
tends toward instability of equilibrium.

Evidently, approached from this standpoint, min-
eralogy and geography elucidate history, for the one
helps to explain the forces which have moved the

seat of empire, the other the obstacles which have fixed its course by determining the path of least resistance. Furthermore, civilization may be examined scientifically. The cause may be deduced from the effect, until the origin of the phenomena of the twentieth century may be traced back to the murky past which preceded the pyramid of Cheops, and human development may be presented as a mechanical whole. For present purposes it suffices to begin with the smelting of the metals.

We know not when Chaldea and Egypt may have emerged from the Stone Age, but nothing indicates that prior to 4000 B.C. either community had achieved opulence. On the contrary, the evidence indicates that both empires rose to fortune through a successful speculation made by the Egyptians in Arabian copper, at the beginning of the fourth dynasty. The richest mines then known lay in the valley of Maghara in the peninsula of Sinai, and though the Egyptian kings appear to have previously invaded the valley, a permanent occupation seems only to have been achieved by Sneferu, about 4000 B.C.

At the mouth of one of these mines Sneferu commemorated his victory by causing his portrait to be cut in the rock, slaying a captive, and, near by, an inscription to be carved relating his triumph. That victory, by making Egypt the chief producer of metals, made her the western terminus of commerce, and the market whose tastes had to be consulted by all who needed the minerals she had to sell. Between Asia, east of the Tigris, and Egypt, lay Mesopotamia ; all trade routes converged there, accordingly Mesopotamia became the central market where the most

important exchanges were effected, and thus was
founded the Babylonian economic system. This
mighty system, which, in its prime, comprised all the
nations bordering the highways connecting the Oxus
and the Indus with the Guadalquivir, flourished for
nearly three thousand years. Culminating about the
siege of Troy, for some centuries it struggled with
the Greek system afterward established along the
cheaper waterways of the north, and finally sank into
ruin under the onset of Alexander the Great.

The evidence that Egypt achieved affluence through
her mines, especially her Arabian copper mines, is
pretty convincing. The Egyptians were good metallurgists and certainly worked gold, iron, copper, and
bronze before the fourth dynasty. The gold and iron
came originally from Nubia. According to Diodorus
the Nubian gold mines, under Rameses II. or in the
fourteenth century B.C., yielded annually bullion to
the value of $650,000,000.[1] Possibly, also, the Nubi-
ans discovered the smelting of iron, and the Egyptians
may in early times have drawn their supply of steel,
especially as a finished product, from the south.
Afterward they mined iron in the valley of Maghara,
near their copper. Yet conceding that iron was used
in Egypt under Cheops, it cost high, and held a
secondary place in the arts. Copper served as the
useful metal.[2]

Except the systematic working of the Maghara
mines, nothing is known to have occurred in Egypt
about the beginning of the fourth dynasty which

[1] *Die Geschichte des Eisens*, Beck, I., 71.
[2] See *Die Geschichte des Eisens*, Ludwig Beck, I., 77, 96. Also
Histoire de l'Art, Perrot & Chipiez, I., 650, 831.

could have caused a social revolution. The relations of the country with Nubia underwent no especial change before the campaigns of Una, five hundred years later; the methods of industry, transportation, and agriculture remained unaltered, and yet, immediately after Sneferu's conquest, Egypt entered her golden age. This fact is established by her architecture.

Egyptian emotion found its strongest expression in the tomb. As tomb builders the Egyptians have had no equal. The pyramid stands alone as an everlasting abode for the dead. Also the era of colossal art opens with Sneferu.

Sneferu reigned for twenty-nine years, between 3998 B.C. and 3969. As he first regularly mined the Sinai copper, so he first built a pyramid. He even built two, one of which survives. Cheops succeeded Sneferu, and Cheops's tomb is still a wonder of the world. Nor, in the expenditure lavished on details of workmanship, have the builders of the pyramids of Gizeh ever been surpassed. The fourth dynasty lasted for 284 years, during which period construction continued on a scale thus described by Flinders Petrie : " The simplicity, the vastness, the perfection, and the beauty of the earliest works place them on a different level to all works of art and man's devices in later ages. They are unique in their splendid power, which no self-conscious civilization has ever rivalled, or can hope to rival; and in their enduring greatness they may last till all feebler works of man have perished." [1]

Egypt must have amassed wealth rapidly to have

[1] *History of Egypt*, I., 67.

borne this burden through near three centuries without exhaustion, and the magnitude of her foreign trade is proved by the rise of Mesopotamia where her commercial exchanges centred. The glory of North Mesopotamia opened with the renowned Sargon, who reigned about 3850 B.C., whose empire is supposed to have extended to Cyprus, if not to Maghara itself, and who stands as the first of that long line of potentates which ended with the Darius who perished in his flight from Alexander.

Centuries before Sargon, Ur of the Chaldeans held the first place in the valley of the Euphrates. Ur stood at the junction of the coast road from India with the camel track leading to Sinai, accordingly the reasonable inference would seem to be that, originally, the chief traffic passed straight from the mouth of the Indus to the mines on the Red Sea, and that the highways converging at Babylon acquired consequence later. Ample explanation of such a growth is to be found in the geography of central Asia.

The combined continents of Asia and Europe have proved impossible to develop as a unit, not only because their different shapes demand irreconcilable systems of transportation, but because of the deserts and mountains in their midst. Still commerce between the East and West has always been a necessity, because the two regions supplement each other. While India, China, and Turkestan have been renowned for agriculture, manufactures, and the production of luxuries and gems, they have failed to compete in the metals; whereas Europe, though dependent on Asia for spices and the like, has surpassed her in mining.

But before there could be commercial exchanges between East and West, avenues of communication had to be opened, and the cheapest of these long presented insuperable difficulties. For ages the voyage from China to India, and from India to Egypt, defied nautical skill.

Although primitive savages use boats, the sail is a later invention, and the art of working to windward modern. Dangerous coasts affright the navigators of frail ships and the open sea appalls them, yet the voyage to Aden, or even the Euphrates, lay over a waste of waters, or along a barbarous and desolate shore.

Even as late as 325 B.C., when Nearchus returned from India with Alexander's army, the Greek general nearly perished. From Pattala, at the mouth of the Indus, it took Nearchus nearly three months to reach the Persian Gulf. There he met Alexander, but so changed by hardship that the emperor did not know him. Although, of course, provided with the best craft, pilots, and stores which were to be obtained, Nearchus lost several ships by wreck, had to abandon others, narrowly escaped death from hunger and thirst, and was assailed by the natives when he landed. If Nearchus fared so ill upon the short voyage from the Indus to the Tigris, the lot of the lonely merchantman bound for Egypt may be imagined. Direct communication between India and Egypt only opened after the Christian era. Therefore merchandise crossed central Asia by caravan, and in ancient times by one of three routes, for the northern plain now traversed by the Siberian railway led to no market before civilization spread to the Baltic. Until the Middle Ages the Mediterranean afforded the only vent.

The heart of Asia from Lake Baikal to India is occupied by the desert of Gobi and the ranges of the Altai, the Pamirs, the Hindu Kush, and the Himalaya, forming together a tremendous barrier. When, after crossing the Gobi, the traveller reached Kashgar or Yarkand at the base of the mountains, he might turn to the south toward the Indus, keep on due east toward the Oxus, or journey north into the valley of the Syr-Daria. If he chose the southern road, he followed the paths described by Wood and Young-husband along the tributaries of the Oxus until he found a pass in the Hindu Kush, leading to India.[1] Once on the banks of the Indus he descended the river to the delta, and, at Pattala, took the southern highway to Babylon, along which Alexander marched. The objections to this route were manifold. It was long, toilsome, and dangerous.

Secondly, merchants utilized the valley of the Syr-Daria. After the fall of Troy caravans passed along the northern coast of the Caspian, to the Sea of Azov, by way of the Volga and the Don; and since the Middle Ages they have sought Moscow, by Tash-kend, Turkestan, and Orenburg. Before the opening of the Hellespont to commerce, these northern outlets were closed, and traffic had to pass by Maracanda, the modern Samarkand. But as gaining the Syr-Daria from Kashgar involved making the Terek pass 12,700 feet high, and closed in summer by melting snow, a more northern track through Siberia, and south of Lake Balkash, seems to have been preferred. It is noteworthy that Maracanda never attained the con-

[1] See the route of Benedict Goës given on Yule's map in *Cathay and the Way Thither*, Vol. 2, Hakluyt Soc. Publications.

sequence of Bactra, the inference being that, before
the Middle Ages, the highway on which the town stood
remained a subsidiary avenue.　In 1218, at the opening of his campaign against Trans-Oxania, Jenghiz
Khan marched through this region on Otrar.　Doubtless he followed what was then the beaten track.　William of Rubruck was carried over the same road in
1253,[1] and in the time of Tamerlane the northern route
seems to have superseded all others.　Friar William
also started from the Sea of Azov, an outlet much used
by the Greeks and also by the Genoese.　Nevertheless, in antiquity, speaking broadly, the bulk of traffic
probably took the path afterward selected by Marco
Polo, who kept as straight as might be across the
Pamirs into the valley of the Oxus, and thence to
Bactra, which we know as the wretched hamlet of
Balkh.[2]　From an economic standpoint Bactra presents phenomena of surpassing interest.　The city was
created by the junction of the main thoroughfare
to China with that which led to northern India by
Bamian, Kabul, and the Khyber.　While the sea presented the terrors encountered by Nearchus, the merchants of Kashmir and the Punjab had the alternative
of descending the Indus and then journeying by land
to Babylon, or of crossing the mountains and seeking
Bactra.　Apparently they preferred the latter, for
the ruins of Bamian still fill the pass, while the remains of Bactra cover a circuit of twenty miles, after
six hundred years of abandonment.

---

[1] See map prepared by Hon. W. W. Rockhill in his edition of *The
Journey of William of Rubruck*, Publications of Hakluyt Soc., Second
Ser., No. IV.

[2] For Polo's route, see Yule's edition of Marco Polo.

When Nineveh and Babylon were born, Bactra, the mother of cities, was already hoary. The legend has it that when Ninus, the founder of Babylon, was besieging Bactra, the ineffable Semiramis joined his camp, and by her intelligence, carried the walls. Ninus, captivated by her wit, her courage, and her beauty, drove her husband to suicide and married her. At all events Bactra long remained the metropolis for the trade of China, the Punjab, Kashmir, and Turkestan; and from Bactra many roads diverged to the sea. Of these roads, according to the legend, Semiramis built the first across the Zagros Mountains to Babylon, a road still used by the traveller from Bagdad to Teheran. A second avenue unites Balkh with Teheran, Mosul, and Alexandretta, and formerly connected the famous cities of Bactra, Ragae, Gaugamela, Nisabis, Haran, and Aradus. From any Syrian port such as Aradus, Tyre, or Sidon, the mariner steered due west to Cyprus, Crete, Carthage, and Cadiz.

Thus, before the opening of the Dardanelles, the lands beyond the Oxus and the Indus were connected with the Mediterranean by three main thoroughfares : —

First, that which leaving Pattala skirted the Arabian Sea and the Persian Gulf, reaching the Nile by Ur.

Second, that built by Semiramis across the Zagros Mountains between Bactra, Babylon, and the coast.

Third, that which joined Bactra, Nineveh, Haran, and Aradus.

Upon each of these thoroughfares a great market was begotten, and if the chronological order in which

these markets grew be examined, it will be found to
indicate a movement northward of the seat of empire
continued through thousands of years, and gaining
constantly in velocity.

The rise of Ur, the most southern of the three
capitals, is lost in the past, but Ur must have been
extremely ancient, since she had culminated when
Sargon reigned in 3850 B.C.

In Sargon's time the centre of exchanges seems to
have been in transit, for Sargon's chief city was,
probably, Nippur, about two-thirds of the way from Ur
to Babylon; notwithstanding which, Babylon only
achieved supremacy fifteen hundred years later, under
Hammurabi, toward 2250 B.C. Compared with such
sluggishness the advance from Babylon to Nineveh
was rapid, for Salmanassar established the preponderance of Assyria in Mesopotamia about 1300 B.C.
Salmanassar chose for the site of his capital the angle
made by the confluence of the Tigris and the Great
Zab, where are now the mounds of Nimrud. His
successors moved to Nineveh, eighteen miles up the
Tigris, but the new city was only an extension of
Calach. Meanwhile, movement had been accelerated, for Nineveh lived fast, even judged by modern
standards. Born in 1300, she perished in 607 B.C.,
just as Athens and Syracuse blossomed.

An impulsion so persistent must have been the
effect of an equally persistent cause. Such a cause
might have been the expansion of the economic mass
occasioned by the opening to commerce of the basins
of the Mediterranean and Euxine. It can be demonstrated in support of this view that these regions
were developed during this interval.

Certainly the assumption is justified that prior to 4000 B.C. Europe was barbarous and poor, and the purchasing power, even of Egypt, limited. The Nile, therefore, formed the terminus of the eastern trade, and offered the single market of consequence west of the Euphrates. Under such conditions only small articles of pure necessity, such as jade axe-heads, could have been transported from China to Europe over the long and costly route by Bactra. Bulky merchandise would have followed the shortest road to Egypt. That road lay through Ur and Arabia straight to Sinai, where copper might be obtained for goods.

The conquest of Maghara worked a social revolution in the west by enlarging its purchasing power, and creating capitalistic accumulations in Chaldea which stimulated expansion. This appears from the annexation of Cyprus by Sargon, and the transference of mining activity from the Red Sea to the Mediterranean. The Phœnicians led in enterprise, and the discovery and development of Cyprian copper was the first of their many industrial triumphs. Another thousand years elapsed before Babylon achieved supremacy, for Babylon's rise was the effect of the extension of exchanges westward until they, probably, reached the Atlantic. That such an extension occurred is proved by the recent excavations in Crete, which show that in 2400 B.C., or before Hammurabi, Crete had become a civilized and opulent kingdom, and a foremost maritime power. Crete could only have prospered because she lay in the track of a lucrative commerce flowing west, and that commerce must have been the Bactra trade which reached Babylon over the highway of Semiramis as soon as Babylon offered a market for costly wares. These wares passed from Babylon to a Phœnician port, such as Tyre or Sidon, and thence were shipped wherever they could be exchanged for metal or slaves.

Who the Phœnicians were, and whence they came, is immaterial. Archæologists incline to the opinion that they migrated from India to the head of the Persian Gulf and thence passed on into Syria, probably always in the wake of the commerce which they loved so well. Nor did their migrations stop at Syria; a few hundred years later they had wandered to Spain by way of Utica, and founded Cadiz. The Phœnicians were the greatest explorers and metallurgists of antiquity. They penetrated every inlet and prospected in every land. They developed the resources of southern Europe and northern Africa west of Egypt, and as the sphere of Phœnician enterprise expanded, the lines of communication changed to correspond. Therefore the route across Arabia to Sinai yielded to those leading to Aradus, Tyre, and Sidon. A glance at the map will explain the situation. Nobody knows where the ancients obtained the tin with which they made bronze in the early times, for tin is not supposed to have been found in any region accessible to them. Primitive workings are, indeed, said to exist near Bamian, but the cost of transporting ore from Bamian to Egypt by caravan must have been prohibitive. A plausible theory is that before the Phœnicians reached Cornwall by sea, they dealt with the natives for tin at the mouths of such rivers as the Rhone, where it had come from England by passing from hand to hand; that they slowly traced the supply to its source, and so discovered the mines.[1]

But wherever they found their ore, the Phœnicians certainly waxed rich by their dealings in metals, and, as capital increased, ships multiplied, energy augmented, and exploration went on faster. The next step was the development of the countries bordering the Euxine, and probably expansion in this direction received its first stimulus from the discovery of gold in Lydia.

When the Lydian gold first permeated the international market can never be ascertained, but, judging by the legends, it must have been during the Babylonian supremacy. According to the myth, certain peasants having found Silenus drunk in a garden belonging to Midas, bound him with garlands of flowers and brought him to the king. Midas entertained him for some days, and then restored him to Dionysus, who in his gratitude granted Midas a wish. Midas wished to turn all he touched into gold. But in eating he turned his food into gold, so that, on the brink of starvation, Midas prayed to be saved from himself. The god ordered him to bathe at the source of the Pactolus, whose sands forthwith became gold. From this sand Crœsus afterward drew his wealth. Lydian gold opened a new market and drew trade north. Doubtless this trade first passed by Nineveh to Tarsus, and then through the Cilician Gates to Sardis by way of Philadelphia, a route which Tavernier mentioned as much used in his time; or else it may have gone up the valley of the Tigris, and over what later became the Royal Persian Road. In

[1] See *Die Geschichte des Eisens*, Beck, I., 184 *et seq.*

either case the journey through Nineveh necessitated
a long detour, the direct line to Sardis and Smyrna
from Teheran passing to the north of Lake Van,
through the modern Tabriz and Erzeroum.   But all
Armenia is mountainous and difficult, and it was the
difficulty of Armenia which ruined the Assyrian empire.   The Caucasus and Urals are rich in minerals,
and once abounded in gold.   Georgia has always
been famous for its slaves.   And as travel drew
northward toward the shortest lines of communication, these regions began to be explored not only
overland, but through such ports as Trebizond and
Sinope.   How rich this region must have been for
the early adventurers is proved by every discovery of
modern times.   Not to speak of the gold ornaments
of Panticapæum, found by the Russians, and which
belong to a later age, Schliemann's treasure would set
doubt at rest.   A generation ago, in searching for
Troy, Schliemann fell upon the lowest of six super-
imposed cities, the last of which was Ilium.   The
town Schliemann unearthed belonged to the Stone
Age, so far as useful metals were concerned, and
must have been extremely ancient, yet in this small
and barbarous community he found the hoard which
made him famous.   Beside the metals, the slaves
of Georgia and southern Russia have always been of
value.   When Chardin visited Persia in 1664, he
sailed in a slaver.

If these geographical conditions be borne in mind
the career of Nineveh is comprehensible.   Nineveh
prospered during the relatively short period when
she served as the centre of the trade passing east and
west, between Bactra, the northern ports of Syria,

Lydia, and the basin of the Black Sea. When that commerce sought cheaper routes, she fell; but while she lived, she lived only on the condition that she could hold and police the avenues running west and north. Accordingly her story is one of perpetual war. Her emperor lived in the field. The campaigns of Tiglat-Pileser I. about 1100 B.C., one of the greatest of her captains, and who achieved a suzerainty over Babylon, are typical of what happened during every reign. Tiglat-Pileser I. passed his life in warfare along the highways diverging from Nineveh toward Syria and Armenia. The fiercest fighting occurred in Armenia, in the same country where Mithradates, centuries afterward, resisted Rome.

The seasons resembled each other, but, according to Winckler, he achieved one of his most brilliant successes in the second year of his reign, when he conquered the Kummuchs, a nomadic and predatory tribe which inhabited the hills between Haran and Amida, and robbed on the road to Antioch.

In the fifth year he marched through north Mesopotamia to Aradus, and celebrated his triumph by sailing upon the open sea.[1] Nevertheless his most important victory was probably achieved in Armenia, — a victory commemorated by a column which still stands. The road from Trebizond to Nineveh skirts the base of the huge extinct volcano called Nimrud, which forms the core of the mountainous region about Lake Van, and Betlis to the south of Nimrud commands the pass leading to the plateau above. For ages the princes of Betlis maintained their independence; the last fell in 1849. Tavernier, who left

---

[1] *Geschichte Babyloniens und Assyriens*, Hugo Winckler, 175.

Paris for Persia in November, 1663, thus described their fortress : —

" Betlis is the principal town of a bey or prince of the country, the most powerful and the most considerable of all; because he recognizes neither the Sultan of Turkey nor the King of Persia, while the others all owe allegiance to one or the other. Both powers are interested in standing well with him, because on whichever side he might range himself, it would be easy for him to close the road to those who wish to take this route from Aleppo to Tabriz, or from Tabriz to Aleppo. For there are no mountain passes to be seen in the world easier to guard, and ten men will defend them against a thousand. In approaching Betlis when one comes from Aleppo, one marches an entire day between high and steep mountains which continue for two leagues beyond. And one has always on one side the torrent and on the other the mountains, the path being cut in the rock in many places, so that the camels and the mules have to walk cautiously to prevent falling into the water."

The castle stood perched on a sugar-loaf hill, so steep that it could only be reached by a zigzag, and was defended by three moats.

" The prince who commands in this place, beside being redoubtable because of this pass which cannot be forced, can put in the field twenty or twenty-five thousand horse, and a quantity of excellent infantry composed of the shepherds of the country, who are always ready at the first command." [1]

[1] *Les Six Voyages de Jean Baptiste Tavernier*, Edition of 1712. Livre 3, p. 375, 6.

To place Nineveh's commercial interests on anything approaching a solid basis, she should have conquered and held Armenia, but more especially the country round Lake Van, where the roads leading west from Tabriz and north from Nineveh crossed. The Assyrians failed; and they paid the penalty of failure.

Among the many commanders who essayed the task, perhaps Tiglat-Pileser fared best, for he not only forced the pass of Betlis, but he met the enemy on the plain of Melazkert above, and routed them at the point where the roads to Trebizond and Kars fork. There he erected the pillar which commemorates his victory.

Had the Assyrian race possessed the energy to continue the movement northward, to conquer Armenia, to extend their power along the coast to the Dardanelles, and to overrun Lydia, as the Persians did subsequently, possibly the life of the Babylonian system might have been prolonged for centuries, and the rise of Greece proportionately postponed. The fate of Asia was not so much decided at Salamis as centuries before at Van.   Assyria produced no greater warrior than Tiglat-Pileser III., and under him she made the supreme effort.   In 735 B.C. he advanced on Van, took the town, and laid siege to the citadel.   He suffered a repulse, and retreated. Then Assyria began to decline, and during the season of her decay the Greeks gained strength to resist the Persian onset when the storm broke three hundred years later.[1]

[1] For an account of the Van country, see *Armenia*, by H. F. B. Lynch, 2, 53 *et seq.*

As long as the Dardanelles remained closed, and
the Greeks were excluded from the Euxine, they lay
too far to the north to participate in the Bactra trade,
or to seriously compete with the Phœnicians. The
question of unchallenged Asiatic supremacy turned
upon command of the straits, and this both sides seem
to have understood. Even hampered as they were
by their inability to hold the roads to the northwest,
the Assyrians appear to have done their best to protect their interests. Diodorus has stated that Troy
received help from Nineveh during the siege; and
apart from Diodorus, the legend of the Argonauts
proves the danger which attended an attempt to
enter the Propontis, and leads to the inference that
Troy must have been an outwork of the Assyrian-
Phœnician combination. On their side the Greeks
showed a patience in attack perhaps unequalled in
their history. Though wonderfully gifted in many
directions, the Greeks usually lacked cohesion. Seldom, even when invaded, could they unite against an
enemy. Yet Agamemnon formed a coalition for an
aggressive campaign, and won a decisive victory.
Nor were they less successful in improving their advantage than in gaining it. All the world has heard
of the deeds of the heroes before the walls of Troy;
but very few have reflected on the genius which
raised the children of these heroes from insignificance
to supremacy in the Orient.

The Greeks excelled not only as soldiers, as artists,
as orators, and as poets, but as colonizers and financiers. Long study alone breeds an appreciation of
their marvellous aptitudes. Advancing steadily for
centuries, they wrought out a system for controlling

the roads converging on Bactra, at once comprehensive and economical. Their scanty numbers precluded extended conquests, their poverty the maintenance of great armies; they therefore limited themselves to seizing and holding the points which commanded trade. But the Greek system deserves to be followed from the beginning.

The Greeks, though intelligent and brave, were scattered and poor. Their sterile hills yielded but a precarious subsistence, their mines were undeveloped, and they eked out a slender livelihood by slaving and piracy. These conditions are reflected in their myths, which teem with their revolt against oppression and their yearning for that wealth which poured past their threshold. The exquisite tale of Theseus, who volunteered to take his place among the victims sent to Crete, that he might fight and slay the Minotaur and deliver his country from the yoke of Minos; of his victory, of his return with the black sail which was to signify his death, and of his father's agony and suicide at the sight, is the tradition of the uprising against Cretan slaving. On the other hand, we have the *Argo* penetrating the Euxine, and Jason bringing back the golden fleece from Colchis, where the Greeks afterward planted Phasis, the door to the Caspian; and last and greatest of all, Hercules, who sought, in the garden of the Hesperides, those golden apples which were to be plucked in Spain.

Stretching east from Sunium, the islands lie so close together that the longest interval of open water between Attica and Ionia is the twenty-five miles separating Myconos from Icaria. At the end of this chain of islands lies Miletus, and it was along

this causeway that Neleus, the son of Codrus, must
have passed when he founded the mother of the
Greek colonies in Asia.   Perhaps, indeed, Neleus
may have come rather as the leader of a reënforce-
ment than as the actual founder of Miletus.   Codrus
lived in 1050 B.C., which is relatively late, and the
Greek tradition seldom went back to the original
settlement, but rather chronicled the events which
dwelt in the popular imagination as the beginning of
the Golden Age.   Nevertheless, the precise date is
immaterial ; the essential fact is that no sooner had
the Greeks planted themselves firmly on the coast
than they spread along the shore, colonizing the more
important points, until at Lampsacus, at Chalcedon,
and at Byzantium they obtained control of the straits.
Probably they had previously explored the Euxine,
for they appear very early to have seized upon all the
avenues converging on the sea, by which trade could
find vent.   They built Tyras, near where Odessa now
stands, and Olbia at the entrance to the chain of
watercourses, by following which, traffic throughout the Middle Ages reached Scandinavia by the
Dnieper, the Lovat, and Lake Ladoga.   Farther east,
in the Crimea, they settled at Panticapæum, the modern Kertch, where recent excavations have yielded
the gold ornaments which are the gem of the Her-
mitage in St. Petersburg.   From Panticapæum merchants travelled to the Caspian by ascending the
Don, crossing the neck between the rivers, and
descending the Volga.   Poti is the terminus of the
Caucasian railway, whence the line leads direct to
Tiflis and Baku; but Poti occupies the site of the
ancient Phasis, as Trebizond, the port of Teheran,

does of Trapezus. Lastly came Sinope, where the roads met which led southeast to Nineveh, or Mosul, and southwest to Sardis, the capital of the kingdom of Crœsus. Yet this was but the half of what the Greeks conceived and executed. To have established connections with the East alone would not have sufficed; a market had to be secured in the West. Accordingly while Athens, Megara, and Miletus girdled the Black Sea, Corinth and Achaia stretched out to Sicily and Italy, and contemporaneously created Syracuse, Sybaris, Croton, and Tarentum — the immortal Magna Græcia.

Before the Greeks navigated the Black Sea, merchandise must have reached Sardis by caravan, probably over the road which crossed the Mæander near Hierapolis, a route described by Xenophon, and afterward by Tavernier. Miletus lay below, at the mouth of the river, and flourished not only on the trade which flowed directly to it, but also as one of the ports of Sardis. The Greeks inhabiting Miletus grew rich fast, and as they prospered pushed forward by sea toward the sources of supply, always seeking cheaper avenues of communication. In their explorations they could not have met with much opposition, for the Euxine had an infamous reputation, and the inhabitants of Asia Minor were timid sailors. Of course no caravan from Teheran can now compete with steamers on the Black Sea, but they did better when ships were frailer, and, even in the seventeenth century, Persians and Frenchmen preferred the sixty days of horseback to facing the perils of the voyage to Trebizond, which is still the port of Teheran.

The best early account of the journey east by
sea is given by Ruy Gonzalez de Clavijo, an
ambassador sent by Henry III. of Castile to Tamerlane at Samarkand. Samarkand lies in nearly
the same longitude as Bactra, only farther north,
on the other side of the Oxus, so that the journey
thither was substantially the same as that to
Balkh.

On Tuesday, the 22d of May, 1403, the embassy
embarked at Cadiz, but they did not finally leave
Spain until the 29th, when they sailed from Malaga.
Although Clavijo travelled in state, he made use of
ordinary merchantmen, so that he underwent the
delays incident to commerce, and his voyage to Trebizond may be taken as typical. From Trebizond he
rode so hard, by the command of Tamerlane, that
several of his suite died of fatigue. No caravan
could have done the like. Nevertheless he only
reached Samarkand a year from the 30th of the following August. Clavijo found both the Mediterranean and the Black seas dangerous, the Black hardly
more so than the Mediterranean, considering that he
traversed the Mediterranean in summer, and only
reached the Euxine in the middle of November. He
consumed five months in gaining Constantinople, and
more than once gave himself up for lost. For example, on July 29th, his ship drifted so near a rock
that "the captain, and some merchants and sailors,
stripped off their clothes; and, when they stood off
the shore, they understood that God had shown great
mercy." At Constantinople the ambassador waited
until November 13th for "a vessel to take them to
Trebizond; and, as the winter was approaching and

the sea very dangerous . . . they took a galliot to prevent further delay."

On the second day out, in the middle of the night, "the wind rose and the sea got up." They were lying within sight of a Genoese carrack and tried to reach her, but it blew so hard that they could not. Then they let go two anchors, but "the gale increased in a frightful way, and every person commended himself to God our Lord, for they thought they would never escape." Meanwhile the carrack "was like to run foul of the galliot; but it pleased our Lord God to succour her, and she passed without touching; and they let go the anchors of the said carrack, but they would not hold, and she drifted on shore. Before day, she had gone to pieces, so that nothing was left of her." The galliot lived through the night, and with dawn the wind changed, "and became fair for the land of Turkey." "There were few to assist in working the sail, as the greater part of the crew were more dead than alive, so that if death had really come, they would not have cared much." Finally they reached shore, but the galliot went aground and "the sea swept into her, and at intervals the swell caused by the tempest broke over her; and in the lulls the men carried the things to the land, and thus all the king's property was saved. In a very short time, however, the galliot was broken up, and her cargo was piled up in a heap."

So Clavijo returned to Pera, where they remained all winter, reaching Trebizond the 11th of April, nearly eleven months after leaving Spain.[1] Even

[1] *Narration of the Embassy of Ruy Gonzalez de Clavijo to the Court of Timour*, 53, Publications of the Hakluyt Society.

within this century, Curzon has estimated that half
the Turkish ships navigating the Black Sea were
lost annually.

Chardin, who visited Persia in 1664, did not like
Black Sea ships. " I pointed out to him that we had
neither provisions nor supplies, that the vessel was
old, that it was filled daily with slaves of both sexes
and all ages, so that one could no longer move on
her. That since morning there had arrived a large
number of Abcas and Migralians who swarmed with
vermin, and brought an infection which would en-
gender the pest, that the vessel would only sail for
Kaffa in two months, that this would be the season
of tempests, and the time when the Black Sea, that
sea so stormy and dangerous, is the most disturbed
by hurricanes." [1]

Tavernier shared these views : " Embarking from
Constantinople, one can arrive there [Trebizond]
with a favorable wind in four or five days. In this
way one can make in ten or twelve days, at slight
expense, the journey from Constantinople to Erzeroum. Some have tried this route, but they have not
found it satisfactory, and have not wished to return.
It is a very dangerous voyage, and rarely made, because this sea is full of fogs, and subject to tempests."

Each race followed its instincts, the more hardy
and adventurous gaining the advantage. Chardin
and Tavernier represented the French; and the
French, on the whole, fell steadily behind in the
Levant, where during the crusades they stood foremost. The Venetians, the Genoese, and afterward

[1] *Voyages de M. le Chevalier Chardin*, Edition of Amsterdam,
1711, 2, 11.

the English, followed the sea, and ousted their rivals who adhered to caravans. When Clavijo returned to Pera after his wreck, he found " six Venetian galleys at the great city . . . to meet the ships which were coming from Tana." And the Genoese were more active than the Venetians. The Persians always shunned the water. Tavernier mentioned that a caravan left Constantinople every two months for Persia, and the one he joined at Smyrna for Ispahan numbered twelve hundred horses and camels. The Greeks in 700 B.C. held the same advantage as the Italians of the Middle Ages, only in a greater degree. The most intelligent and enterprising of all the ancient races, they faced the danger of the voyage to Trebizond in order to benefit by its economy; and they earned their reward. In those early days central Asia was more flourishing than it ever has been since, for then none of its commerce had been diverted. When Clavijo lived, the routes were being abandoned, and yet he visited a land which, although it had been invaded, devastated, and superseded as a thoroughfare, still impressed him as opulent. For instance, the Spaniard described Nishapoor as " very large, and well supplied with all things. . . . the neighborhood is very populous and fertile " . . . where one of his suite named Gomez was lodged in a good house, and attended by the best doctors; " but it pleased God that the said Gomez should end his days at this place." Nishapoor is now a ruinous village with a population estimated at eight thousand. Tabriz, though decayed, still remains one of the most prosperous cities of Persia. " The city of Tabriz is very large and rich, owing to the quantity of merchandise that passes

through it every day.   They say that in former days
it was more populous; but even now there are more
than two hundred thousand inhabited houses.   There
are also many market-places, in which they sell very
clean and well-dressed meat, cooked in a variety of
ways, and plenty of fruit. . . .   In this city there are
many very rich and beautiful mosques, and the finest
baths that, I believe, can be seen in the whole world." [1]
Two hundred thousand inhabited houses indicated a
population approximating a million; but about 1680,
though Chardin spoke of Tabriz with enthusiasm "as
a really great and powerful city, whose commerce
extended through Persia, Muscovy, Tartary, India,
and the Black Sea," he computed that she possessed
no more than fifteen thousand dwellings, or, in other
words, that the population had shrunk to less than
one hundred thousand.   At present the buildings of
Tabriz are mean, the only remains of former grandeur
being the ruins of the Blue Mosque and the citadel.

The movement northward of the current of travel
to the road leading across Siberia to Moscow on the
one hand, and the discovery of the ocean voyage
round the Cape of Good Hope to India and China on
the other, killed this ancient civilization.   In the fifteenth century, though the revolution was in progress,
it had not been completed.   A remnant of the Indian
trade still survived.

At Sultanieh, Clavijo found that each year "very
large caravans of camels arrived, with great quantities
of merchandise. . . .   Every year many merchants
come here from India, with spices, such as cloves, nut-
megs, cinnamon, . . . and other precious articles

[1] *Embassy to Timour*, 90.

which do not go to Alexandria." [1]   When the eastern
trade split, and, to avoid the Pamirs, either passed
by sea to Europe or else went north by Siberia,
the civilization of central Asia died. Therefore,
to judge of Bactra in her prime, our only resource
is to recall what remained at Samarkand, just as
the age of splendor closed. Thus Clavijo described
a lesser palace of Tamerlane. "In the centre of the
garden there was a very beautiful house, built in the
shape of a cross, and very richly adorned with ornaments. In the middle of it there were three chambers,
for placing beds and carpets in, and the walls were
covered with glazed tiles. Opposite the entrance, in
the largest of the chambers, there was a silver gilt
table, as high as a man, and three arms broad, on the
top of which there was a bed of silk cloths, embroid-
ered with gold . . . and here the lord was seated.
The walls were hung with rose-colored silk cloths, orna-
mented with plates of silver gilt, set with emeralds,
pearls, and other precious stones, tastefully arranged.
. . . In the centre of the house, opposite the door,
there were two gold tables, each standing on four legs,
and the table and legs were all in one. They were each
five palmos long, and three broad; and seven golden
phials stood upon them, two of which were set with
large pearls, emeralds, and turquoises, and each one
had a ruby near the mouth. There were also six round
golden cups, one of which was set with large round
clear pearls, inside, and in the centre of it there was a
ruby, two fingers broad, and of a brilliant color. The
ambassadors were invited to this feast by the lord." [2]

Thus the prize for which so much blood was to be

[1] *Embassy to Timour*, 93.   [2] *Ibid.*, 136.

spilled, and the paths along which that prize had to be sought, become visible. Twelve hundred years before Christ, Asiatics and Europeans began their struggle for the control of the avenues of the eastern trade which radiated from Bactra. The Assyrians met defeat in Armenia and perished. The Greeks forced the Dardanelles and opened the Euxine. The gold of Lydia drew commerce overland toward the Mæander, at whose mouth, near where the caravans halted, the Greeks made their first lodgment on the continent. From Miletus, spreading north and eastward, always reaching out toward the sources of supply, the Greeks girdled the basin of the Black Sea until they held every outlet in their hands, the whole system of traffic converging on the isthmus of Corinth.

Toward the end of the seventh century before Christ the work appears to have been completed, and when the complex yet elastic mechanism operated, its shock proved resistless. Forthwith Nineveh and Babylon, being undersold, languished, and by 650 the prophet Nahum pronounced his diatribe: "Woe to the bloody city! Nineveh is laid waste; who will bemoan her?" In 606 Nineveh fell, never to rise again; and when, two hundred years later, Xenophon passed her crumbling walls, her very name had been forgotten. Babylon fared little better. In 538 Belshazzar, when feasting, read the handwriting on the wall; that same night he died; and thenceforward the Persians ruled in Chaldea. Thus the vitality of Mesopotamia ebbed, for the life-blood no longer ran through the arteries which centred at her heart. But as the same life-blood which had once invigorated Asia permeated Greece, she blossomed like the rose, and as no doom has ever quite had the terror of the doom of Nineveh, so no bloom has ever equalled the flowering of Hellas. Almost within a generation the peninsula stood transfigured. During the Mycenæan Age, Greece, like other predatory communities, had been subject to a military caste, whose castles dominated the towns, — grim strongholds like Tiryns, the lairs of the pirate and the slaver. With the opening of the trade routes east and west, the aspect of civilization changed. Tradition has preserved the memory of the so-called Doric invasion; but this invasion may not improbably have been the democratic revolution, which, beginning in the north, swept gradually through the Peloponnesus. Certainly a social upheaval followed upon the rise of a trading class; and as this class waxed rich and powerful, the palace vanished from the acropolis, and in its stead appeared the temple, that exquisite civic decoration, which transformed the warriors' donjon into the public pleasure-ground.

As usual, in Greece as elsewhere, architecture, for him who will read the language of the stones, tells the tale of civilization more eloquently than any written book. When thus read, among all the stones of Greece, none speak more movingly than those noble columns which still stand upon the shore of the Gulf of Corinth. On either side of the isthmus, Ægina and Corinth were the two ports where ships discharged their freight, and these two towns were accordingly the first in Hellas to feel the exhilaration of success. Therefore, at Ægina and Corinth the oldest temples still stand to reveal to us the secret

of their birth.   Long before Athens dreamed of supremacy at sea, Corinth had achieved maritime greatness, and the Corinthians furnished the Athenians
with the ships to destroy their enemy Ægina, an
enemy whom Corinth afterward would gladly have
resuscitated.   Originally, doubtless, like Mycenæ,
Corinth had a king who lived in a castle perched
upon the mountain which overhangs the bay.   Certainly a castle stood there for ages after classic Corinth
died, and probably ruins of the archaic fortress would
be found embedded amidst the walls of the mediæval
keep, could the Acro-Corinth be excavated.   Were
those remains found, what must now be presented as
an historical theory would be demonstrated as a fact.
The first effect of the democratic revolution at
Corinth must have been to bring down the population from the mountain to the shore, then the castle
crumbled, and in its stead arose those monolithic
columns, which remain one of the most impressive
memorials in the world.   For, from the building of
that temple we must date the birth of the civilization
we now behold about us, and with the building of
that temple opened the struggle for survival of
Babylon, Tyre, and Carthage, with Greece and Rome,
which only ended with the victory of Alexander over
Darius, and of Scipio over Hannibal.

When the temple of Corinth arose, Mesopotamia
was already sinking, and Darius, when he succeeded
Belshazzar, could no more withstand his destiny than
a log can withstand the torrent of the Mississippi.
When two economic systems compete, they are apt
either to consolidate or to fight; and between Greece
and Asia commercial rivalry had reached an inten-

sity which engenders war. The convulsion which was to last two centuries began, in 546, B.C. with the attack of Cyrus on Lydia and the defeat of Crœsus. The Persians succeeded where the Assyrians failed, and absorbed Asia Minor. Then Darius invaded Russia, an expedition only to be accounted for on the theory that he intended to cut off the Greek cities on the northern coast of the Euxine from the interior. To accomplish this, he perhaps attempted to occupy the narrow neck of land between the Volga and the Don,[1] for by ascending the Volga and descending the Don, commerce passed from the Caspian to the Sea of Azov. From this source Pantica-pæum, the chief of these northern cities, drew her wealth.

Defeated in Scythia, Darius invaded Greece. In 505 B.C. he overran Imbros and Lemnos, captured Chalcedon, and occupied both shores of the Bosphorus. Then the Ionian cities revolted, and Miletus was sacked. In 490 B.C. Darius pushed forward a reconnaissance to Marathon, and met with a reverse. Appreciating the gravity of the crisis, he withdrew, and began those preparations which recall the effort of Philip II. to fit out the Armada. In the midst of his labor he died. His death, however, altered nothing. Herodotus ascribed to Xerxes only the conviction of his contemporaries, when he made him answer in these words the remonstrance of Artabanus against the prosecution of his father's enterprise : —

" It is not possible for either party to retreat, but

---

[1] See the maps and comments in *The Geographical System of Herodotus*, James Rennell, 1, 133 *et seq.*

D

the alternative lies before us to do or to suffer; so that all these dominions must fall under the power of the Grecians, or all theirs under that of the Persians; for there is no medium in this enmity." [1]

In 485 B.C., when Xerxes came to the throne, the Babylonian economic system formed, as it were, a segment of the periphery of a vast ellipse, of which the Greek markets at the isthmus of Corinth and at Syracuse were the *foci*. Along the periphery of this ellipse were ranged many peoples inhabiting the region stretching from the Oxus to Gibraltar, and including Bactra, the Punjab, Persia, Mesopotamia, Phœnicia, Egypt, North Africa, and part of Spain; practically the Saracenic dominions of the Middle Ages, only more extended toward the east. This vast mass, though politically unconsolidated, was sufficiently stimulated by a common danger to cast itself, at a given moment, on its foe. The Persians invaded Greece Proper, the Carthaginians attacked Sicily, and the battles of Salamis and Himera are said to have been fought upon the same day. Certainly they formed parts of a single campaign, and the defeat of Xerxes by Themistocles, and of Hamilcar by Gelon, pierced the centre of the coalition. Then the wings fell asunder, and the work of destroying the vanquished in detail began. As between the two wings, the Babylonian and Carthaginian, the latter showed more vitality, for Carthage drew her nutriment from the mines of Spain, while Mesopotamia existed solely as a centre of exchanges. How rapidly Asia sank may be measured by her loss of military energy. The Greeks thought their success

1 Herod. vii. 11.

at Platæa in 479 extraordinary, although they admitted putting in the field upward of 110,000 men, of whom 39,000 were hoplites, against the 300,000 light-armed troops led by Mardonius, and the Greeks did not underestimate their prowess. Likewise, the Persians were exhausted by a painful journey, and a winter in an inhospitable land. Only eighty years later Xenophon marched with 10,000 mercenaries from Sardis to Babylon, and from Babylon to Trapezus.

During this period of eighty years the fortunes of Hellas culminated. Greece failed to consolidate at this juncture, and expand vigorously westward, partly, no doubt, because of the Greek inaptitude for political administration, but chiefly because of her physical conformation. The lines of trade crossed her diagonally and not longitudinally, so that her provinces had few or no common material interests. Furthermore, while her commercial centre lay at the isthmus of Corinth, which was the cheapest point in the basin of the Ægæum for the distribution of cargoes bound west, her industrial centre was situated at the silver mines of Laurium, near Cape Sunium. Accordingly, the interests of Athens and Corinth were antagonistic, as the Athenian commerce lay to the east and the Corinthian to the west, and formed two distinct and competing commercial systems.

Moreover, Athens could not conquer Corinth, not only because Corinth occupied a strong position on the other side of the isthmus, almost unassailable by Athens either by land or water, but because Corinth served as a rampart to Sparta; and Sparta could not let her be destroyed for fear of disaster to

herself.   Therefore, two irreconcilable economic systems overthrew each other.   Athens impinged on
Corinth; and Corinth, retaliating, allied herself with
Sparta.   The Peloponnesian War ensued as a logical
effect, and the expedition against Syracuse formed
an episode of the Peloponnesian War.   The loss
of the army of Nicias in 413, and the defeat of
Ægospotamus in 405 B.C., together with the gradual
failure of the silver of Laurium, exhausted the
Athenian vitality, and with the decline of Athens the
dream of Greek expansion toward the west ended.

But although the vitality of ancient Hellas flickered
low after the Peloponnesian War, Macedon retained
her vigor, largely because she possessed richer mines
than Attica.   In 356 Philip annexed Thrace up to
the Nestus, founding the city of Philippi in the heart
of the region about Mount Pangeus, where lay the
gold.   This gold Philip worked so successfully that
he obtained a yearly revenue of 1,000 talents, or tenfold the return of Laurium to Athens at the time of
Salamis; and before the death of Alexander the total
yield had exceeded 30,000 talents.   Fortified with
this treasure, Alexander invaded Asia.   Alexander is,
perhaps, the highest specimen of the Greek intellect,
astonishing alike in its strength and weakness.   Unrivalled as an economic conception, his empire failed
as an administrative mechanism.   In approaching his
task he showed a profound knowledge and appreciation of the geographical conditions which governed
the relations between Asia and Europe, but in execu-
tion his structure, like all efforts of classic Greeks at
centralization, lacked cohesion.

Of the five avenues in use at Alexander's birth,

between central Asia and the Mediterranean, Persia controlled all but the Euxine, for the ocean voyage to Egypt had not been attempted. All of these Alexander undertook to concentrate in a single system, and, besides, to open direct communication between India and the Nile by sea.

Starting from his base upon the Hellespont Alexander's first task was to isolate Persia by crushing Phœnicia, the ancient maritime rival of Greece, who had made Persia formidable at Salamis by furnishing her with ships. This he accomplished, after defeating Darius at Issus, by the siege and capture of Tyre, possibly the most extraordinary feat in his extraordinary career. After subjugating Phœnicia he proceeded to the Nile, examined the delta, and selected Alexandria as the best outlet for the southern water-route which he contemplated. The experience of two thousand years has justified his judgment. This done, he turned toward the interior. His problem was to consolidate the avenues of communication; to do so he marched entirely round the vast triangle in central Asia whose base is formed by a line drawn from Bactra to Pattala and whose apex lies at Babylon. Crossing the Euphrates at Thapsacus, he moved on Nineveh by Haran, over the ground which had been disputed for centuries by the Assyrians; and having defeated Darius at Arbela, he advanced south as far as Persepolis. Thence turning north, he marched by Ecbatana on Ragae, finally reaching Samarkand. He passed the winter of 328 at Bactra, and, in the spring, ventured to invade India by the series of passes which begin with Bamian and end with the

Khyber, following the road by Kabul, even yet imperfectly known to Europeans. Incredible as it seems, he gained the Indus with small loss, and, having vanquished Porus on the Hydaspes, pacified the Punjab, and in 326 B.C. descended the river to the delta. There dividing his force, he sent Nearchus to explore the Arabian Sea, while he proceeded to Babylon by way of Susa. He established police by building cities at strategic points along the roads, sometimes but a day's journey from each other.

Nothing can be more fatuous than to regard the campaigns of soldiers like Alexander, Cæsar, or Jenghiz Khan as the result of ambition or caprice; for the soldier is a natural force, like the flood or the whirlwind. He breaks down obstructions otherwise insuperable. Alexander's battles were but an incident in a process which only ended with Actium. His function was to centralize; and that he understood his destiny is clear from his answer to the embassy sent him by Darius during the siege of Tyre: "As it would be impossible for order to reign in the world with two suns, so it is impossible for the earth to be at peace with two masters."

Alexander dealt with converging economic systems which, because they converged, could be consolidated. As usual under such circumstances, social amalgamation preceded political unification, and a fusion of commercial interests laid the basis of the Roman Empire. This is proved by the voluntary reform of the coinage under Alexander, as well as by the spread of the Greek language throughout the Levant.

Among the many debts which civilization owes the Greeks, none is deeper than that due for the invention of the coinage; for whether money was first struck in Lydia or Ægina, the conception of a currency is Greek and not Asiatic. Indeed, the Asiatic races never accepted the coinage kindly, for the Asiatics have always been slow; and perhaps the introduction of a currency accelerated social movement more powerfully than any innovation during the historic period of antiquity. By a currency commercial transfers are made cheap and rapid, and international banking on a large scale becomes possible. To work well, however, the currency should be uniform, as the fluctuations of various standards entail loss in exchange. Under the archaic system each city struck its own money, — the disadvantage whereof the Greeks soon perceived; and one of the greatest triumphs of the Greek mind was the adoption of a common standard of value under Alexander; an achievement to be attributed to voluntary and intelligent coöperation, and not to physical force.

Throughout Alexander's nominal dominions, many of the most opulent cities retained their privileges, the coinage among the rest; especially in Thrace, Asia Minor, and Phœnicia. These cities struck the imperial tetradrachma, by their own authority, and for their own convenience, and maintained the standard long after Alexander's death.[1] Modern Europe has not yet done as much.

Under the conditions which prevailed in ancient times, expansion ended with the establishment of the Roman Empire, and with the termination of expansion an equilibrium between the East and West could not be long maintained. The reason is obvious. The

[1] *Numismatique d'Alexandre le Grand*, L. Muller, 91.

Romans, though great soldiers and administrators, were uninventive. They never learned to manufacture any article which commanded the Oriental market and served as a means of balancing their purchases. Neither did they explore, or improve their ships. Therefore the Mediterranean remained always, for them, a closed ellipse, not rich enough in metal to sustain a prolonged drain, especially under the wasteful Roman methods. This ellipse, divided into three basins by the peninsulas of Greece and Italy, varied in resources, the central basin being poor. Development, accordingly, began at the extreme east, probably first in Cyprus and afterward in Lydia, and for many centuries remained in the hands of Asiatics. At length the Greeks began to compete, and, settling at the mouth of the Mæander, they gradually concentrated transportation in their hands.

If a line be drawn north and south through Miletus, it bisects the ancient civilization according to its aptitudes. To the east of that line lay the lands which led in agriculture and industries; to the west, those producing minerals and soldiers. Egypt, for example, grew grain at a profit, at prices which exterminated the Italian farmers; Egypt, Phœnicia, India, and China readily undersold Europe in manufactures; while spices, gems, and perfumes were a natural monopoly of Arabia, India, and Ceylon. These commodities were coveted by Greeks and Romans; but Greeks and Romans could offer nothing in exchange which Orientals would accept, save metals, and consequently metals flowed eastward; a fact proved by the abundance of Athenian coins found in Asia, as well as by the statements of Pliny.

Under such conditions the basin of the Ægæum
became the seat of empire, because it not only afforded,
for several centuries, the most convenient market for
merchandise consigned westward, but it furnished
metals for exchange and soldiers for police.

Copper came from Cyprus, close at hand; iron
from the Euxine, from Bithynia, Pontus, and the
Caucasus. The Urals, then as now, were rich in
minerals, and every Greek city east of the Azov sent
caravans into the interior to buy.[1] Herodotus stated
that for such an expedition ten interpreters were
needed. More important still, the whole coast of the
Ægæum teemed with gold and silver. Lydia yielded
gold and electrum, Attica silver, and Macedon gold.
Therefore, commerce tended to discharge through
the Dardanelles in a stream which, passing over the
isthmus of Corinth, flowed west by Sicily toward
north Italy, Gaul, and Spain.

These conditions lasted until the demand on the
resources of the country became too great to be supplied by the mines of so limited a region, and recourse
was had to Spain.

Then, as mineral production moved westward, the
central market moved to correspond. Conceivably,
it might have grown up at almost any point in the
middle basin; at Carthage, at Syracuse, or at Rome.
Rome probably prevailed, not only because of the
superior military quality of her people, but because
of the relatively large territory tributary to her; a
territory which even then may have extended to the
North Sea. The bronzes found along the roads indicate an extensive trade. Yet wherever the central

[1] *Die Geschichte des Eisens*, Beck, I., 275, 6.

market might have been, there could have been
but one, for the lines of transportation converged
at a single point in Spain, and Spain could not have
remained under a divided ownership. The cost would
have been too great. One rival or the other must
have perished. Even the burden of one empire
proved too heavy to be borne. It had hardly come
into being before decay began.

A single administrative system, with a machinery
complex enough to police roads, administer justice,
and unify the coinage, is an economy provided the
revenue to be administered is commensurate with the
charges of administration. But the expense of centralized administration, always great, in ancient times
was crushing because of the narrowness of commercial
exchanges. The resources of the East were exhaust-
less, those of the West limited because of industrial
incapacity and the failure to expand beyond the
Rhine in search of metal. Had rivalry in Spain
necessitated a double political organization, the decay
of the West would have been almost immediate,
possibly as rapid as the collapse of Alexander's empire.

In fact, the Romans expelled the Carthaginians
from the Iberian peninsula in 207 B.C., and thenceforward hardly met with serious resistance, because
they alone had the means of organizing a competent
army. Then Rome gradually culminated. She appears to have reached her meridian before she had
spent all the plunder brought from Gaul by Cæsar, or
near the opening of the Christian era. The precise
date is immaterial, for the period of equilibrium was
short, and the decline, once begun, rapid. In the

year 9, after the defeat of Varus, Augustus could not replace the army the Germans had destroyed; and under Trajan, toward 100, an agricultural crisis prevailed, which lasted until the end. A century later silver had grown so scarce that the currency could not be sustained, and toward 220 A.D. the government of Elagabalus repudiated. In 284 A.D. Diocletian withdrew the capital to the shore of the Propontis, and Rome ceased to be a general market.

The dominant market receded, precisely as it had advanced, in the wake of commercial exchanges; and commercial exchanges ceased to be possible, on a large scale, in the Mediterranean countries after the mines had failed. When no income remained to be administered, the machinery of administration passed out of existence. There was no barbarian conquest. There was a resolution of an economic consolidation into its elements.

Lastly, as the cohesive energy waned and the provinces fell asunder, the archaic conditions revived. Competition reopened, and three empires once more appeared upon the three main highways leading from east to west. One rose on the Tigris, one on the Bosphorus, and one on the Nile, and amidst the wars between the Persians, the Byzantines, and the Saracens the Middle Ages dawned.

CHAPTER II

THE Western Empire died because the predominant race in the basin of the Mediterranean failed, after the opening of the Christian era, to develop the qualities necessary for survival under the conditions which then prevailed. The struggle for supremacy, among the Phœnicians, the Greeks, and the Romans, had lasted for upward of one thousand years. The Phœnicians had succumbed rather early in the conflict; the Greeks, though highly gifted in many directions, lacked the administrative energy which alone creates social cohesion; while the Latins, excelling as administrators and soldiers, were intellectually inflexible.

This rigidity wrought their destruction. Although, soon after their career of plunder closed, it became evident that nothing but expansion and industries could save them from annihilation, the Latins made no serious effort. On the contrary, when their armies met with a decisive check in Germany, they resigned themselves to starvation, without relaxing their contemptuous intolerance of the arts as a means of subsistence for freemen. As explorers they did little more than tread in the footsteps of their predecessors; and though they worked the Spanish ores for six hundred years, it is doubtful whether they ever improved the methods bequeathed them by the Carthaginians.

44

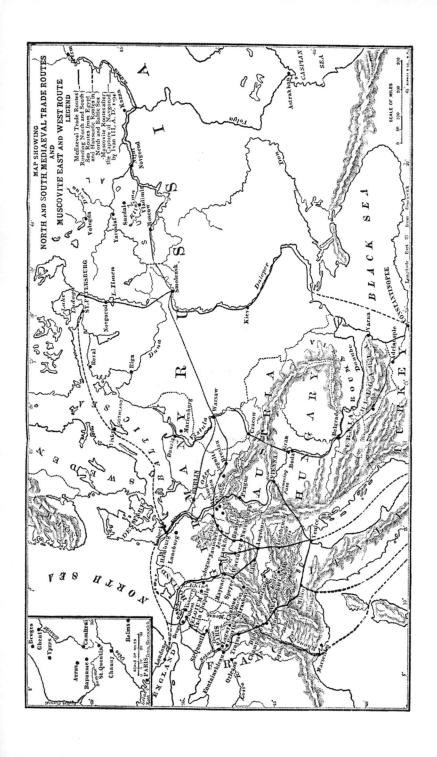

MAP SHOWING
NORTH AND SOUTH MEDIAEVAL TRADE ROUTES
AND
MUSCOVITE EAST AND WEST ROUTE
LEGEND

Mediaeval Trade Routes
Running North and South ━━━
Sea Routes from Egypt
and Hanseatic Routes in
North and Baltic Sea ━ ━ ━
Muscovite Routes after
the Capture of Novgorod
by Ivan III, A.D. 1494 ┄┄┄

There could have been no reason, save incompetence, why England should not have yielded wool as fine under the Cæsars as under the Carlovingians; the Gauls wove good cloths, although no one put them on the eastern market. Pliny, and the men of his generation, knew and lamented the drain of metal to the East, and yet no one could suggest a commodity wherewith to make exchange. A civilization thus wasteful fell, a race thus incapable perished, and Nature addressed herself to developing a new type. In about six centuries she achieved her task; but, as the mediæval mind was moulded by the conditions which created it, a glance at European geography should precede a survey of European history.

Throughout the Middle Ages very small streams were used for transportation, because of the cost of land carriage; therefore the flow of the rivers determined the lines of travel and the shape of empires.

In reality Europe and Asia form but a single continent, Europe being a long, narrow, and indented peninsula, thrust out from the vast mass of Asia. The almost imperceptible rise of the Urals can hardly be considered a scientific boundary, but, assuming that Europe stretches eastward as far as the modern maps indicate, the core of the continent will be found to be divided into three transverse sections by waterways which do not converge.

First, a network of rivers connects the Caspian and Black Seas with the Arctic Ocean and the Baltic. The same rivers, with their lateral branches, may be navigated almost as conveniently east and west, and taken thus they unite the Urals with the Gulf of Finland. This region is Russia.

Second, from the mountains which form the backbone of Europe, four streams flow north into the Baltic and the North Sea; the Oder, the Elbe, the Weser, and the Rhine. As the valleys of these rivers are nearly parallel, the inhabitants during the Middle Ages had no very intimate relations with each other because relatively little commerce passed from valley to valley. Consequently Germany did not centralize before the invention of the locomotive.

Lastly, at the end of the peninsula, the Seine, the Rhone and Saône, and the Loire, emptying into the English Channel, the Gulf of Lyons, and the Atlantic, converge toward their sources. Therefore France early consolidated.

Spain and England lay isolated, and, for present purposes, may be ignored. It suffices to observe, that neither Spain, England, nor Italy were so situated that amalgamation was possible, either among themselves, or with the economic systems of the rest of the continent.

Scientifically speaking, with the Vistula begins the isthmus which connects Europe with Asia. This isthmus comprises the region between the rivers which join the Black Sea and the Baltic; that is to say, the region between the Danube, south and east of Buda, and the Vistula, or the Dniester and the Vistula, on the west, and the Dnieper, the Lovat, the Volkhoff, Lake Ladoga, and the Neva, on the east. This isthmus, shaped somewhat like a triangle, has its apex on the Black Sea between Odessa and Kherson, with a base extending from Dantzic to Petersburg. It contained, if the Dniester be taken as the western boundary, Poland, Lithuania, the possessions of the Teutonic knights, and Novgorod, to which must be added Hungary, as far as Pesth, if that boundary be extended to the Danube.

To the east of the Dnieper and the Lovat stretched the wastes of Russia, closed to the north, and traversed by the network of rivers which, emptying into the Azov, the Caspian, or the Arctic, may be navigated almost without interruption as far east as Lake Baikal. Russia, therefore, between the Volga and the Vistula, but more especially between the Dnieper and the Vistula, may be regarded as a debatable land sometimes adhering to Europe and sometimes to Asia.

Men expressly evolved to replace others who have perished through incompetence usually display strength where their predecessors have been weak, and so it proved in the Middle Ages. No modern nation like the Latins has won supremacy purely by arms; modern success has been achieved rather by technical ingenuity, genius for exploration, and mental flexibility.

These characteristics appeared at the outset. The mediæval city grew from the guild, and the first efforts to accumulate capital took the shape of manufacturing for export. Long before the discovery of the German mines Flemings wove the English wool, and Flemish cloths sold in Bagdad. Charlemagne advertised them throughout central Asia by sending them as gifts to Haroun-al-Rashid. He did nothing for other manufactures. He chose horses and dogs for the remainder of his presents.

The probability is that most of the revenue which Charlemagne relied on to support his administration came from the woollen trade, and that the industry could not bear the taxation is demonstrated by the collapse of the empire. The raw material, grown in England, crossed the Channel to Bruges, and the manufactured product either passed up the Scheldt and through Champagne to the Rhone, or else reached Cologne by land and Mayence by the Rhine. At Mayence the Flemings established their chief selling agency, and sent their goods into Italy, either up the Rhine to Basel and Lausanne, and over the Great St. Bernard to Genoa or Milan; or else by Constance, Coire, and the Septimer. Little or nothing went by Ratisbon before the crusades, as the Huns closed the Danube.[1] The line of the imperial custom-houses ran through Magdeburg, Erfurt, Hallstadt, Forchheim, Pfreimt, Ratisbon, and Lorch. The heart of the organism lay at Aix-la-Chapelle, about midway between the French and the Rhenish waterways. It could hardly have done so had not the Flemish industries been the chief source of wealth, and the Rhine and the Meuse the chief arteries of commerce.

The vices of such a consolidation speak for themselves. In the first place, the length of road to be guarded was out of all proportion to the traffic. In the second, as the lines of communication diverged, centralized defence was impossible. Each province needed its own army, for all were exposed. The Elbe could not be fortified, and yet beyond the Elbe roved the Huns, the Wends, and other ferocious Slavs, while, to the north, Scandinavia poured forth

[1] *Histoire du Commerce du Levant*, Heyd, French translation, I., 86.

fleets of pirates, who sailed up the rivers, robbing and burning to the gates of Paris. Yet even the Vikings were less alarming than the Saracens, who swarmed in the Mediterranean, and penetrated to the heart of the Alps, where they put all commerce to ransom. Even as late as 970, during the reign of Otho the Great, when a relatively wealthy government labored to suppress marauding, the Moslems attacked strong caravans. In that year Majolus, abbot of the famous convent of Cluny, had travelled to Italy over the Septimer, rather than run the risk of brigands on the western passes. In haste to return, he made the Great St. Bernard, and, in his descent into France, had reached the bridge of Orsières, when the Saracens overtook him and carried him and all his suite into captivity.

No one understood the situation so well as Charlemagne, who dealt with it, and the monk of St. Gall has described him weeping, on the coast of the English Channel, at the sight of the Norse ships. He wept at the thought of the woes to fall upon his posterity, for he knew that, with the resources at hand, resistance would be futile.

Civilization could only receive an adequate impulsion from the discovery of minerals, which would balance exchanges and place production upon a firm basis, and no metals could be obtained until the line of the Elbe should be guarded. The core of Germany lies between the Rhine and the Elbe, for there have been found the chief of the metals which have made her wealth. Close to the Elbe, and exposed to any sudden raid, stand the Harz Mountains, in whose midst rises the Rammelsberg, long the richest silver-

bearing region of Europe ; while on the higher Elbe,
just where the river forces its way through the Bohemian Mountains, are the Erzgebirge, the district of
which Freiberg is the capital, and which by the twelfth
century had attained its highest relative importance.
In the silver and copper mines of the Tyrol, also,
thirty thousand miners are said to have found employment at about this period.

Nobody knows precisely when the Rammelsberg
was opened.   According to the legend a huntsman of
Otho the Great, who had ridden a restive horse from
Harzburg, noticed that the animal had uncovered a
vein of ore by his pawing.   The emperor, afterward
hearing of the discovery, became convinced of its
value, and sank the first shaft.   He then founded
Goslar.   The probability is that the industry was
older, and that it lent Henry the Fowler the energy
to garrison his frontier.   For the mediæval city was
at once a factory and a garrison.   Every burgher
belonged to a guild, and yet every burgher was also,
by necessity, an excellent soldier, at least in all that
touched the defence of his walls.   The Harz formed
the heart of Henry's new kingdom.   He turned the
clump of hills into a citadel.   After he had done so,
modern civilization dawned.   When, in 912, Henry I.
succeeded his father as Duke of Saxony, society
seemed sinking into chaos.   In 924 Henry fortified
Quedlinburg, which afterward served as his capital,
and fifty years later his son died emperor of Germany, the greatest sovereign of his age.

Goslar, which lies on the northern slope of the
Harz, and which owed its consequence to the Rammelsberg mines, was certainly one of the oldest free

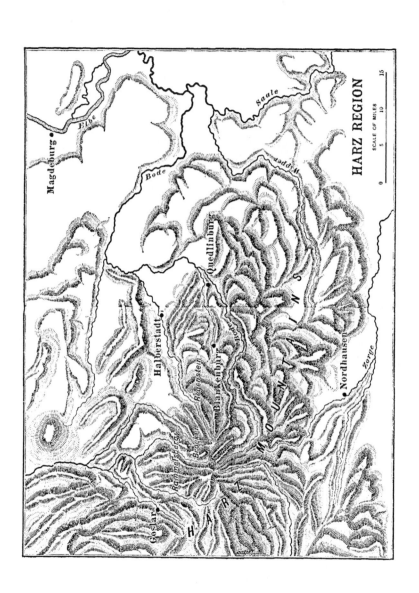

HARZ REGION

SCALE OF MILES

0   5   10   15

Magdeburg

Elbe

Saale

Bode

Wipper

Quedlinburg

Halberstadt

Blankenburg

Regenstein

Nordhausen

Zorge

Bodethal

Rammelsberg

Goslar

H A R Z

M O U N T A I N S

imperial cities of Germany. Possibly it may have
been nominally founded by Otho; but, if no mining
existed there earlier, it is difficult to comprehend his
father's policy. Henry planted a castle at Goslar,
he built a tower at Regenstein in 919, toward the east,
and he constructed the stronghold of Nordhausen, on
the southwest, guarding the approach to the Rammelsberg along the Zorge; while directly in the face of
the Wends he planted his capital of Quedlinburg,
the centre of his military organization, from whence
he conducted his campaigns. His policy was to
make good the line of the Elbe as far as the Erzgebirge, and to this end he invaded Bohemia, and reduced the duke to a tributary. He also defeated the
Slavs toward the Oder, and established two fortresses, one at Meissen and one higher up the river, to
overawe southern Saxony. Before the death of his
son, a chain of cities from Lüneburg to Freiburg commanded the frontier, the mines were regularly worked,
the Elbe could be used as a highway, and the rest was
but a matter of time.

The sequence of cause and effect is plain. When
virgin mines of precious metal began yielding plenti-
fully, Europe came into possession of a portable
commodity of universal exchangeable value, at a comparatively low cost. Consequently Europeans could
trade at a profit, and, as capital augmented and industry
gathered energy, the cost of policing the thoroughfares bore a regularly diminishing ratio to the profit
earned by the traffic passing over them. The process
was automatic, and can be gauged by the growth of
the ports, and the cities at the cross-roads.

Otho the Great died in 973, and assuming that the

mines of the Rammelsberg came into full operation
during his life, the stimulus should have been felt
within about a generation, or toward 1000.   Of course
the movement would have been most sensible at
Venice, the port of Germany, whence the streams of
commerce diverged which passed down both the Elbe
and the Rhine.   This *a priori* theory corresponds
with the facts.

Venice rose to the dignity of a considerable maritime power under Pietro Orseolo II., in 991.   Orseolo
not only negotiated commercial treaties with the
Saracenic courts at Aleppo, Cairo, Damascus, and
Palermo, but he forced the Greek emperor to reduce
the tax on vessels passing Abydos.   In the year 1000
he defeated the Croatian pirates, and thenceforward
Venice held undisputed control of the Adriatic.   In
the tenth century, also, Augsburg, the converging
point of the roads between South Germany and Italy,
first built a wall.   A low wall, it is true, and without
towers, but strong enough to twice bid defiance to the
Huns.   In 1050 occurs the earliest reference to Nuremberg, when the Emperor Henry III. held a diet
there.   Had Nuremberg been wealthy, it would have
been famous long before.   About the same period
Leipsic came into notice, but seems to have grown
rather slowly, for it was not until 1170 that the town
obtained her first considerable grant of privileges.

According to Beck,[1] German weapons were exported to India.   Cologne was the base of the trade
to the west, as Lübeck was of the trade to the east.
The commerce of the Rhine was, of course, always
more important than the commerce of the Elbe, in

[1] *Geschichte des Eisens*, I., 745.

proportion as Flanders and England outweighed
Sweden and Russia ; Cologne, accordingly, developed
early. By 1000 A.D. she had her guild-hall in London, which formed the nucleus to which other German
cities, especially Regensburg and Bremen, adhered.
From this counter as a core grew the German guild-
hall, called the Steelyard, in upper Thames Street,
near London Bridge, which long continued one of
the most powerful of the London corporations.[1]
The Hanse merchants for several centuries almost
monopolized the carrying trade of the kingdom, besides being very influential bankers. Before 1016
the emperor's subjects had secured the rights of
Englishmen in the courts. About 1040 the English
wool trade raised Bruges to the rank of a universal
market, and weaving spread over the north of France,
St. Quentin acquiring a charter near 1089. Equal
activity reigned in the Baltic. Although the Germans
did not obtain undisputed control of the lower Elbe
until after the founding of Lübeck in 1143, and possibly even of New Hamburg in 1189, commerce flowed
through such Slavish ports as Jumne on the Oder
and Dantzic on the Vistula. Written records fail, but
the quantity of coins found buried in Sweden, and
more particularly at Wisby in the Island of Gotland,
prove the diffusion of the new silver. Not less than
ten thousand German coins have been found in these
regions, belonging to the century and a half which
followed the opening of the Rammelsberg mines,
those of the reign of Otho III., from 983 to 1001,
predominating.[2]

[1] *Die Geschichte des Eisens*, Beck, I., 745, 746.
[2] *Die Hensestädte und König Waldemar von Dänemark*, Schäfer, 39.

An energetic social movement is usually equivalent
to expansion ; and as the Atlantic barred migration
westward, Europeans invaded Asia, both by way of
the Mediterranean and the Baltic. The age being one
of faith, the movement took a religious shape, beginning with the Council of Clermont in 1095, and last-
ing upward of two centuries. As a civilizing agent,
the importance of the crusades cannot be overesti-
mated ; since, though the Franks finally met with defeat, the war proved a powerful intellectual stimulant,
and also exceedingly profitable.

The Saracens had advanced farther in the arts
than the Latin Christians, and served as schoolmas-
ters, besides learning to be excellent customers. The
wealth of Egypt threw upon her the chief burden of
the Frankish wars, but Egypt produced neither iron,
nor timber for ships, nor a martial population, and she
had to buy all this material from her enemies. The
caliphs lowered their tariffs, making special rates
for Christians ; and, though the avarice which
tempted the Venetians and the Genoese to succor
their enemies roused the scorn of Moslems, they nevertheless recruited their Mamelukes with Christian
slaves, armed them with swords forged by Italians
and Germans, and built their navies with Dalmatian
timber.

Germany served as Egypt's base of supplies.
At Venice the Germans established their southern
counting-house, corresponding to the Steelyard in
London, and called the Fondaco dei Tedeschi. In
the magazines of the Fondaco the merchants of
Nuremberg, Augsburg, Ulm, Constance, and Vienna
stored their wares, consisting largely of iron, copper,

and woollens for export; and spices, silks, carpets, and the like for import. In the courts were loaded caravans for the Brenner or the St. Gotthard. The industries of southern Germany and Italy flourished. The fame of Nuremberg as a manufacturing town spread far and wide. Her smiths had no superiors north of the Alps. They forged not only weapons but peaceful implements, and through the technical skill of her metal workers Nuremberg made her chief contribution to civilization. Yet Nuremberg yielded to Milan in industries, and, during the first crusade, no soldier thought himself perfectly equipped without a Milanese sword and armor.

Although this estimate of the effects which followed the working of the Harz and Saxon mines may seem exaggerated, the evidence is overwhelming that, down to the close of the Middle Ages, minerals lay not only at the base of the German industrial system, but at the root of German wealth. In the last quarter of the fifteenth century the capitalists of southern Germany outranked even the Italian, and in Augsburg and Nuremberg all men of enterprise speculated in mines. The famous patrician house of Welser owned shares in the silver works at Schneeberg, near the Bohemian frontier; the Nuremberg families of Führer and Schlüsselfelder carried on the copper works of Eisleben, between Halle and Nordhausen, and, in conjunction with these, a refining establishment near Arnstedt in Thuringia; Peter Rummel held silver mines in Tyrol, Lucas Semler, smelters in Silesia. In 1482 George Holzschuher and Ulrich Erkel of Nuremberg obtained the monopoly of supplying Bern with the silver for coinage, while Holzschuher managed the

mint.[1]   The list might be prolonged, but to little purpose, for these names, though once noted, have been
forgotten.   One family of Augsburg bankers is, however, still remembered ; and, to prove the part played
by metals in finance down to the Reformation, it is
only needful to tell the story of the Fuggers.   To
do them justice requires a review of above two
hundred years.   Old Hans Fugger, the first known
of the race, being a journeyman weaver, left his village of Graben, in 1367, to seek his fortune in
Augsburg.   By thrift and diligence he advanced in
the world, and died, in 1409, worth 3000 florins.
None of his sons particularly distinguished themselves.   Andrew, at one time the most prosperous,
left descendants who became bankrupt.   The founder
of the renowned house was Jacob Fugger II., the
grandson of Hans, and it was probably through the
maternal grandfather of Jacob the younger, who
settled in the Tyrolese mining district, that the opportunity came which led to fortune.

Jacob II. went into business in 1473, when fourteen
years old, and learned his trade in the Fondaco dei
Tedeschi in Venice.   For some time he and his
brothers dealt in the old way, in silks and woollens
and spices, but presently Jacob entered on the
" more profitable business of exchange and mining."[2]
Mines were then mostly crown property, and the
best security which the sovereigns had to pledge ;
therefore a great money-lender became, almost of
course, a mine owner.   For example, in 1487, as
security for a loan of 23,627 florins made to the Arch-

[1] *Das Zeitalter der Fugger*, Ehrenberg, I., 189.
[2] *Ibid.*, I., 89.

duke Siegmund, Jacob received the silver mines of
Schwarz.   The next year, for 150,000 florins, the
Fugger brothers obtained the grant of the entire
yield of the Schwarz mines until repayment of the
debt, — a good bargain in the opinion of the business
community.   In 1495, as part of an extensive investment in copper, the Fuggers secured the copper
works in Neusohl, eighty miles north of Budapest
in Hungary.   To maintain the price of copper they
organized, in 1498 and 1499, with other Augsburg
firms, a syndicate for cornering the Venetian market.
To effect this purpose they shipped their Hungarian
copper to Antwerp by Cracow, the Vistula, and
Dantzic.[1]   To pursue the subject further would be
tedious, but the statement made by the firm, in 1527,
shows how mining property and minerals predom-
inated among the assets.[2]

In mines and mining shares they had invested . . . 270,000 flrs.
In real estate in Augsburg, Antwerp, and elsewhere 150,000 flrs.
Merchandise . . . . 380,000 flrs.
Loans . . . . 1,650,000 flrs.
Cash . . . . 50,000 flrs.

The merchandise consisted mainly of metal.   The
copper in Antwerp alone was valued at above 200,000
florins, besides silver and brass.   They held little
cloth, damask, or other wares.   The loans were large,
often secured by pledges of mines.   In this generation the Fuggers touched their zenith, when in
the words of the old chronicle of Augsburg, "the
names of Jacob Fugger and his nephews were known
in all kingdoms and lands, even in heathendom.

[1] *Ibid.*, I., 89, 90.   [2] *Ibid.*, I., 122.

Emperors, kings, princes, and nobles have sent embassies to him, the Pope has saluted and embraced him as his beloved son, cardinals have stood before him. All the merchants of the world have called him an enlightened man, and the heathen have wondered at him. He has been the jewel of Germany."[1] With the Fuggers, Germany also culminated, and German cities attained to a size in the fifteenth century which they did not surpass until the middle of the nineteenth. Many, like Lübeck, actually declined, while Cologne occupied an area which sufficed her until the introduction of railways revolutionized the valley of the Rhine. This prosperity came in the main, probably, from the scientific development of minerals, but it also depended in great degree on commerce. During the Middle Ages, the path of commerce lay across Germany, and it was the gradual abandonment of the thoroughfares over the Alps, for the voyage to Flanders, that wrought havoc with such cities as Augsburg, Nuremberg, and Lubeck. With the founding of Lübeck, in 1143, German commerce may be taken to have passed through its tentative period, and to have determined on the lines which offered least resistance in passing overland from the Mediterranean to the northern seas. Speaking generally, Venice proved to be the cheapest base, and the Rhine or the Elbe the best avenue.

Leaving Venice, one route followed the Semmering to Vienna and Prague, gaining Lubeck and Hamburg by the Elbe; the Brenner, likewise, fed the Elbe by way of Nuremberg and Leipsic. The bulk of the travel over the Brenner, however, flowed to the

[1] *Das Zeitalter der Fugger*, I., 116.

Rhine, descending the Main, and building up Wurz-
burg, Frankfort, Mayence, and Cologne. Less com-
monly merchants crossed Lombardy to the Septimer,
and so north by Coire and Ulm to Speyer; or they
may even have preferred the St. Gotthard and Basel;
but whichever route the Germans chose, the great
.highways finally ended in well-established termini,
both to the east and west, where Hanseatic counting-houses of capital importance flourished. The
thoroughfare of the Rhine led through Cologne to
Bruges and London ; that of the Elbe through Lübeck
to Novgorod, which was reached by the Gulf of Finland, the Neva, and the Volkhoff.

As Schäffer has remarked, " He who follows with
watchful eyes the bloom of these mediæval communities will recall the drama of those world cities which,
in our own days, have suddenly from nothing sprung
into being on a newly cultivated soil." [1] Lübeck
only became a German town in 1143, and Vienna
a capital in 1156, yet both were famous at the close
of the century. No story is better known than
that of Cœur de Lion, who chose the Vienna route
to London, on his return from Palestine in 1192,
and was arrested at Erdberg between Vienna and
Prague. He excited suspicion by sending his servant
with his ring to the capital to buy food, while he
remained at the village disguised.

Lübeck owed her consequence to the development
of the whole basin of the Baltic, but particularly of
northern Russia. For centuries Novgorod had been
a considerable market. From its foundation Constantinople had imported grain, — at first from Egypt,

[1] *Die Hansestäate*, 50.

but after the advent of the Saracens, from the Euxine.
Amru occupied Alexandria in 640, and from the
cessation of the distribution of African wheat by
Heraclius, the demand was transferred to the valleys
of the Danube and the Dnieper.   The Eastern Empire
had two periods of grandeur, one under Justinian,
about the beginning of the sixth century; the other
toward the close of the tenth.

The Byzantine Empire, which, after the reign of
Justinian, had languished, fell to the lowest depth of
indigence under Heraclius; but from the beginning
of the eighth century a steady recovery set in, which
brought Constantinople to high prosperity about 950.
As the wealth of the Greeks grew their expenditure
increased, and the Jew, Benjamin of Tudela, was
lost in admiration at the magnificence of their
garments.   Such a population not only bought food
on a vast scale, but the more costly furs, and
the region from which they drew their supplies
flourished proportionately.   The Bulgarian kingdom,
bordering the Danube, rose from barbarism to affluence
and refinement, and the waterway which led through
Russia from the Black Sea to the Baltic became
studded with flourishing cities.   The chief of these
were Kieff and Smolensk on the Dnieper, and Novgorod on the Volkhoff.   Novgorod the Great, lying
at the point where the Volkhoff enters Lake Ilmen,
having connection with the Gulf of Finland by Lake
Ladoga and the Neva, and being the point where
traffic, ascending the Volga and the Dnieper, and
seeking an outlet on the Baltic, converged, was an
emporium open alike to the north, south, east, and
west.   As it flourished when it supplied the Byzan-

tines and the Asiatics with sables and ermines, so it
flourished when the market moved northwestward and
established itself near Paris.

The prosperity of the Fairs of Champagne is, perhaps, the capital phenomenon of mediæval history,
for it indicated the transfer of the focus of wealth
and energy from the borders of Asia to a spot
adjacent to the Atlantic, a greater economic revolution than had ever happened previously. The
rise of Champagne and the fall of Constantinople
were precisely contemporaneous. The earliest mention of the fairs is in a deed by Hugh, Count of
Troyes, dated in 1114. The plundering of Constantinople by Alexius Comnenus took place in 1081,
and may be accepted as the beginning of the end.
About 1200 the Fairs of Champagne reached their
prime, and the wealth which poured into the adjacent
provinces is attested by the unparalleled splendor of
the architecture of the period. No monuments so
superb as the French cathedrals of the early thirteenth century have ever been constructed in Europe.
At this precise moment, in the year 1204, Constantinople fell before the arms of the crusaders, and her
people were plunged in ruin.

This migration of the dominant market from the
Bosphorus to the Atlantic altered the whole social and
political complexion of Russia. Her customers lived
no longer in the south, to be reached only by the highway of the Dnieper, but to the west, through the Baltic
and the North seas. The Baltic is a dangerous and
stormy sea, and the cost of its navigation was increased
by the risk and delay of passing through the sound,
and also by the toll there collected from shipping.

It so happens, however, that on either side of the isthmus, where the promontory of Denmark joins the mainland, two rivers have their outlet, — the Trave entering the Baltic, and the Elbe the German Ocean. The portage between these rivers is short, and accordingly two of the most famous cities of mediæval Germany grew up side by side, forming for many purposes a single corporation.   These cities were Lübeck and Hamburg, and they flourished exceedingly, since they served as the distributing point, not only of the merchandise which descended the Elbe from Venice, but of the coasting trade between Russia and the ports of Flanders.   That trade was considerable in volume and of high value.   All mediæval society luxuriated in fur, "as I believe for our damnation," said Adam of Bremen, "since, *per fas et nefas*, we strive for a garment of martin, as though for our eternal salvation."   Nor could the fashion have been otherwise, since furs in northern Europe were not only essential to comfort but to health itself.   The climate was cold and damp, the streets of the towns narrow and dark, and the houses built without means of warming. Therefore furs played a part in indoor life foreign to all modern ideas.

Suzdal, a province of central Russia, the predecessor of modern Moscow, was long overshadowed by Kieff.   To the Suzdalian, Kieff represented all that was sacred and splendid, and the highest ambition of the Suzdalian prince, George Dolgoruki, was to ascend its throne.   This ambition he finally gratified in 1155. The rapidity of the movement of the age is shown by the divergence of view between two generations. What excited the father's reverence only roused the son's cupidity.   When Andrew succeeded George, far from wishing to abandon the Volga for the Dnieper, his instinct was to plunder his father's sanctuary and carry the spoil home.   Accordingly, in 1169, Andrew attacked Kieff, and after a short siege carried the walls by storm.   Then he gave the city up to sack, plundering not only private houses, but convents, churches, and even Saint Sophia itself.   Kieff never recovered, and Andrew, returning to Suzdal, established his administration at Vladimir on the Klyasma, midway between where Moscow and Nijni-Novgorod now stand.   Vladimir remained the capital of the Grand Duchy until 1328, when Moscow gradually superseded her.   In 1220 Nijni-Novgorod came into being, at the confluence of the Oka and the Volga, at the heart of the river system of which the Volga forms the trunk.

Nothing could mark more pointedly the automatic processes of nature than the conversion of the ancient Greek Russia of the Dnieper into the modern Asiatic Russia of the Volga.   In the year 1000, Constantinople being the dominant market, the regions tributary to that market were organized to correspond. Merchandise from Russia moved southward, and to avoid the navigation of the stormy Euxine, men used, when possible, the Dnieper instead of the Don. Novgorod served as the port of entry for the furs and amber of the Baltic, and also as the depot for furs from the valley of the Petchora, which reached the Volkhoff by the Volga and Rybinsk, the thoroughfare still in use.   The wares collected at Novgorod were conveyed by the Lovat and the Dnieper to Kieff, where Greek merchants congregated to buy grain, and thus Kieff became the leading local market. But leading local markets are the natural seats of administrative systems. So it came to pass that Russia in the tenth century was administered from Kieff; and the causes which made Kieff a capital, kept it a capital until the direction of trade changed.

Between 1000 and 1200 A.D. the development of German minerals, and the consequent industrial prosperity of all northwestern Europe, propelled the seat of commercial exchanges toward the English Channel; and when the market thus shifted, all civilization readjusted itself to conform to the change. As the purchasing power of Constantinople waned, and that of the Hanse towns waxed, the core of Russia, revolving on Novgorod as on a pivot, passed through the segment of a circle, abandoning the thoroughfare of the Dnieper, which led north and south, and travelling to the valley of the Volga, which, with its branches, the Mologa and the Kama, forms an almost complete system of waterways from the Ural on the east, and the Petchora, which empties into the Arctic on the north, to the Volkhoff on the west. At Novgorod, on the Volkhoff, the Germans fixed their counting-house.

As a consequence Kieff decayed, and with it the Greek civilization; while Moscow, Vladimir, Nijni, and Kazan rose, and with them came the Tartars. Meanwhile, German replaced Greek as the commercial language, German enterprise penetrated the recesses of Russia wherever trade promised a profit, and by 1200 the Novgorod merchants had extended their stations throughout the valley of the Petchora, and perhaps also the valley of the Obi. This was commercial expansion, and, as often happens, war followed.

Christianity had previously been preached to the heathen Slavs, but until the German merchants perceived the value of the basin of the Baltic, the Church had not been awakened to the necessity of armed conversion.   Religious enthusiasm for conquest grew with the prosperity of Lübeck and Hamburg, and in 1198 Innocent III. proclaimed a crusade against northern Russia.   Bishop Albert of Buxhoewden led his flock in twenty-three ships, and, entering the Duna, soon baptized the multitude and settled Riga, which quickly developed commercial importance and became the capital of Livonia.   During the thirteenth century, two military crusading organizations, which were afterward fused under the name of the Knights of the Teutonic Order, conquered East Prussia and the region now known as the Baltic Provinces of Russia.   They founded many towns, among others, Revel, Venden, once the residence of the Grand-Masters, Volmar, Marienburg, where the celebrated castle still stands, Konigsberg, and Thorn.   In 1310 they acquired Dantzic.   The Hanse held sway in Novgorod.

When, during the eleventh century, trade, surmounting the Alps, flowed down the Rhine and the Elbe and across the northern seas, pirates on the water, and robbers in foreign lands, threatened the life of every traveller.   To protect their citizens, some of the German ports early coalesced; and though this coalition did not earn the name of the Hanseatic League until a comparatively late date, the corporation existed, probably, from the beginning.   Had the

F

German trade routes converged, so as to give all Germany a community of interest, such a league could hardly have been evolved, for the purposes for which it was established could have been more cheaply accomplished by a centralized government, as in France or England.

As German commerce flowed in two great streams to the Baltic and the North Sea, being split in twain by the peninsula of Denmark, the interests of the cities lying along these trade routes diverged, and in consequence the methods of administration remained rudimentary. The imperial government developed little energy, and the allied cities only acted together within a restricted sphere. They agreed to pursue pirates, to police the rivers as far as possible, and to support the rights of their citizens abroad, but for aggression they were helpless. To resist a powerful enemy, a separate treaty had to be made which might include other towns than those of the Hanse. Such a treaty, negotiated in 1367, organized the Cologne confederation which overthrew Waldemar of Denmark, and it was after this war that the league reached its maturity. Imperfect as it was, the Hanse proved the most effective instrument Germany employed to extend her influence; and it was through the energy and adroitness of her merchants, rather than through the arms of the crusaders, that mediæval Germans colonized Russia.

The League intrenched itself at Novgorod, and when all allowance has been made for hyperbole, Novgorod if semi-barbarous must have been both populous and wealthy. Gilbert of Lannoy, who visited Novgorod in 1413, described it as a prodigious town, surrounded by forests, lying low and subject to inundations, and fortified with mean clay walls and stone towers. The merchants lived the lives of a garrison amidst savages. The guild brethren occupied large buildings, with separate rooms set apart for the use of the master, the servants, and the members. Saint Peter's church served as the main warehouse, goods being stored in its vaults. They also stacked wine casks about the altar, only on the altar itself nothing could be placed. Part of the duty of the guild members was to guard the church, day and night, particularly against fire. When supper ended, visitors left, the doors were locked, and all went to bed. At night the houses lay like fortresses, within strong wooden palings, to climb which was criminal; while, to insure discipline, warders regularly made the rounds and fierce dogs roved in the yard. For such privations the merchants sought indemnity from the Russians. Russians were excluded from the company, and Russian commerce, therefore, vanished from the Baltic.

To sustain prices in Russia, the Novgorod counter restricted imports; and all Europe paid tribute to the Hanse for furs, and the wax from which the Church made her candles.

Under such conditions Lübeck and Hamburg, serving as the outlet of the commerce both of the Elbe and of the Baltic, should seemingly have risen to be a chief international market; and that they did not do so must be attributed to the physical conformation of Germany, which set her at a disadvantage.

No error can be greater than to regard the barons,

who held the castles on the roads, as public enemies,
or even as the enemies of commerce. Without police,
roads would be closed by robbers, and, in an age of
decentralization, local castles protected travellers.
The great work of the early Saxon emperors lay in
the erection of strongholds along the line of the Elbe,
to keep the Slavs in check. In fine, a guard must
always be maintained and paid ; the only question is
one of price, and the trouble with Germany was that
her castles were too small and too numerous, and the
tolls needed to support the garrisons too high.

Thomas Wikes, in 1269, complained that "the mad
Germans," perched on their inaccessible rocks above
the Rhine, and restrained neither by fear, nor respect
for the king, exacted intolerable dues from all passing
vessels, by reason of which merchants were ruined.
In the first fifteen miles above Hamburg on the Elbe
there were no less than nine of these tolls. The
total number between Hamburg and Vienna may be
estimated. To reach Champagne, on the other hand,
after leaving Switzerland, only the government of
Burgundy had to be dealt with, which collected six
tolls.[1] Therefore, the route by Genoa and the St.
Bernard, or by Marseilles and Lyons, to Paris, came
cheaper than the Semmering or the Brenner and
the Elbe to Hamburg, and accordingly the Fairs
of Champagne undersold Lübeck. The sea, however, cost less than any land journey, once the
difficulties of navigation had been overcome, and by
the middle of the twelfth century sailors had learned
much. In 1147 a fleet of two hundred Flemish ships

---

[1] On this subject see *Études sur les Foires de Champagne*, Félix
Bourquelot, 320.

reached Venice, which was perhaps the first time that a Flemish vessel had been seen in the Adriatic.[1] Thenceforward the Italians always preferred the ocean when practicable.

But, for ships bound from Venice, or Genoa, to the north of Europe, Hamburg and Lübeck were inaccessible. In those days vessels were slow, and it would have been impossible to reach the Elbe and return the same year. Therefore, the Italian fleets stopped in Flanders. The Germans and Italians met in Bruges or Antwerp, and the Germans sent their purchases farther east, either in coasters or else by land, to Cologne, and so up the Rhine and the Main. As sea freights gained on land freights, the constant tendency was for the thoroughfares through the Alps to lose importance, and had it not been for mining, south Germany would have sunk into comparative poverty at a relatively early period. Such facts seem to show that the inventive and industrial faculty which first brought German metals on the international market, and afterward threw central Europe into excentricity by substituting water for land transportation, kept western civilization in ferment from the opening of the crusades to the Reformation. Nevertheless, on the whole, Europe prospered. A catastrophe, induced by the same causes, fell on central Asia, under which it sank, never to revive.

The ancient trade from China and India had converged at Balkh, and from thence had reached

[1] *Les Relations commerciales des Belges avec le Nord de l'Italie et particulièrement avec les Vénetiens, depuis le XII jusqu'au XVI Siècle*, Alexandre Pinchart, 11 *et seq.*

the Mediterranean by Babylon, or by Tabriz and
Trebizond.   Consequently, commercial activity had
centred in Persia and Mesopotamia, and these countries had been the richest, the most populous, and
the most polished in the world.   No such cities
could be found elsewhere as Samarkand, Bokhara,
Merv, Herat, Bamian, Tabriz, Hamadan, Mosul, and
Bagdad.   When Haroun-al-Rashid lived, about 800,
Bagdad was indisputably the first capital, and her
caliph the chief monarch, of the earth.

The change came with the introduction of the mag-
net in navigation.   From about the third century
the Chinese appear to have sailed as far as the
Persian Gulf, but the dangers of the Red Sea long
protected Bagdad.   Already in the age of Haroun this
bulwark was failing.   Those interested in the early
voyages will find the authorities collected by Heyd
in his work on the *Commerce of the Levant*, but for
ordinary readers the story of Sindbad the Sailor is
equally convincing and more amusing.   The tales of
Sindbad are accurate descriptions of travel, with only
enough exaggeration for popular consumption.   To
the east, Sindbad reached Malacca, to the south,
probably, Madagascar.   He made his last voyage to
Ceylon, by the command of the caliph, as ambassador to the king of the island, and the noteworthy
part of the tale is the small importance Haroun
attached to the mission.   In his sixth voyage Sindbad
had been wrecked, and escaped by a subterranean
river, carrying with him many jewels.   On awakening
on his raft he found himself in Ceylon, whose king sent
him home with a letter and presents for the caliph.
After his fatigues Sindbad proposed to remain in

Bagdad for the rest of his life, but one day he received a message that the caliph wished to speak with him. On reaching the palace, Haroun announced his intention of sending him to Ceylon with an answer to the king, and a return of presents. When Sindbad remonstrated he observed: "It's only a question of going to Ceylon to acquit yourself of my commission. After that you can return." The difference between Haroun's standpoint and Alexander's explains all that followed.

In ancient times, although navigation improved sufficiently to admit of voyages from India to Egypt, and Alexandria, accordingly, gained upon Babylon, ships never became powerful enough, and ocean freights cheap enough, to supersede the caravans of central Asia. The revolution came with the introduction of the magnetic needle, probably about the time of Sindbad, or a little later, and then events moved very rapidly. When a voyage to Ceylon from Bagdad counted for no more than it did in the mind of Haroun-al-Rashid, it evidently would no longer pay to make the Persian Gulf a stopping-point on the way to Egypt. Nor when Chinese junks could sail direct from Nanking or Canton to Aden, would it be profitable to send merchandise by camels across the Pamirs to Bactra, far less from Delhi or Lahore into the valley of the Oxus, as an avenue to a Mediterranean market. Consequently the caravan, for through traffic, fell into disuse, and central Asia lapsed into excentricity. The inevitable result followed. Energy declined, and the Saracenic empire dissolved.

According to Gibbon, the caliph El Rahdi, the

twentieth of the Abbassides, "was the last who de-
served the title of commander of the faithful. . . .
After him the lords of the eastern world were reduced
to the most abject misery, and exposed to the blows
and insults of a servile condition."[1] Conversely,
Egypt rose to almost incredible splendor and power,
and became at once the centre of wealth, of refinement, and of learning. Her progress is marked in
many ways. El Rahdi reigned from 934 to 940.
Nicephorus Phocas, emperor of the East, came to the
throne in 963; and Phocas and his successor, John
Zimisces, taking advantage of the weakness of the
Moslems, devastated the valley of the Orontes, and
closed Syria as a thoroughfare. In 969 the first
Fatimite caliph of Egypt laid the foundations of
Cairo, in 1176 Cairo was walled, and "from the year
1176 to our days Cairo has had no notable increase,
if it be not the prolongation of the quarter El-
Hasanyeh. In two centuries it acquired its actual
limits."[2] Moreover, Cairo's architectural splendor
belongs to the interval between the decline of Bagdad, which began in the ninth century, and the discovery of the sea route to India, in 1497. One of
the earliest and most beautiful of her mosques, Tey-
loun, "a model of elegance and grandeur," dates from
876 A.D.,[3] sixty years before the final wreck in
Mesopotamia after El Rahdi. Her noblest gate, the
Bab-el-Nasr, is a work of the eleventh century.
The Gama-el-Azhar, destined to be the greatest of
universities, and finished in 972, is said, in its prime,
to have sheltered twelve thousand students who daily

[1] *Decline and Fall*, Chap. LII.
[2] *L'Art Arabe*, Prisse d'Avennes, 74.   [3] *Ibid.*, 94.

received instruction in medicine, theology, philosophy, mathematics, geography, and history. In 1359 the Sultan Hassan completed his famous mosque, costing $3,000,000, equivalent to more than ten times that sum in our money, and which ranks among the masterpieces of the world.

The Egyptian court was most gorgeous, the Egyptian empire largest, and Egypt's fame highest under Saladin, who defeated Philip Augustus and Cœur de Lion in Palestine, and who will always remain an heroic figure in history. From these facts the inference is justified that, toward the year 1200, the old economic system, which had been based on the caravan routes across central Asia, had been superseded by the modern system, which is based upon the sea. The track commerce followed was simplified. Starting from the Chinese and Indian ports and the spice islands, cargoes were often consigned to Aden, where they changed hands, and, crossing the Red Sea and Egypt to the Nile, were floated to Cairo and Alexandria, where they were sold to Europeans. At the mouth of the Nile the stream branched to Venice, Genoa, and Marseilles, the Venetian section being, probably, the most considerable. The Venetian traffic also was, in the main, that which emerged at the mouths of the Elbe and the Rhine. In the North Sea and the Baltic another maritime system prevailed, controlled by the Hanseatic League. This system struck its roots into Russia at Novgorod, and stretched out to Sweden on the north, the Urals and the Arctic on the east, and to London on the west, its base being Lübeck, Hamburg, Cologne, and Bruges. Thus it would appear that the old and new economic systems were divided from each other by a sharp line of demarkation. The ancient system comprised the interior of China, the whole of central Asia and northern India, Syria, and most of Europe east of the Adriatic; the new, all of Africa and Europe west of a line drawn from Aden to Suez, and thence to Venice through the Adriatic. From Venice the frontier followed the trade route north to Vienna, Prague, and the Elbe, until it reached East Prussia, where, turning east, it ended with Novgorod. In fine, as far as the Western Empire extended, this division almost coincided with its boundary save in regard to Egypt; and the cause which produced the division led to the Mongol invasion.

Wherever commercial exchanges centre, movement is rapid, because men's minds are highly stimulated; when a region falls into excentricity, the stimulant is reduced, and proportionate languor supervenes. This law seems to be universal. Therefore communities which have been abandoned by their trade routes, though often retaining wealth for long periods if undisturbed, lose their energy, and offer temptations to pillage. Such was the case with Rome, and such was the fate of this unfortunate region which had been discarded between the eleventh and the thirteenth centuries. Constantinople fell first.

In 1198 Innocent III. preached a crusade against the Saracens, and the Byzantine Empire had then been languishing for upwards of a century. If the fortification of the Harz by Henry the Fowler be taken as the point of departure, all these events fall into a regular sequence. In 924 Henry built his first tower at Quedlinburg. In another generation the

mines had come into operation, and before the close
of the century western Europe had responded to the
impetus. The effect had been the diversion of trade
from the Bosphorus to the Adriatic, and Venice had
prospered while Constantinople had declined. In the
Byzantine Empire all went ill. Disorder prevailed,
and in 1081 Alexius Comnenus, having bribed a body
of Germans to open a gate, entered the capital with a
body of ruffians, and pillaged as though in a hostile
land. Proclaimed emperor, he dared not fight Robert
Guiscard with his own navy, but abandoned the
defence of Durazzo to the Venetians. Thenceforward the administration degenerated apace, trade fell
off, the coinage deteriorated, and, when Innocent's
crusaders met at Venice, in 1202, to take ship for the
Holy Land, Constantinople offered the fairest prize
to the spoiler that had been known since Alaric took
Rome. Henry Dandolo, the greatest of Venetian
statesmen, saw his opportunity. He held the crusaders
in his power, for they owed the Republic for transportation sums they could not pay. Dandolo proposed to
them to aid him to sack Constantinople, to divide the
proceeds, and thus meet their obligations, suggesting
that afterward enough would remain to enrich them
all.

The event proved Dandolo's sagacity. On April
12, 1204, the soldiers of Christ carried the tremendous battlements of Byzantium, which had been
deemed impregnable, and slaughtered, almost without
loss, a garrison outnumbering them about five to one.
The sack which followed has lived in human memory,
even amid the multitude of such awful tales. Neither
age nor sex escaped. Nothing was so sacred as to

command immunity, and the ecclesiastics who accompanied the army found an incalculable treasure in the relics with which the convents and churches were filled. The prices these fetched in the mediæval market may be estimated by the sum paid for the Crown of Thorns by Saint Louis, which could not have been far from a million of our money.

Mark that Constantinople stood just to the east of the line which separated the old from the new economic systems, and consider the success of Dandolo; then turn to Cairo, which lay as far to the west, and ponder the fate of those who attempted a similar raid. In 1249, forty-five years later, Saint Louis, at the head of the finest force ever organized in Europe, landed in Egypt and advanced to Mansurah; there, meeting a decisive defeat, on April 5, 1250, he and his army surrendered. Instead of bringing home infinite wealth, he exhausted France in furnishing a ransom.

Doubtless, Europeans won sporadic successes during the crusades; but, notwithstanding these, they never, like the Greeks under Alexander, penetrated the recesses of Asia. The destruction of the ancient civilization of the interior was reserved for hordes of nomadic barbarians. The Mongols had been deemed by their civilized neighbors to be "among the most wretched of mankind, wandering in an elevated region of Tartary, and under an inclement sky, and so poor that Rashid tells us only their chiefs had iron stirrups." [1] There is nothing to show that thirteenth century Mongols differed materially from their ancestors. True, they produced a great soldier, but the greatest

[1] *History of the Mongols*, Howorth, I., 108.

of soldiers is naught without an opportunity; and the opportunity of Jenghiz Khan came to him, not from his own strength, but from the weakness of his victim. The fact seems established that the Mongols seldom or never prevailed against a united and determined foe; their successes were won against organisms resembling the Byzantine Empire, and their victories recall the sack of Constantinople.

Probably in the year 1162, on the banks of the river Onon, which rises to the east of Lake Baikal, and which finally merges in the Amur, a certain Mongol chief had born to him a boy whom he named Temudjin, after a Tartar khan, whom he had defeated. Temudjin was but thirteen when his father died, and that he survived is evidence of his adaptation to his surroundings. At one time he sank to the depth of misery, was captured, tortured, escaped, was recaptured, and only saved from death by the pity of his pursuer, who hid him in his house. For many years Temudjin waged war upon his neighbors, nor was it until the year 1206, that, having destroyed his rivals, he assumed the title of Jenghiz Khan, or "Very Mighty Khan."

At this time China was divided into two empires, a southern with a capital at Hangchow, and a northern, ruled by the Kin emperors, who resided near Peking. In 1209 the Kin emperor sent to Jenghiz Khan to collect the regular tribute, but Jenghiz, relying on rumors of disaffection which came to him through refugees, scornfully told the envoy that the "Son of Heaven" was an imbecile, and, mounting his horse, rode off. War followed, and Jenghiz obtained his first success through the treachery of the garrison of the great wall, who deserted. At a favorable point the Kin generals awaited him with a vast army, but Jenghiz learned their plans from the commander of their advance guard, who went over to him, and found means to crush one of their divisions. Then the Chinese fell back, the fortress which covered the capital was abandoned in panic, and the Mongols took the town. In August, 1212, Jenghiz besieged Tai-ton-fu, but meeting with a stout resistance he retired into the desert.

In these campaigns the Mongols could have accomplished little without the aid of the Chinese themselves, for the Mongols were not engineers, and relied on deserters to conduct their siege operations. But China was rotten to the core. In 1213 the Kin dynasty collapsed. A certain general named Hushaku conspired against the emperor, murdered him, and raised a creature of his own to the throne. He then defeated the Mongols, but, being wounded, a rival cut off his head and sent it as a present to the new potentate, who rewarded the mutineer by making him commander-in-chief. Yet China, broken as it was, fought valiantly compared to central Asia. In 1217 Jenghiz reached Kashgar, his dominions then becoming coterminous with those of Mohammed the Khuarezm Shah, whose empire stretched from the Pamirs to Mesopotamia, and from the Indus to the Aral. Soon a quarrel broke out. Certain agents of Jenghiz, nominally employed in purchasing for him, were arrested and executed as spies at Otrar. Receiving no satisfaction, Jenghiz, in 1218, marched from Karakorum in two columns. The southern, moving by the Terek Pass and Usch, encoun-

tered Mohammed's forces, ill disciplined and disorgan-
ized.   Mohammed himself, a debauched poltroon, fled
to Samarkand.

The northern column, following the valley of the
Irtysh and Lake Balkash, attacked Otrar.   In April,
1219, the garrison, being somewhat pressed, deserted.
Otrar taken, Jenghiz overran the valley of the Syr-Daria
and marched on Bokhara, one of the magnificent and
cultivated cities of Asia.   Garrisoned by 20,000 men,
it was surrounded by two walls, one about four miles in
circumference, the other nearly fifty, the interval between the two being filled with palaces, parks, and
gardens, and traversed by the river Sogd.   In a few
days the troops in Bokhara fled, but were cut to pieces,
and then the chief men surrendered.   Jenghiz addressed the people, saying: " I am the scourge of God.
If you were not great criminals, God would not have permitted me to have thus punished you."   The inhabitants were then driven from the gates, that the pillage
might be the easier, and the Mongols burned the
town.   "It was a fearful day.   One only heard the
sobs and weeping of men, women, and children, who
were separated forever ; women were ravished while
many men died rather than survive the dishonor of
their wives and daughters." [1]   Von Hammer has
compared the accounts of the sack of Bokhara given
by the Moslems, with those given by the Greeks of
the sack of Constantinople.   Samarkand fell next.
Samarkand was not only the capital of Trans-Oxania,
but an opulent market.   Its garrison consisted of
110,000 Turkomans and Persians.   The Turks at
once deserted.   Then the town surrendered.   Besides

[1] *History of the Mongols*, I., 78.

plundering the place, 60,000 citizens were reduced to slavery. The troops were massacred. Next the Mongols fell upon Khorasan, the garden of Asia. Merv, the "king of the world," and extremely ancient, was rich and populous. The governor, after a couple of sorties, decided to surrender. Tempted by promises, he visited the Mongol camp with his relations and friends, when all were massacred. The Mongols entered the gates, and the inhabitants were made to march out with their treasures. The procession lasted four days. The Mongol prince, raised on a golden throne in the midst of the plain, caused the chiefs to be decapitated as a spectacle. Then a general massacre ensued. It is said that " Seyid Yzz-ud-din, a man renowned for his virtues and piety, assisted by many people, was thirteen days in counting the corpses, which numbered 1,300,000." [1] The ferocity of the invaders can be judged by their slaughter of 5000 victims who had hidden in holes and corners and afterward came out for food.

Nishapur fell in April, 1221, two months after the death of Sultan Mohammed. In two days the walls were breached. The carnage lasted four days. To prevent the living hiding beneath the dead, Tului, the Mongol general, ordered all the heads to be cut off, and separate heaps made of those of the men, women, and children. Only 400 artisans escaped, who were transported into the north. Years afterward the Sultan Jelâl-ud-dîn farmed out the right to seek for treasure in the ruins of Nishapur for 30,000 dinars a year. Sometimes as much was found in a single day.

Herat surrendered, afterward rebelled, and was

---

[1] *History of the Mongols*, I., 87.

captured because of dissensions among its garrison. For a whole week the Mongols ceased not to kill and burn, and 1,600,000 people are said to have perished; the place was depopulated and made desert. The Mongols then retired. Soon after they returned to destroy any of the inhabitants who yet lived. They slaughtered over 2,000. When the scourge ended, "forty persons assembled in the great mosque—the miserable remnants of its once teeming population." [1]

Balkh, Bamian, every town of importance in central Asia, shared in the ruin. All men knew the fate awaiting the conquered, and yet all historians have remarked on "the miserable decrepitude of the opponents of the Mongols," and have cited astonishing examples. "A Mongol entered a populous village, and proceeded to kill the inhabitants one after another, without any one raising a hand. Another, wishing to kill a man, and having no weapon by him, told him to lie down while he went for a sword; with this he returned and killed the man, who in the meantime had not moved. An officer with twenty-seven men met a Mongol, who was insolent, he ordered them to kill him; they said they were too few, and he actually had to kill him himself; having done which all immediately fled." [2]

Inertia invariably accompanies a slackening in the velocity of social movement. This inertia was conspicuous throughout the whole zone of the Mongol conquests, which comprised the entire ancient economic system. It is true that Jenghiz himself did not erect a principality in the valley of the Indus, but Tamerlane some generations later laid, at Delhi, the

---

[1] *History of the Mongols*, I., 91.   [2] *Ibid.*, I., 131, 132.

G

foundations of the empire of the Great Mogul. Jenghiz and his immediate successors expended their energy in the north. In Asia Minor they swept through the Van country; in Syria they pillaged Antioch, and occupied Damascus; in Mesopotamia they slew, according to report, 800,000 people in Bagdad alone.

In 1237 the Mongols assailed Russia. At Ryazan the prisoners were impaled, or shot with arrows for sport, or flayed alive. Priests were roasted, "and nuns and maidens ravished in the churches before their relatives." Invading Suzdal, they immolated Moscow and Vladimir and many other cities. At Kieff the fugitives collected in the cathedral, where numbers ascended to the roof, carrying with them their wealth. The roof, being flat, gave way, when the Mongols, rushing in among the ruins, slaughtered without mercy; "the very bones were torn from the tombs and trampled under the horses' hoofs." [1]

Advancing into Poland, the Mongols crossed the Oder, and, on April 9, 1241, fought a famous battle at Liegnitz, about one-third of the way between Breslau and Dresden. Outnumbering the Christians nearly five to one, they defeated them, but at such a cost that they turned south and entered Hungary. Several noble Silesian and Moravian families still bear the Mongol cap as a memento of their ancestors' prowess in this action. In Hungary the Mongols met with slight opposition, as "the Hungarian nation was disintegrated and dissatisfied." [2] Therefore Batu forced the line of the Vistula and the Danube, as he had forced the line

---

[1] *History of the Mongols*, Howorth, I., 141.   [2] *Ibid.*, I., 147.

of the Dnieper and the Lovat. The story of the
invasion is like the story of the conquest of China
and of Persia. Cracow had been previously burned,
and Batu marched direct from Russia on Buda.
The enemies met on the heath of Mohi, near Tokay.
Batu attacked at night the Hungarian army, which
would no longer obey its leaders. The Templars,
indeed, fought as beseemed their order and their
fame, but the Huns, as a body, first refused to leave
their camp, and then fled. Their pursuers strewed
with their corpses a space of two days' journey.
Sixty-five thousand men are believed to have fallen.

On December 25, 1241, Batu crossed the Danube
on the ice, to storm the rich city of Gran. He encountered little resistance from the inhabitants, many
of whom he roasted to discover hidden treasure. He
then tried the citadel, but the citadel was held, not by
a Hun, but by a sturdy Spaniard, and Batu suffered
a defeat. Nor did the Duke of Austria fail to raise
an army with which he made good Vienna. As
usual, when they encountered a serious obstacle, the
Mongols moved in a direction where the resistance
would be less, and turning south from Austria, they
marched along the eastern coast of the Adriatic to
Scutari. There they stopped.

Thus the limits of the barbarian inroads are well
defined. Starting from near Pekin, they followed the
caravan routes to Kashgar, and thence across the
Terek Pass to Usch, Khokam, Samarkand, and Bactra.
There, still following the highways, they branched.
One division crossed the Hindu Kush by the Pass of
Bamian, and erected the empire of Delhi; another,
marching along the highway of Semiramis, sacked

Bagdad; still another, using the thoroughfare by
Tabriz and Lake Van, attacked Mosul, Aleppo, and
Damascus. Advancing into Russia they ascended
the Volga to Vladimir, and descended the Dnieper
to Kieff. They devastated Poland and Hungary,
and swept bare the valleys of the Vistula and the
lower Danube; but when they overstepped the boundary between the old economic system and the new,
their triumphs ended. Egypt defied them. Germany, both north and south, repulsed them, and they
recoiled from before the walls of Novgorod. The
cleavage was the same as that which, eight hundred
years earlier, split the domain of Rome into an Eastern and a Western empire, and for the same reason.

Nature is consistent. The fit survive, the discarded perish. As the destruction of Rome, in one
age, supervened because a martial race could not develop into mechanics and explorers, so, in another
age, the annihilation of what had been the eastern
supplement to Rome followed upon the propagation
of more versatile competitors in the west, who revolutionized exchanges and altered the paths of trade.

Rome decayed and fell, because she could neither
provide other commodities than metal to barter with
the East, nor improve her metallurgy and discover
fresh mines. The men of the Middle Ages, bred to
fit the emergency, not only supplied what the Latins
lacked, but cheapened navigation, until ships sup-
planted the caravan, and central Asia lost the international eastern traffic. Then the eastern half of the
ancient economic system sickened and died of in-
anition, even as the western half had already died;
and sorry bands of barbarians wandered through the

Persian gardens, as the Goths and Vandals had wandered through Italy and Gaul.   Cæsar's legions would
have scattered the rabble of Genseric like chaff, had
Cæsar's legions lived in the fifth century; and the
hordes of Jenghiz would have fared hardly on the
plains of Mesopotamia, had they met there warriors
such as Saladin.   Yet none can avert their fate;
Egyptian splendor and Egyptian prowess survived
not the discovery of Vasco da Gama.   In 1517 the
Turks stormed Cairo, and Egypt degenerated into an
Ottoman province.

CHAPTER III

PROSPERITY has always borne within itself the seeds of its own decay. Piloti remarked that the master of Cairo was master both of Christendom and India, because Cairo commanded the road from the Red Sea to the Mediterranean. The French understood the situation in the thirteenth century, and Saint Louis led the crusade of 1248, not only with the view of recovering Jerusalem, but also in the hope, by conquering the Sultan of Egypt, of obtaining the key to the Orient. His defeat left the West helpless, and the Arabs profited by their advantage. They taxed the traffic crossing to Alexandria, up to the limit at which spices could be delivered at Constantinople or Beyrout by caravan from Samarkand or Bagdad. Rapacity produced its inevitable effect. The most ingenious and enterprising race which had ever been developed was stimulated to elude the enemy whom they could not vanquish. The result was the discovery of America by Columbus, in 1492, and of the passage round the Cape of Good Hope by Vasco da Gama, in 1497. Thereafter in a single decade a disturbance of the social equilibrium occurred, greater, probably, than had ever before taken place in many centuries.

From time immemorial eastern merchandise had entered the Mediterranean by the Levant, and from thence had percolated through Europe, enriching the cities on the avenues leading toward the Atlantic. In one age it had been Corinth and Syracuse; in another, Antioch, Alexandria, and Rome; in a third, Venice, Augsburg, Nuremberg, and Lübeck; or Genoa, Lyons, and Paris; but at the beginning of the fifteenth century this order abruptly closed, and commerce, avoiding the Mediterranean altogether, passed directly toward the North Sea through the ocean.

On the northwest and southwest the British Islands and Spain jut out into the Atlantic from the continent like two promontories. When the eastern trade moved to the Atlantic, the effect was to transfer the competition, which theretofore had gone on between river systems, into a struggle between Spain, England, and France, who alone had ports which could be utilized as centres of exchanges for ocean traffic.

The intensity of the struggle for supremacy was heightened during the sixteenth century by a financial crisis of the first magnitude. Europe's vulnerable point has always been her metals. Rome fell because the Spanish mines proved inadequate to meet the demands upon them, and at the time of the discovery of America a similar catastrophe threatened the civilization of the Middle Ages. Though population, industry, and trade had all increased since the reign of Saint Louis, the yield of the precious metals had, probably, not augmented, even if it remained constant; therefore, relatively to commodities, the value of money rose, and debtors suffered correspondingly.

Long ago Thorold Rogers pointed out " the significant decline in prices " which took place in England between 1461 and 1540.[1] In reality the decline began earlier, and extended throughout Europe.

The French manufacturing towns which, at the close of the twelfth century, built cathedrals such as Chartres, Amiens, and Rheims, toward the year 1260 fell into insolvency.[2] Louis IX. had coined the mark of silver into 2 pounds, 15 sous, and 6 pence. Under Philip the Fair, in 1306, the same weight sufficed for 8 pounds, 10 sous. In England, at the close of the thirteenth century, the penny weighed $22\frac{1}{2}$ grains of standard silver; in 1546, the penny contained but 10 grains of metal, two-thirds of which were base. And yet values, if anything, tended downward. Thorold Rogers marvelled. He could not explain why, with such a debasement, the bushel of grain should have cost as much during the first forty years of the sixteenth century as during the last fourteen of the thirteenth.[3]

Silver bought more because scarcer, and this scarcity may be attributed both to an increased demand for money without a proportionate supply of bullion, and also to a larger export of gold and silver to the East.

As long as the caravan trade nourished central Asia, the Persians and other neighboring communities bought liberally of woollens, because of the severity of the winter climate. After the devastations of the Mongols the people being poorer bought less. Jenkinson, in 1559, could barter no English cloth of any kind in Bokhara.[4] Egypt purchased

---

[1] *Agriculture and Prices*, IV., 454.

[2] *Les Communes Françaises*, Luchaire, 200, 201.

[3] *Agriculture and Prices*, IV., 200, 292.

[4] *Early Voyages and Travels to Russia and Persia*, by Anthony Jenkinson, Publications of Hakluyt Soc., I., 88.

iron, copper, and tin, besides timber and slaves, but India and China took few commodities from the West, and, on the whole, Europe had to face a heavy adverse trade balance, which she settled with cash. Heyd has estimated the annual export of the precious metals, in 1497, at 300,000 ducats. The Venetian ducat contained 3.559 grammes of gold, or about the weight of $2.13; the equivalent of 300,000 such ducats to-day might be $7,500,000.

Everywhere the suffering was acute, and everywhere it broke out in discontent, chiefly against the Church; a discontent which can be understood in view of the weight of her exactions.[1] A document of the sixteenth century has estimated that, in 1415, at the time of the Council of Constance, France sent annually to Rome 900,000 crowns to pay for annats, bulls, dispensations, and the like, which vast sum contributed nothing toward the maintenance of worship in the kingdom. The English parliament passed a series of statutes to obtain relief; in short, all Christendom, even Spain, betrayed symptoms of resistance. It was just at the moment of crisis that the Spanish struggle for predominance opened. That struggle began with the election of Charles V. as emperor of Germany in 1519, the year in which Luther denied the Papal supremacy, and closed with the defeat of the Armada in 1588; a period of almost precisely two generations. During the interval Cortez conquered Mexico and Peru, the mines of Potosi were discovered, a flood of silver poured across the ocean, and in 1561 Elizabeth restored the shilling to its original fineness.

[1] For the economic aspect of the Reformation see the chapter on The English Reformation in *The Law of Civilization and Decay.*

Nevertheless relief came too late. In 1588 the wars of the Reformation were raging, both France and Spain had repudiated, the Netherlands had been driven to revolt, Antwerp had been sacked, and on the ruin of the economic system of the continent England was preparing to lay the foundations of her empire.

The rise of Spain must always appear marvellous. Castile and Aragon only united in 1479, the Moors were not expelled until Granada fell in 1492, the year in which Columbus reached Hispaniola, and yet in 1520 Spain touched her zenith. And when the evidence is analyzed, it will be found that she owed her high fortune not so much to the valor of her soldiers or the wisdom of her statesmen, as to that chain of cause and effect which for a fleeting moment made the Iberian peninsula a centre of commercial exchanges between America, Europe, and Asia.

On July 10, 1499, the first ship of Vasco's fleet returned. On that day Venice held control of the eastern trade, and was the chief commercial state of Europe. In 1502 the Venetian galleys brought but four bales of pepper from Beyrout, and from Alexandria little more. In a few months, between 1501 and 1502, the price of a cargo of pepper advanced from 75 to 100 ducats on the Rialto, and Venice stood face to face with ruin.[1] On the other hand, Lisbon rose to eminence, and the German merchants, who had been the fountain of Venetian prosperity, left their Fondaco, and hurried westward to Portugal, where spices could be bought for half the price they brought upon the Adriatic. In September, 1503, Vasco da Gama re-

[1] *Histoire du Commerce du Levant*, Heyd, 2, 519.

turned from his third voyage with a rich cargo, part
of which had been bought with the proceeds of a prize
worth 24,000 ducats, or possibly $550,000 of our
money.   The value of the whole consignment touched
1,000,000 ducats, while the cost of the expedition had
not exceeded 200,000.   It was then the great fall took
place in pepper, for the cantar, which had previously
cost 40 ducats, could afterward be had for 20.   And
yet the Portuguese made liberal profits, for the spice
they sold in Lisbon for 20 ducats they bought in India
for two or three.   In 1509, precisely a decade after Da
Gama's return from Calicut, the Portuguese admiral
defeated the Egyptian fleet in the Arabian Sea, established a fortification in the island of Sokotra, and
closed the Straits of Bab-el-Mandeb to the eastern
trade.   Thus Venice was cut off.

What ruined Venice made Antwerp.   From the
middle of the fourteenth century, when the   British
moved the woollen trade from Bruges, Antwerp
gained, but it only reached its bloom after the centralization of the eastern import trade at Lisbon
permitted capitalists to concentrate sales in Flanders.
The great houses bought cargoes of spices afloat from
the Portuguese government, sent them to the Scheldt,
and, by combination among themselves, usually succeeded in regulating prices, from year to year, well
enough to avoid violent fluctuations.   Then Antwerp
became not only the chief port of Europe, and the
dominant market for merchandise, but the clearing-
house for the world.   All governments which needed
money looked to Antwerp; Thomas Gresham, Elizabeth's financial agent, tarried there.   Evidently such
a sudden and considerable increase of the trade to

tropical countries, and the elimination of all the temperate regions of Asia, greatly stimulated the export of specie, and for fully half a century the yield of Mexico imperfectly balanced this loss. Charles abdicated in 1555. In 1550, five years after the discovery of the mines at Potosi, he was estimated to have received annually only 400,000 ducats from America. Not before 1570 did the Spanish fleets bring very great treasures to Cadiz. Also this date is suggestive, for Drake sailed on his buccaneering expedition to Panama in 1572.

Charles I. of Spain, who afterward was chosen emperor, owed his election, and most of his other successes in life, to the credit he enjoyed as Count of Holland, or head of the first financial state in Christendom. This credit won for him his first success over his rival, Francis I. of France, and enabled him to continue his wars long after Spain, had she stood alone, would have been bankrupt.

" The choice of Charles of Spain to be King of the Romans is without question the event of the period which has brought out most clearly the power of money at that time. It is an event which alone suffices to justify the title, ' The Age of the Fuggers.' Never would the German electors have chosen Charles had not the Fuggers intervened for him with their cash, and especially with their overpowering credit." [1]

Charles was the child of Philip the Fair, Archduke of Austria, and Joanna, the daughter of Ferdinand and Isabella. The son of a German, born in Ghent in 1500, he lived in the Netherlands until he inherited

[1] *Das Zeitalter der Fugger*, Ehrenberg, I., 100.

the crown of his grandfather Ferdinand in 1516, and was Spanish only by half-blood, and not at all by training. He first visited Spain in 1517, and found Madrid uncongenial. He was, indeed, the product of the most commercial atmosphere in the world. His affiliations with the leading bankers were close. They trusted him, as they never did his son, and they bought for him the imperial crown. They supported him in his schemes of conquest, and when he admitted failure by abdication, the great financial houses were tottering to their fall.

They fell in an effort to consolidate antagonistic economic systems. The valley of the Rhine is divided from the valley of the Rhone by the ranges of the Jura and the Vosges. In Champagne, on the flanks of the Vosges, rises the Meuse, which flows north to Namur, where it unites with the Sambre, and then easterly until it joins a branch of the Rhine above Dordrecht. To the north the hills sink into the plain, and, on the confines of Flanders, the watershed is almost imperceptible, so much so that the district in which the Scheldt, the Sambre, and the Oise rise was once probably a marsh. Yet this watershed, inconsiderable though it be, has always determined the direction of trade, and by so doing has fixed the frontier of France. At the beginning of the thirteenth century, Bruges, Ghent, and Ypres, lying within the narrow province between the Scheldt and the sea, were the three most important cities beyond the Alps and are supposed to have contained from 150,000 to 200,000 inhabitants each. Their main industry was weaving English wool, and they sold their cloth over all Christendom, Egypt, and

central Asia, the chief brokers being the Italians.
The commercial interests of Flanders, therefore, did
not harmonize with the interests of the region centralized at Paris, though possibly most of the merchandise shipped south passed through Paris because of
the flow of the rivers. This trade-route made the
Fairs of Champagne.

From the Mediterranean, the Rhone, Saône, and
Ouche lead to Dijon ; or, if the road be taken from
Genoa, across the St. Bernard, it also ends at Dijon.
Dijon, in the valley of the Rhone, is about one
hundred miles distant from Troyes, in the valley of
the Seine, and Troyes and Bar-sur-Aube, close by,
are the southernmost of the four towns at which the
famous Fairs were held. The other two were Provins
and Lagny-sur-Marne. All these towns are in the
valley of the Seine above Paris; and just below Paris
the Oise offered a waterway leading northeast as far
as Chauny, about twenty-five miles from St. Quentin. The interval between the Oise, the Sambre, and
the Scheldt is now traversed by canals, but in the
Middle Ages portages had to be made, and it was
because St. Quentin stood on the Somme, between
the Oise, the Scheldt, and the Sambre, that it early
achieved fortune. St. Quentin was the first French
town to receive a communal charter. Ghent lies
a little less than one hundred miles from St.
Quentin, down the Scheldt, and Ghent was the
capital of Flanders, the heart of the manufacturing
region which bought its raw material in England,
and sold the chief of its product to Lombards.[1] On

[1] That Flemish trade did actually pass into France by the Scheldt is
demonstrated by the position of Bapaume, the most noted custom-house

this combination of trade-routes the social and political equilibrium of western Europe reposed down to the accession of Philip the Fair in France in 1285.

When Philip came to the throne, France was centralizing rapidly. By the marriage of Philip with Jane of Navarre, the heiress of the Count of Champagne, Champagne became absorbed in the kingdom, and then forthwith the organism, of which Philip was the head, stretched out along the highways leading to the east, in the effort to reduce under one administration all the region between the Scheldt and the ocean, which used the Scheldt as an avenue to the Fairs.

Flanders, though a fief of the French crown, was, in reality, an independent state, enacting laws, coining money, administering justice, and making war and peace without reference to her feudal superior. When Philip began his reign, Guy of Dampierre was Count of Flanders, and it was not long before

of the kingdom, which "was the point of transit of the merchandise exchanged between the north and south of all western Europe." (*Étude Historique sur les relations commerciales entre la France et la Flandre au Moyen Âge*, Jules Finot, 68.)

Cambrai stood on the Scheldt just beyond the French border, and Bapaume is nearly midway between Cambrai and St. Quentin, only somewhat to the west of both. The ancient road seems here to have diverged from the direct line because of the dangers of the forest of Arrouaise, which extended from Albert to the Sambre. (*Ibid.*, 1, 2.) The main highway, from Arras to Rheims, passed through Bapaume and St. Quentin. Therefore when the merchant from Flanders, travelling to the Fairs of Champagne, arrived at Bapaume, he chose his route south, according to circumstances. He might go, for the most part, by boat, or he might go by pack-train, but as even in the eighteenth century the cost of travel by road was estimated at tenfold that of travel by canal or river, it is fair to conclude that he ordinarily preferred the Oise and Seine.

matters came to a crisis between him and the king. The fiscal agents of France spread themselves over Flanders, practically setting aside the local administration. As Philip's historian has observed : " Gui de Dampierre thus witnessed the progressive and increasingly rapid invasion of the county of Flanders by the authority and influence of the crown of France. Flanders was enveloped in its turn in the assimilating movement, which was the mission of the royalty forming the unity of the French nation, and the Count was not slow to comprehend that it was the independence, not to say the very existence, of his crown which was at stake." [1]

Like Athens and Corinth, wherever two contiguous economic systems thus come in collision, the effects ramify infinitely. In this case they warped all western civilization. War broke out, and Philip was defeated at Courtrai on July 11, 1302, when the whole nobility of France was annihilated. It was said that 20,000 Frenchmen fell, and but 100 Flemings. Then a long period of confusion followed, ending with a prohibition of intercourse by Louis X.

The routes across Champagne being closed, commerce was obliged to seek new channels, and it took to the sea. About 1330 a document, addressed by the officials of the Fairs to the king, stated that merchandise which previously had passed through Champagne then went by ships.[2]

A social revolution supervened. The Fairs of Champagne decayed, as did the Flemish cities.

[1] *Philippe le Bel en Flandres*, Funck-Brentano, 128.
[2] *Études sur les Foires de Champagne*, Première Partie, Bourquelot, 319.

Their impoverishment drove many weavers to England, whose emigration stimulated English manufactures ; more important still, Flanders, to resist France, entered into the English alliance. It was from Van Artevelde that Edward III. drew much of his strength. " The struggle of the Flemish communes, therefore, constituted the first act of the long social drama which unrolled itself through a whole century, and which historians have named the Hundred Years' War." [1]

When the ocean route to Italy had once been established, it undersold the French highways, and the Fairs ceased to be held. The result was a great relative decline in the French influence in Flanders, and a proportionate increase in the German ; an increase which made possible the movement toward consolidation which took place under Charles V. Like Philip, Charles failed, but his effort caused the long wars of the first half of the sixteenth century. The rise in taxation following thereon occasioned the revolt of the Netherlands, and the English buccaneering, which, by seizing Spanish treasure, precipitated the mutiny of the Spanish army; the sack of Antwerp; and, finally, the Armada. Thus the Rhine and Main, and the Rhone and Seine, competing, crippled each other, and drove the seat of international exchanges into England.

In the year 1500, although the routes through Germany from Venice were not frequented as of old, they had not been abandoned, and the mines of Hungary, Bohemia, and the Tyrol were still productive. South Germany, therefore, was opulent, and

[1] *Philippe le Bel en Flandres*, 678.

Augsburg and Nuremberg were its financial capitals. In especial the bankers of Augsburg were famous. Their affiliations with Brabant were close, they had counting-houses in Antwerp which were often more important than those in the parent city, and their speculations in the metals and in eastern wares were enormous. They also formed the most important group of financiers with whom governments dealt.

Although Charles had lived in a mercantile community from his birth, he little appreciated, on his accession to the crown of Spain, the difficulties which confronted him in satisfying his ambition. Charles coveted the Empire as the first step toward a consolidation such as had been conceived by Charlemagne, and resolved to buy the crown of the King of the Romans. Had those who honored his drafts recognized the dimensions of the undertaking, they might have hesitated. Charles betrayed his inexperience. On his way to Spain, in 1517, he gave his ambassador drafts on the Fuggers for 94,000 florins to pay the electors ; the money only to be delivered when the choice had been made. His paternal grandfather, the old Emperor Maximilian, understood his countrymen better. Toward the end of his life Maximilian fell into such bitter poverty that Jacob Fugger had to lend him 3000 florins in 1518, because, "literally his Majesty had nothing to eat"; accordingly no one esteemed money more than he, or felt less inclined to waste it; nevertheless Maximilian wrote to Charles reproving him for his parsimony, and warning him to forward forthwith 450,000 florins in cash, to be spent on the spot, else he would be defeated.

Francis would have been a more formidable competitor had he inspired confidence, but no one would trust him. In Genoa he could obtain nothing, and in Lyons he actually found the leading capitalists lending to the Hapsburgs. Ultimately he received a handsome gift from his mother, the Duchess of Angoulême, who advanced a sum inadequate to content the electors, it is true, but large enough to raise the price of votes to Charles.

When Charles, in his eagerness, declared that he would be King of the Romans, "cost what it might," he passed from stinginess to recklessness. He squandered in the contest 850,000 florins, substantially all of which he had to borrow, nearly four-fifths of the whole amount coming from the two Augsburg houses, the Fuggers and the Welsers. The Fuggers lent 543,000 florins, and the Welsers 143,000. The Genoese and Florentines together contributed only 165,000 florins. As Jacob Fugger afterward wrote : "It is well known and as clear as day that your imperial Majesty could never have obtained the Roman crown without my help." [1]

This election was the first trial of strength between France and Germany, and though Germany prevailed, it was at a vital sacrifice. To overcome the French king, Charles had to mortgage his means unduly, and the burden he then assumed impaired his military energy throughout his life. To maintain his armies he needed a large revenue. Spain, a poor country, and without manufactures, suffered from a constant deficit ; Italy yielded little ; the Holy Roman Empire cost more than it paid, therefore the chief

[1] *Das Zeitalter der Fugger*, I., 112.

burden fell upon the Netherlands, which, though rich, saw no profit in hostilities. The discontent, afterward culminating in general revolt, broke out early. In 1539 Charles undertook to collect from Ghent a subsidy of 400,000 florins, which the citizens maintained had not been lawfully granted.

On February 9, 1540, the emperor marched from Brussels with 10,000 men, and a vast train of cardinals, archbishops, bishops, and other Church dignitaries, besides " dukes, princes, earls, barons, grand masters, and seigniors, together with most of the Knights of the Golden Fleece." The cortege was reckoned at 60,000 men and 15,000 horses, yet the city accommodated all.[1] Charles made an example. He first executed nineteen ringleaders ; then he annulled the municipal charters, collecting not only the 400,000 florins, but 150,000 more by way of fine, and imposing a subsidy of 6000 yearly forever. Finally, he caused the deans of the guilds and chief burghers, in their shirts, with halters round their necks, to appear before him and pray for mercy. In all that touches the economic aspect of the Dutch revolt, Motley's view is interesting, as he regarded the revolution as a religious phenomenon, and therefore minimized the effect of the pressure of taxation. Yet even Motley perceived that Charles was a financier rather than a theologian. " Charles was no fanatic. It was the political heresy which lurked in the restiveness of the religious reformers under dogma, tradition, and supernatural sanction to temporal power, which he was disposed to combat to the death." [2] If Charles had continued to reign,

[1] *Rise of the Dutch Republic*, ed. of David McKay, I., 69.
[2] *Rise of the Dutch Republic*, I., 123.

affairs might have turned differently, could he have
controlled them.   Perhaps he felt his grasp relaxing,
and for this reason withdrew.   As early as 1550 the
world recognized that consolidation had failed, and
the bankers, with one accord, sought to liquidate.
As the Spanish influence gradually obtained the
upper hand, the financiers grew uneasy.   In 1553
Anthony Fugger complained of the methods at
Madrid.   He detested and distrusted Erasso, the
Spanish financial agent, intimating that if Erasso
still found means of doing business, it could only be
on ruinous conditions.   He did not hesitate to declare
that if the Court broke faith when payment had been
solemnly promised, a gift to Erasso of 1000 florins
" would make things go."   He added : " I have little
taste for such business ; having had enough of it." [1]

When things reached this pass, Charles convened
the Estates of the Netherlands on October 25, 1555,
and surrendered the crown to his son Philip, who was
a true Spaniard.   Doubtless the public regret was
sincere ; " there beyng in myne opynion not one man
in the whole assemblie, stranger or another, that
dewring the tyme of a good piece of his oration
poured not oute abondantly teares ; some more,
some less." [2]   The community instinctively comprehended its danger.   The bulk of the population of
the Netherlands was not Protestant, nor did it object
to the extirpation of heresy, provided business remained unmolested.   What the Dutch resisted was
oppressive taxation whether by Church or State.

[1] *Das Zeitalter der Fugger*, I., 155–6.
[2] Despatch of Sir John Mason, *Life and Times of Sir Thomas
Gresham*, Burgon, I., 175.

Motley also has admitted that of the seventeen provinces, as late as 1576, "fifteen were, on the whole, loyal to the king; while the old religion had, of late years, taken root so rapidly again, that perhaps a moiety of their population might be considered as Catholic." [1]

Holland and Zealand were of the Reformed Faith, but they were poor and maritime, and even in Holland the capital sided with Philip. The Prince of Orange thought that the defection of Amsterdam injured the patriots more than the campaigns of Alva. Most modern authorities, therefore, agree that financial distress, rather than religious persecution, occasioned the war. Mr. A. J. Crosby, the editor of the British State Papers relating to this period, is a good example. "Brabant and the rest of the provinces which depended on their manufactures and were infinitely more wealthy and pleasant to live in [than Holland and Zealand] were for the most part Catholic, and it was on account of its avarice and tyranny that they disliked the Spanish rule, and not through its interference with their religion, which was probably not so great as is usually imagined." [2]

The abdication of the emperor, therefore, a Fleming who understood the material interests of his native country, and enjoyed the confidence of the conservative class, caused regret. While he ruled, the revolution might be postponed, with his abdication the catastrophe began. Like Charlemagne he foresaw the magnitude of the crisis.

Charles V. left so serious a deficit, that Philip after-

[1] *Rise of the Dutch Republic*, III., 60.
[2] Calendar of State Papers, Foreign, 1575–1577.   Preface, xiv.

ward declared that he could never have paid the
floating debt, though he would gladly have done so
" even with his blood." During the next two years
difficulties thickened; panic prevailed in Antwerp,
and the Fuggers, whether they would or no, were
forced to intervene. By a contract dated February 1,
1556, Anthony Fugger agreed to deliver to Philip, in
Spain, 400,000 ducats in cash, to pay his troops and
relieve his other necessities, taking as security there-
for such personal obligations as the king could find
in the Netherlands, beside the pledge of the first
" aid " which should be voted by the Estates. Only
three months later the Fuggers made another advance of 600,000 ducats, and in the beginning of
1557 Oertel, the Fuggers' agent in Antwerp, lent
an additional 430,000 ducats, to be repaid with the
next bullion which should come from America. Yet,
in spite of favors, the Spaniards hated their creditors more every day. Oertel wrote to Anthony Fugger: "I doubt whether I shall succeed in making
Erasso our friend, for I have never met his like; one
who always flatters you before your face and vilifies
you behind your back." "He and his say to whoever will listen to them, that one has with nobody so
much vexation and so little advantage as with us." [1]
Such expedients could only be temporary, and in the
summer of 1557 Philip suspended payments. At the
moment, he happened to be forwarding two invoices
of specie to the amount of 570,000 ducats to the Fuggers in Flanders, and the stoppage of the shipment
filled Anthony with wrath. Oertel implored the king
to keep his word, and intimated that he would inter-

[1] *Das Zeitalter der Fugger*, I., 162.

cede with the firm to assist him further, but Erasso
retorted that Anthony Fugger had already begged
the Emperor Charles not to worry him about more
loans, for he wished to be left in peace.   In vain Oertel indignantly declared that his employers had not
left the king in his need, but in eighteen months had
advanced a million and a half of gold; the king twice
told the factor "that he did it as unwillingly as he
ever did anything, but necessity constrained him, since
he could not fall into discredit with the soldiers."
Philip realized his danger.   Of all the peoples of the
modern world the Spanish retained most of the Roman characteristics.   They possessed the same courage, the same military qualities, the same patience
under hardship; but they inherited also the same
cruelty, the same incapacity for industry and the
higher branches of finance, and the same intellectual
rigidity.   The Spaniards could not assimilate new
ideas.   They could not think otherwise than they
had always thought.   They were a primitive type.
Being orthodox, they could not compound with
heresy, however heavy the cost of persecution; and,
when confronted with insolvency, instead of making
a bargain with the Dutch by way of compromise,
their instinct, like the instinct of all archaic mankind,
was to plunder.   To them it seemed cheaper to
rob.   Philip determined to send Alva to Brussels
to replenish his treasury by confiscations and to
reduce the population so low they would submit to
taxation at the discretion of the cabinet at Madrid.
Alva arrived on August 22, 1567.   Even before his
coming, the measures taken had stimulated emigration on a large scale.   On the twenty-ninth of the

previous March, Richard Clough, Thomas Gresham's agent, wrote: " It is marveylus to see how the pepell packe away from hens; some for one place and some for other, so well the papysts as the protestants; for that it is thought that, howsomever it goeth, it cannot go well here; for that presently all the wealthy and rich men on both sydes, who shuld be the stey of matters, make themselves away."[1]

Alva promised Philip that he would not only make the Netherlands self-supporting, but yield annually at least 2,000,000 ducats.   He proceeded to raise the money as Milo would have done.   He organized a supreme tribunal, afterward called the Council of Blood, to take cognizance of all offences which had been committed since the troubles in the Netherlands began.   " The greatest crime, however, was to be rich, and one which could be expiated by no virtues, however signal.   Alva was bent upon proving him-self as accomplished a financier as he was indisputably a consummate commander, and he had promised his master an annual income of 500,000 ducats from the confiscations which were to accompany the executions. . . . Every man, whether innocent or guilty, whether Papist or Protestant, felt his head shaking on his shoulders.   If he were wealthy, there seemed no remedy but flight."[2]

Such severity provoked an emigration to England, which ended in transferring thither many of the most lucrative trades of the continent.   As early as July, 1567, Clough noted the movement, and wished to encourage it.   He wrote: " They that were wont

[1] *The Life and Times of Sir Thomas Gresham*, II., 209.
[2] *Rise of the Dutch Republic*, II., 152.

to live by making of powdyr, are now undone: wishing that and if they would come into Englande they might have a place appointed to make powdyr . . . Which if they had, I wolde not doubt but they wolde go into Englande; and where they go, the great quantity of salpeter and brymstone wyll follow." [1] The same year the Bishop of London took a census of the strangers in the capital, and found, of 4851 foreigners, 3838 to be Dutch. This occurred before the creation of the Council of Blood. The publication of the British State Papers [2] leaves little room for doubt that Alva represented tolerably exactly the views of Spanish society, and Alva's mental processes were those of such a race as that which produced Jenghiz Khan. On returning to Madrid he boasted that he had executed 18,600 persons, and confiscated their property; and, on relinquishing his government, he recommended the burning of all Dutch cities save such as might be needed for barracks.

Men of this type can hardly administer successfully a commercial or industrial community, but they often make good soldiers, and the Spanish would have found little difficulty in subduing Holland, could they have guarded their communications. The resistance they met in the field was contemptible. All the evidence shows that Brabant and Flanders bred but sorry material for armies. In the maritime provinces alone, where a hardy seafaring population throve, was there any fighting worthy of the name.

Spain's vulnerable point lay in her decentralization. Like Charlemagne's empire, pirates could cut

---

[1] *Life and Times of Sir Thomas Gresham*, Burgon, 2, 241.
[2] See Calendar of State Papers, Foreign, 1575–1577, No. 1165.

her asunder. Conducting a war upon the German Ocean, Philip had to transport his supplies by sea from Cadiz to Antwerp, and his treasure from Mexico to the Scheldt. He had not the funds to maintain both an adequate army and navy, and in making the attempt to do so each suffered. The English proportionately prospered, for the English worked their factories with fugitive Dutch labor, and laid the foundation of their opulence with American silver won by buccaneering.

The sequence of dates is suggestive; when Elizabeth came to the throne in 1558, England possessed only about 50,000 tons of shipping, while Spain and Portugal held a substantial monopoly of the trade both to India and America. Alva reached Brussels in August, 1567, just at the moment when the export of Peruvian silver was assuming large proportions, and offering a correspondingly strong temptation to pirates. During Alva's residence in Flanders, competition at sea steadily gathered intensity, until, at its close in 1573, it had reached the ferocity of war. Drake's expeditions were distinctly naval campaigns. This competition caused the mutiny of the Spanish army. The mutiny forced Philip to protect his lines of communication by attacking his enemy's base, and Philip's attack took the form of the Armada, which was destroyed in 1588. Spain eliminated from the trade-routes, her rivals occupied them. The British organized their East India Company on December 31, 1599, with a capital of £80,000; the Dutch theirs in 1602 with a capital of 6,600,000 florins, or about £316,000; and these sums, probably, pretty nearly represented the relative resources of London and Amsterdam.

The Spanish ships were large and slow, high out
of water, and incapable of beating to windward.
They were therefore easy to attack and unable to re-
taliate. They were laden with goods, bullion, and men.
A mixed fleet of privateers, sailing under commissions
issued by the Prince of Orange, used Dover as a
base, and there, on certain market days, these Dutch,
French, and English rovers sold Spanish gentlemen at
auction for their ransom. They brought about £100 a
head. Alva passed six years in Brabant, from August,
1567, to December, 1573, and during his regency the
losses must have been enormous. The Spanish merchants set their damages at upwards of 3,000,000
ducats, and finally declined to contract to supply the
army, but, aside from this, tons of bullion fell into English hands. In 1568 Philip's credit was bad; nevertheless, he succeeded in obtaining 450,000 ducats
in Genoa, which he despatched to Alva to pay his
troops. French privateers chased the ships bearing
the treasure into south of England ports, where Elizabeth appropriated it. Sir Thomas Gresham coined
it for domestic use, "and so with the said monney,
her Majestie maie paie her debtes both here and in
Flaunders, . . . to the great honour and credit of her
Majestie throughout all Christendom." Shortly afterward Gresham announced to Cecil, "I left order
with my servant, Hew Clowghe, to deliver at his
comyng, V sackes of new Spannyshe Ryalls; . . .
at the Towre . . . in good secreat order," willing
his man "to saye . . . that the more expedyssone he
did use in the coinage, the more profytable servyze
he shuld doo to the Queene's Majestie." [1]

---

[1] *Life and Times of Sir Thomas Gresham*, Burgon, II., 305–306.

As the American silver trade grew in value, the onslaught waxed hotter. In 1572 Drake sailed on his famous voyage to Panama, where he surprised, on the isthmus, a mule train loaded with silver. The silver he buried, as of inferior value, but freighted his ships with gold and jewels. What he realized no one ever knew. And Drake was only one of scores who sucked the Spaniard's blood. After six years of service Philip recalled Alva, not because he objected to Alva's methods, but because Alva failed to make the provinces pay. In spite of confiscations and sacks, the budget, instead of showing a surplus, showed a chronic deficit. When Alva left Brussels the arrears due to the troops amounted to 6,500,000 ducats, the payment of one-half of which would have maintained discipline. Probably Spain lost annually at least 3,000,000 ducats by piracy. In Holland, not only private soldiers but officers high in rank were straitened. Alva himself kept his bed during the last weeks of his government to escape his creditors. The arteries being cut, the organism bled to death. Therefore, "after the arrival of a fleet at Seville the American silver flowed through the land like water, not fertilizing, but, on the contrary, wasting it, and leaving even sharper dearth behind." [1]

At last the blow fell suddenly. Toward the beginning of August, 1576, news reached Madrid that affairs in the north had reached a crisis. A mutiny had broken out. The soldiers threatened to sack the whole country. Philip felt the supreme moment had come, and appealed to the Fuggers to save him.

The Contador, Garnica, demanded of Thomas

---

[1] *Das Zeitalter der Fugger*, II., 150.

Muller, the Fuggers' agent, that he should send
200,000 crowns to the Netherlands; "the Fuggers
must not abandon the king in his need." If the
troops were not satisfied, the provinces would be
lost, and the Fuggers would be responsible. As soon
as the soldiers saw the Fuggers' bills, Garnica declared, they would wait with patience until the ducats
came. An answer must be given in the morning.
Nevertheless, he sent again the same night to say
that the Fuggers must pay, else Müller knew what
would happen to them. When Müller replied that
the Fuggers had truly served the king, and that he
knew not what could befall them, Garnica pulled out
a cross, kissed it, and said, "I swear by the holy
cross if Flanders is lost for want of money it will
be their fault." The factor then visited President
Hopper, and asked his advice; but Hopper took the
part of Garnica, and adjured Müller for the love of
God to prove what true servants of the king the
Fuggers were. By so doing, they would put not
only Philip, but the whole Netherlands, under an
eternal debt of gratitude.[1]

That same night the king wrote to the factor, and
declared in council, that no one but the Fuggers
could help him in this pinch, and that this should be
the last service he would ask of them. Müller was
harassed; for, though feeling no confidence in Spain,
he feared to alienate Philip, lest he should include
the Fuggers' loans in a second declaration of insolvency which he had issued in 1575. These loans
exceeded 5,000,000 ducats. Therefore, in order not
to "spill the broth altogether," he agreed to send the

[1] *Das Zeitalter der Fugger*, I., 180,

200,000 crowns. Philip, overjoyed, thought the danger past, and expressed his gratitude ; but the loan
came too late. On November 4, 1576, the garrison
of Antwerp sacked the town. That they succeeded,
and succeeded almost without loss, displays the military inaptitude of the population. The citizens had
full notice of the plans of the mutineers, they had the
support of the government, abundant funds, arms,
and competent officers. They even undertook to
reduce the citadel where the troops were quartered.
Yet at the first onset of their enemy they fled in such
disgraceful rout that, during the whole day, but two
hundred Spaniards fell, while more Flemings were
slaughtered in the streets than were Huguenots in
the streets of Paris in the massacre of Saint Bartholomew. All told, the mutineers numbered less than
6000 men.

Antwerp itself was partially burned and altogether
ruined. Capital fled, and the town ceased to be a
dominant market. The experience of the Fuggers
shows how business suffered, and explains what
Garnica meant when he urged them to befriend the
king lest worse should befall them. During the sack
the Fuggers' factor was taken and had to pay 11,000
crowns as ransom ; furthermore the firm lost £2000
which it had placed on deposit, and lastly one
Colonel Fugger, a relative of the family, who had
gone to Flanders to serve under Alva, in command
of an Augsburg regiment, presented himself and demanded 50,000 crowns as the price of his protection.
As the officials in Madrid had foreseen, the mutiny
proved decisive. A brilliant campaign had just ended
in Zealand. The town of Zierickzee, in the heart of

Protestant Holland, had fallen after a long siege, but when the troops deserted, the Prince of Orange quickly recovered all that had been lost. For the Fuggers, too, the end had well nigh come. Although they escaped being included in the decree of September 1, 1575, suspending payments to creditors, they were too deeply involved to extricate themselves.

And now all men saw that either Spain or England must succumb. The mutiny illuminated the future even to Spanish eyes. If Spain were to remain the heart of an organism of which Mexico and the Netherlands were the members, she must protect the arteries through which her life-blood flowed. England had cut those arteries, and hence a convulsion which portended dissolution.

Philip, like Xerxes, comprehended at last that, for his country to live, his rival must be destroyed; but, like all Spaniards, he thought too slowly. Already capital had migrated, and long before 1588 the British owned the means at home to repel attack. The nation had ceased to be dependent upon foreign loans for funds to maintain an armament. Until the overthrow of credit upon the continent, the English government had borrowed abroad, latterly in Flanders, and Sir Thomas Gresham had managed their negotiations with skill; but, as the resources of Antwerp sank, Gresham observed that those of London rose, until he became convinced that domestic accumulations had reached the desired point. Accordingly he advised Cecil to apply to the "Merchant-Adventurers." " Assuring you, Sir, I do know for certain, that the Duke de Alva is more trowblid with the Queene's Majestie's gret credit, and with the

vent of her highness' commodities at Hamborough,
than he is with anny thing else, and quakes for feare :
whiche is one of the chifest things that is the let
that the said Duke cannot com by the tenth penny
that he now demaundeth for the sale of all goods,
anny kind of waye, in the Low Country (which, Sir,
I beleve will be his utter undoing.) Therefore, Sir,
to conclude, I would wishe that the Queene's Majestie in this time shuld not use anny strangers, but
her own subjects; wherbie he, and all other princes,
maie see what a Prince of power she ys." [1]

It would be needless here to repeat the story of the
Armada, which is known to every child. It suffices
to say that with Drake's victory off Calais, on
August 9, 1588, a readjustment of the social equilibrium began, which gradually moulded that mighty
economic system whose heart, for more than two
hundred years, lay upon the Thames. On that day,
also, the organism which had centred at Venice and
in Flanders, which had given birth to the Augsburg
bankers and the Hanseatic League, received its death
wound, and the long strife opened between Holland,
England, and France for the command of the oceanic
eastern trade.

These facts seem to justify the conclusion that the
centre of energy was forced from the continent of
Europe into England because of the physical structure of the peninsula, which precluded consolidation,
and therefore encouraged war. War is economic
competition in its sharpest aspect; but parallel economic systems connecting common termini must
consolidate or compete. The continent of Europe,

[1] *Life and Times of Sir Thomas Gresham*, II., 340.

cut into transverse sections by trade-routes which did
not converge, could not consolidate, and therefore
has been subject to such catastrophes as the sack of
Antwerp.

I have elsewhere attempted to describe the rise of
the English Empire,[1] and accordingly need here only
indicate the form which that empire has assumed.
It is an economic system connecting Asia and America by way of the Red Sea and the Cape of Good
Hope. In other words, England accomplished on a
great scale, by means of water communications, what
Alexander failed in doing on a small, because of the
cost of overland routes. From Hindustan the English system stretches, by way of Egypt and South
Africa, the two stopping-places on its two lines of
travel, to the British Islands, which have served not
only as a centre of exchanges, but as a focus of
industry, because of their minerals. Thence it
spread over North America, which afforded an expanding market. The United States was politically
severed from this system by the Revolution of 1776,
but continued economically to appertain to it until
of late it has begun to assume the aspect of the
heart of a new organism. It is also worth observing
that the success of the American Revolution, like the
success of the Dutch, hinged on European rivalries.
Had not England and France been competing for
the same trade between the same termini, and had
the colonies been unaided by French money, troops,
and ships, England might probably have suppressed
the rebellion.

The loss of the American colonies accentuates the

[1] See *The Law of Civilization and Decay.*

fact that England rose slowly to supremacy, and that until she developed her minerals she did not reach maturity. It may well be doubted whether she would have prevailed against imperial France had she relied solely upon commerce as the source of wealth, or even upon such manufactures as she could conduct without fully utilizing her iron and coal. Her high fortune came with the "industrial revolution," which began in 1760, and which, by 1800, enabled her to undersell Sweden and France in iron and steel, and India in cotton. It was this combination of advantages which gave England the energy to conquer and retain under a single administration that system of trade-routes, of bases of supply and markets, which encircled two-thirds of the globe, and which raised her, during the nineteenth century, to an eminence unequalled since the disintegration of Rome.

Yet, in spite of all the advantages attending ocean transportation, land traffic between Asia and Europe never wholly ceased. It probably fell lowest during the Mongol domination, but with the migration of energy to the shores of the North Sea it received a stimulus which, slowly gathering strength, has created another vast empire based on the continental thoroughfares which connect China, Turkestan, and Persia with the Atlantic. In fine, the growth of Russia was supplementary to the growth of England, and obeyed similar laws.

CHAPTER IV

SPEAKING broadly, the modern Russian Empire is formed by the consolidation of a series of river valleys running north and south, but connected through their branches in such a manner as to make an almost unbroken waterway from St. Petersburg to Lake Baikal. From Baikal the Amur completes the system to the Pacific. Centring at Moscow, these natural trade-routes radiate like the spokes of a wheel. To the north, by way of the Volga and Vologda, the Dwina, Archangel and the Arctic are reached; while from Vologda the Suchona and Witchegda lead to the Petchora and the fur-bearing region of the Samoieds. To the south the Oka and the Don stretch to the Sea of Azov. To the southwest the Oka and the Volga flow to the Caspian; while directly eastward the Volga communicates with the Kama, and the Kama by an easy portage with the rivers of Siberia.

Under such geographical conditions commerce flows as readily to a northern as to a southern market, and, since the opening of the Middle Ages, the social system of the empire has adjusted itself to both. Until about 1150 A.D., when the countries bordering upon the North Sea acquired a certain opulence, the Euxine and the Bosphorus afforded the only outlet for exchanges. Accordingly, Kieff, upon the Dnieper, became the seat of administration, and merchants journeyed to Constantinople along the

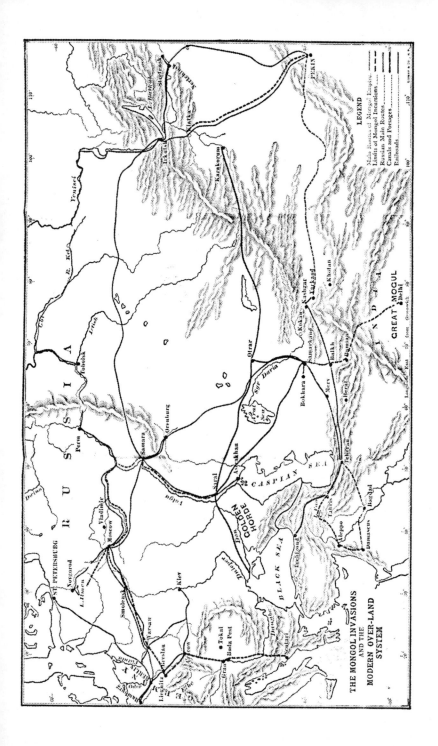

THE MONGOL INVASIONS
AND THE
MODERN OVER-LAND
SYSTEM

LEGEND

Main Routes of Mongol Empire . . . . .
Limits of Mongol Incursions . . . . . .
Russian Main Routes . . . .
Canals and Portages . . . .
Railroads . . . .

avenues which offered the least resistance. These avenues were the three rivers flowing south, the Volga, the Don, and the Dnieper, the Volga being utilized through the short portage at Zaritzin which connects it with the Don, and by which the Sea of Azov is easily reached.

The chronology thenceforward tells the story with absolute clearness. The first dated document relating to the Fairs of Champagne, which became the northern centre of exchanges, is of 1114 A.D. Lübeck was founded in 1143. Therefore, by 1150, the thoroughfare through the Baltic was established. According to Gibbon, Constantinople reached her zenith during the third quarter of the tenth century, under Nicephorus Phocas and John Zimisces. Zimisces died in 976. Contemporaneously, Kiev's great era opened with Saint Vladimir in 972, and ended with Iaroslaf the Great, who reigned until 1054. After 1100, or with the rise of the Fairs of Champagne, Kieff's decline set in, and in 1169, twenty-six years subsequent to the foundation of Lübeck, the town was sacked by the Prince of Suzdalia, the predecessor of the Czars of Moscow. This proves that the northern routes had then acquired an importance equal to the southern. Nevertheless, they did not decisively preponderate, for Venice and Genoa were as good customers as Lübeck and Bruges. Therefore a period as it were of slack-water intervened, when, in the words of Rambaud, " Russia ceased to have a centre about which she gravitated as a mass."[1] Not having a central administration, Russian society disintegrated, and the Mongol domination ensued. The

[1] *Histoire de la Russie,* 90.

battle of the Kalka was fought in 1224, toward 1285 the Golden Horde permanently established themselves in the south, and Batu built Sarai.

The Mongols controlled the southern route from Lake Baikal to the Black Sea by Samarkand and Trebizond, as well as the one which leads by the Syr-Daria to Sarai and the Azov. From the earliest times these roads had thus debouched, and the traffic upon them had made the fortune of the Greek cities of the Euxine of the sixth and seventh centuries before Christ. The Mongols adhered to the ancient paths. Friar John of Pian de Carpine, who in 1246 carried to the Grand Khan a letter from the Pope, went close to the head of the Sea of Azov, then passed near Sarai, then, skirting the Aral and following the Syr-Daria, he rode almost due east to Karakorum. William of Rubruck was taken over much of the same ground, only he crossed the Don higher up, and left the Volga not very far from Zaritza.[1]

The books of travel all show that the Mongol transportation was good, and that they moved rapidly. Timour's posting service was famous, and Gonzalez de Clavijo, in 1404, found the road from Trebizond to Samarkand better equipped than Russian highways have usually been up to the introduction of steam.

Russian society remained in this fluid condition until it received an impulse toward centralization through the rise to supremacy of the markets on the German Ocean. The movement in this direction began after

---

[1] *Journey of Friar William of Rubruck to the Eastern Parts of the World*, 1253–1255. Edited by Hon. W. W. Rockhill, Hakluyt Soc. Publication, Second Series No. IV.

mariners had overcome their fear of the ocean voyage beyond the Straits of Gibraltar.

In 1317 a regular packet service was established between Flanders and Venice, and the following table of receipts of the fairs of Saint John of Troyes shows the diminution of revenue, through a series of years.

In 1275 the fair yielded	1300 livres.
In 1296 the fair yielded	1375 livres.
In 1297 Philip invaded Flanders.	
In 1317 packet service established.	
In 1320 the fair yielded	250 livres.
In 1340 the fair yielded	180 livres.

About 1322 the merchants of Champagne submitted to the government a series of propositions for legislation, "to prevent the ruin of the fairs"; and in 1433 Henry VI. of England, who was then in possession of Paris, granted the town of Provins an exemption from taxes because her cloth works could no longer maintain her craftsmen, who were obliged to labor in the fields. The extinction of the Fairs of Champagne represented a fundamental alteration in the social equilibrium. The trade-routes having abandoned France, the French connection lost importance to the Netherlands, and the Flemish cities, Bruges, Ghent, and Ypres, which had prospered because of their convenience to Champagne, sank in relative consequence.[1] Energy migrated to Brabant, for the trend of exchanges thenceforward for a century was toward Germany, and Brussels and Antwerp had the advantage. Antwerp especially, not

[1] *Le Siècle des Artevelde, Vanderkindere,* Chapter VI.

only surpassed Bruges in its harbor, but afforded landlocked navigation to the Rhine.

The revolution, nevertheless, moved at first slowly. During the Hundred Years' War the Netherlands were paralyzed. Misery prevailed, for communications were cut both by land and sea; on land by marauding, and on the sea by piracy. Nothing prospered until toward the return of peace. The turning-point seems to have been the recapture of Paris by the French in 1436. In 1443 Charles VII. officially admitted the collapse of the Fairs of Champagne by establishing other fairs at Lyons.[1] The year previous the same cause had produced a movement eastward in the Low Countries. In 1442 a great migration to Antwerp occurred of the foreign merchants domiciled at Bruges. Merchants sought the Scheldt, for nearly the whole of the business which had been transacted in Champagne was transferred to Antwerp, and in less than sixty years the favored town received an even stronger stimulus. By the discovery of the sea passage to India the eastern trade was drawn from the Mediterranean to the Atlantic, and the fortune of Genoa and Venice followed in the track of the fortune of Champagne. The exchanges of the whole world were, for a season, centralized in Brabant, and the vibration of this accretion of energy penetrated the recesses of Asia. Thenceforward the development of Russia followed step by step the development of Antwerp, Amsterdam, and London.

Antwerp dated the advent of her high fortune from the migration of 1442, and within a generation the

---

[1] On the decline of the Fairs of Champagne see *Études sur les Foires de Champagne*, Félix Bourquelot, Deuxième Partie, 301 *et seq.*

impulsion had been felt upon the Volga and the Kama.

In 1462 Ivan III., who first took the title of Autocrat of all Russia, ascended the Muscovite throne. He refused to pay tribute to the Tartars, and when, in 1480, Akhmat Khan attacked him, he held the enemy on the river Urga until winter destroyed them. That repulse ended the Mongol domination.

In 1499 Vasco da Gama returned from his first voyage, and in 1502 Venice was already losing trade in favor of Lisbon and the North Sea. In 1505 Ivan III. died, having extended the Muscovite influence over the system of trade-routes which debouch on the Baltic, from the Urals to Novgorod. By 1533 Antwerp enjoyed an uncontested supremacy, and in that year Ivan the Terrible succeeded his father. All authorities agree that the organization of the modern Russian Empire dates from the reign of Ivan IV. In the year 1688 the revolution broke out which exiled the Stuarts, led to the English coalition with the Dutch against the French, and laid the foundation of British ascendency. Parliament incorporated the Bank of England in 1694, and in 1703 Peter the Great laid the corner stone of the citadel of St. Petersburg.

Ivan the Terrible came to the throne in 1533, when three years old. In 1554 he took Astrakhan, and consolidated the valley of the Volga to the Caspian; also at this juncture the Russians first opened direct relations with the English, through the White Sea. In 1553 Richard Chancellor, who had been sent with Hugh Willoughby by the merchants of London to seek for a northeast passage to Cathay, came "to

the place where he found no night at all, but a con-
tinuall light and brightnesse of the Sunne shining
clearly vpon the huge and mighty Sea." Finally, he
entered the port of Nenoksa, at the mouth of the
Dwina, journeyed to Moscow, was welcomed by the
Czar, and returned home with the promise of liberty
to trade. In consequence Mary granted a charter to
the Russia Company in 1555, and sent Chancellor
back to establish relations in Moscow, and also "to
learne how men may passe from Russia either by
land or by sea to Cathaia." [1]

Chancellor discharged his mission and sailed for
England with furs worth £20,000 and a Russian ambassador. After a voyage of four months,
his ships split on the rocks of Pitsligo Bay, and
Chancellor perished. Undiscouraged, the Company
appointed Anthony Jenkinson to the command of
four vessels freighted with cloth, cottons, sugar, and
the like, together with artisans to set up a rope-
walk. Jenkinson unloaded his cargo in the Dwina,
and then, following the road which is still travelled,
he ascended the river to Vologda, and thence crossed
by land to Moscow.

On April 23, 1558, Jenkinson left Moscow for
Persia with the hope of ultimately penetrating to
China. Descending the Moskva to the Oka, he
passed into the Volga and waited at Nijni-Novgorod
for a military convoy of five hundred boats bound
for Astrakhan. On the 29th day of his journey he
came to Kazan, which he described as "a fayre towne,
. . . with a strong castle, . . . and was walled round

[1] *Early Voyages and Travels to Russia and Persia*, by Anthony
Jenkinson, Hakluyt Soc. Publications, Introduction, Vol. I., ii, iii.

about with timber and earth, but now the Emperour of Russia hath giuen order to plucke downe the olde walles and to build them againe of free stone."[1]　On July 6 he reached Perevolog, or the neck of land between the Volga and the Don, eight miles across, and now traversed by a railway, but then "a dangerous place for theeues and robbers, but now it is not so euill as it hath beene, by reason of the Emperour of Russia his conquests."　Astrakhan he found but a sorry abode, having "such abundance of flyes . . . as the like was neuer seene in any land;" the buildings "most base and simple" and the town walled with earth.　There was a plague raging and also a famine, and the Tartars "dyed a great number of them for hunger, which lay all the llande through in heapes dead, and like to beastes, unburyed, very pittifull to beholde; many of them were also solde by the Russes."　"There is a certaine trade of merchandize there vsed, but as yet so small and beggerly, that it is not woorth the making mention, and yet there come merchantes thither from diuers places."[2]

From Astrakhan Jenkinson sailed along the coast of the Caspian to Koshak Bay, the voyage taking nearly a month, and on September 14 started with a caravan of a thousand camels for Bokhara.　On this journey Jenkinson met with treatment which explains why these caravan roads could no longer be profitably used.　Police had ceased to exist, the deserts swarmed with robbers, and the governments of the communities through which they passed connived at

[1] *Early Voyages and Travels to Russia and Persia*, by Anthony Jenkinson, Hakluyt Soc. Publications, I., 49.
[2] *Ibid.*, 55, 57, 58.

plunder. For example, the "Soltan of Kayte" provided the caravan with an escort of eighty men, who
travelled with them two days and ate "much of our
victuals." The morning of the third day "hauing
ranged the wildernes for the space of foure houres,
they mette vs coming towardes vs, as fast as their
horse could runne," declaring that they had found
tracks of the enemy, "and asked us what we would
giue them to conduct vs further, or els they would
returne. To whome we offered as we thought good,
but they refused our offer, and would haue more, . . .
and went backe to their Soltane, who (as wee coniec-
tured) was priuie to the conspiracie." After which
they were set upon, fought till morning, and en-
camped upon a hill cut off from water "to our great
discomfort, because neither we nor our camels had
drunke in 2 days before." Finally the merchants
paid a ransom and marched on, but being again
attacked in their camp in the middle of the night,
"we immediately laded our camels" and fled to the
Oxus. At length, on December 22, Jenkinson arrived
at Bokhara, just eight months after his departure
from Moscow.[1]

Jenkinson had little opinion of the Tartars as cus-
tomers, or of central Asia as a market. "There is
yeerely great resort of Marchants to this Citie of
Boghar, which trauaile in great Carauans from the
Countries thereabout adioyning, as India, Persia,
Balke, Russia, with diuers others, and in times past
from Cathay, when there was passage, but these
Marchants are so beggerly and poore, and bring so

[1] *Early Voyages and Travels to Russia and Persia*, by Anthony
Jenkinson, Hakluyt Soc. Publications, Vol., I. 76, 78.

little quantities of wares, lying two or 3 yeeres to sell
the same, that there is no hope of any good trade
there to be had worthy the following." Worst of all
Jenkinson found no demand for his cloths. The
Indians brought muslins, "but gold, siluer, pretious
stones and spices they bring none. I enquired and
perceiued that all such trade passeth to the Ocean
Sea." "I offered to barter" with them, "but they
would not barter for such commoditie as cloth." As
for the king, "he shewed himselfe a very Tartar,"
for he left for the wars without paying the Englishman his debts, and Jenkinson had to compromise and
take part payment in goods, "but of a begger, better
paiment I could not haue, and glad I was so to be
paide and dispatched." [1]

On his return Jenkinson took back ambassadors
with him, but embassies were also sent from central
Asia to Moscow to negotiate commercial treaties in
1557, 1558, 1563, 1566, and 1583. That commerce
was flowing strongly northward during the reign of
Ivan the Terrible is therefore manifest, yet the movement must have been new, for Jenkinson stated emphatically that, in his time, Bokharans knew nothing
of Russia. On the whole, Jenkinson lost no money;
for "although our iourney hath bene so miserable,
dangerous and chargeable with losses, charges and
expenses, as my penne is not able to expresse the
same; yet shall wee bee able . . . to answere the
principall with profite." [2]

During the next twenty years the Russia Company
regularly prosecuted its business, establishing counting-houses wherever trade justified the investment,

[1] *Ibid.*. 86–88.   [2] *Ibid.*, I., 108.

and soon it had factories at Cholmogory, Vologda, Yaraslav, Novgorod, and Moscow, beside agencies at Kazan and Astrakhan.   If the situation of these towns be examined, it will be found that the English followed the thoroughfares along which the Czar had extended his jurisdiction.   The movements were identical, both being effects of an identical cause.

The weak point of the Russian Empire has been that the travel on its interminable highways has never paid for their maintenance and protection, and therefore the community as a whole has not prospered.   Perhaps the Russians were relatively wealthier under Ivan the Terrible than they are now. Giles Fletcher, who was sent to Moscow as ambassador by Elizabeth in 1588, wrote a description of Russia, which certainly was not flattered, as, when he returned, he sent for his friend Mr. Wayland, prebendary of Saint Paul's, "with whom he hastily expressed his thankfulnesse to God for his safe return from so great a danger."   Ulysses was not "more glad to be come out of the den of Polyphemus than he was to be rid out of the power of such a barbarous Prince; who, counting himself by a proud and voluntary mistake *Emperor of all nations*, cared not for the law of all nations; and who was so habited in blood, that, had he cut off this ambassador's head, he and his friends might have sought their own amends, but the question is, where he would have found it."   The book was published in 1591, but suppressed upon the remonstrance of the Russia Company, who feared its freedom might injure business. Fletcher, notwithstanding his prejudice, found Moscow a very considerable place.   "The number of

houses (as I have heard) through the whole citie
(being reckoned by the emperour a little before it
was fired by the Crim) was 41,500 in all. Since the
Tartar besieged and fired the town (which was in the
yeare 1571) there lieth waste of it a great breadth of
ground, which before was well set and planted with
buildings, specially that part on the south side of
Moskua. So that now the citie of Mosko . . . is not
much bigger than the citie of London." Fletcher
thought that even under Ivan the people had begun to
suffer. He remarked, after speaking of Novgorod,
Kazan, and one or two cities beside, that "the other
townes have nothing that is greatly memorable, save
many ruins within their walles. Which sheweth the
decrease of the Russe people under this government."
Still even Fletcher admitted that "three brethren
marchants of late, that traded together with one stocke
in common, . . . were found to bee worth 300,000
rubbels in money, besides landes, cattels and other
commodities;" one item being "5000 bondslaves at
the least." And these men lived by the Urals.[1] As
for Ivan himself he was reputed to be enormously
wealthy. Michael Lock, in a letter to the Company
in 1572, observed "that he is the moste rytche prynce
of treasour that lyvethe this day on earthe, except
the Turk." Having occasion to move part of his
property at the time of the Tartar invasion, "he did
layde fouer thowsande greate carts with treasur of
jewells, gold, silver and silk, and yet left the same
two castles still furnyshid with his ordenary howsolde
stuffe."[2]

[1] *Russia at the Close of the Sixteenth Century*, Hakluyt Soc. Publications, edited by E. A. Bond, 17, 62.   [2] *Ibid.*, Introduction, xi, xii.

Perhaps the history of Russia illustrates more strikingly than any other the inexorable exigencies of competition. The shifting of the market to the north stimulated movement along the Russian rivers. Growing commerce led to police, and the extension of the imperial administration; but when the semi-barbarous Slavs came in contact with Europeans they had no alternative but to be conquered or to accept western standards. From the reign of Ivan III. all the Czars strove to import foreign inventions, artisans, engineers, and officers, with the effect of increasing the expenditure disproportionately, because of the social inertia arising from slow and costly transportation.[1]

Nevertheless, although the result might be obtained at a prodigious sacrifice, Russia could become formidable as a military power, and this the Swedes and Poles soon perceived. In 1556 Gustavus of Sweden sent a special embassy to remonstrate with Queen Mary against the trade carried on by Englishmen at the port of St. Nicholas, and in 1569, when Ivan had occupied Narva, King Sigismund of Poland flatly told Elizabeth, when she protested against certain seizures of ships, that by reason of "our admonition divers princes already content themselves, and abstaine from the Narve. The others that will not abstaine from the said voyage shall be impeached by our navie, and incurre the danger of losse of life, liberty, wife and children." He explained to Elizabeth that English commerce with Muscovy in munitions of war

---

[1] For a criticism of Russian finance during the last century, see an exhaustive article by W. C. Ford in the *Political Science Quarterly*, March, 1902, "The Economy of Russia."

was "full of danger, not onely to our parts, but also to the open destruction of all Christians and liberall nations." Isolated, Ivan could not obtain the arms, the engineers, and the material to be highly formidable, but by commerce he organized an effective force. "We know and feele of a surety the Muscovite . . . dayly to grow mightie by the increase of such things as be brought to the Narve, while not onely warres but also weapons heretofore unknowen to him, and artificers and arts be brought unto him; by meane whereof he maketh himself strong to vanquish all others. . . . We seemed hitherto to vanquish him onely in this, that he was rude of arts and ignorant of policies. If so be that this navigation of the Narve continue, what shall be unknowen to him?"[1]

To make inventions profitable, however, they must be had early and used intelligently, else they are superseded where they originated, and competitors maintain their relative advantage. Early in the sixteenth century Sigismund von Herberstein noticed that the Russians lacked the mechanical genius to keep abreast of the age, even when given improved implements: "The prince [Vassili IV., 1505–1533] has now German and Italian cannon-founders, who cast cannon and other pieces of ordnance, and iron cannon balls such as our own princes use; and yet these people, who consider that everything depends upon rapidity, cannot understand the use of them, nor can they ever employ them in an engagement. I omitted also to state, that they seem not to compre-

[1] *The Treatise of the Russe Commonwealth*, by Giles Fletcher, Hakluyt Soc. Publications, Introduction, xvii.

hend the different kinds of artillery, or rather I
should say, what use to make of them. I mean to
say, that they do not know when they ought to use
the larger kind of cannon which are intended for destroying walls, or the smaller for breaking the force
of an enemy's attack." [1]

Thus, whether they would or no, the instinct of
self-preservation forced the Russians during the
fifteenth and sixteenth centuries into the vortex of
competition.   The market had migrated from the
south to the north, therefore the ancient avenues
which had sufficed them when Byzantium held
supremacy, sufficed no longer, and a new network
of waterways came into use by the beginning of the
eighteenth century, which consolidated into the existing trans-Siberian economic system.

When at Bokhara, Jenkinson had found the road
to Cathay closed by a war between the Kirghiz and
the cities of Tashkend and Kashgar.   For three
years no caravans had reached the Syr-Daria, but
merchants whom he met gave him information, which
he appended to his report in the form of an itinerary
of routes.   He described three roads, two by Kashgar, and a third, mentioned by an inhabitant of Perm,
through the north of Siberia, and, seemingly, south
by the Lena.   Jenkinson wrote of the year 1559, and
not impossibly the growing anarchy in central Asia
may have hastened the opening of the outlet to Peking across the Siberian plain.   During the fifteenth
century the Russians reached the Urals, and in 1499
they even sent a force into the valley of the Obi.

---

[1] *Notes upon Russia*, by the Baron Sigismund von Herberstein, Hakluyt Soc. Publications, 98.

Among the early settlers at Perm were the Stroganoffs, probably wealthy Tartars, who enjoyed large
privileges and in return kept order. They guarded the
passes of the Ural at their own expense, built blockhouses, bought guns, and hired men. About 1573 the
Stroganoffs decided to conquer the rich fur country
of the Obi, and to this end they employed a certain
Cossack pirate of the Volga named Yermak. Yermak,
with a mixed band of 800 adventurers, armed and
equipped by the Stroganoffs, started to cross the
Urals on September 1, 1581. The story of the
conquest of Siberia deserves to be read in detail
because of its bearing on the opening of new
trade-routes.[1] Here only a summary is possible.
Yermak followed the rivers, ascending the Tchussa-
waya and the Serebrianka as far as the boats would
float, when an easy portage brought him to the Jara-
vli, an affluent of the Taghil, which, through the
Tura and the Tobol, enters the Irtish at Tobolsk;
the whole system forming part of the valley of the
Obi. Near Tobolsk lay the Tartar capital Sibir,
from whence the name Siberia. Yermak attacked
and defeated the Tartars and occupied Sibir. He
then sent one of his robber comrades, who had been
condemned to death by Ivan the Terrible, to Moscow
with sables and the news of his victory. Ivan is said
to have created Yermak a prince. He certainly
made him the first governor of Siberia, and sent him
his own mantle. Sibir became shortly a famous
market, merchants flocking thither from far and near,
but on Yermak's death in action the Tartars regained

[1] A very good account of Yermak and his successors is to be found
in *Russia on the Pacific and the Siberian Railway*, Vladimir.

the town.   The Russians thereupon removed to
Tobolsk, about twelve miles distant, and Sibir slowly
disappeared.

The Russians were few in number, and the conquest of Siberia amounted to little more than guarding the more exposed portions of the streams with
blockhouses.   Between the Ket and its tributaries,
which belong to the system of the Obi, and the Kas
and its tributaries, which belong to that of the Yenisei, there is only an interval of five miles.[1]   Near the
junction stood Yeniseisk, which is supposed to have
been founded in 1618.   It probably consisted of a
palisaded enclosure of a hundred yards or so square,
with a church, magazine, and storehouse.   Like Tobolsk, Yeniseisk became a centre of the fur trade,
and from thence men wandered farther into the interior, seeking always the path of least resistance eastward.   In this case that path proved to be the portage
from the valley of the Yenisei to the valley of the
Lena, by the neck of land between the two rivers
across which the road from Ilimsk to Mukskaya now
runs.   This portage, defended by blockhouses, gave
the Russians control of the upper waters of these
streams, `and with them the approaches to Lake
Baikal.   Hitherto their progress had been rapid, but
in the neighborhood of the lake itself they met with
stubborn resistance, nor was it before 1651 that they
succeeded in establishing a permanent settlement at
Irkutsk.   The Russians crossed Lake Baikal, explored the Amur, and wandering eastward about five
hundred miles, in 1654, fortified Nertchinsk, at the
junction of the Nercha and the Shilka.   At Nert-

[1] See itinerary given in full in *Russia on the Pacific*, 72.

chinsk the road from Peking debouched, and they accordingly held the place tenaciously. They afterward settled at Albazin; but here the Chinese onset proved too cogent. In 1689, by the treaty of Nertchinsk, they abandoned Albazi and the whole valley of the Amur.

The result was logical. Trade to China passed by Nertchinsk, but the Pacific offered no outlet. Hence the Muscovite economic system followed the trade route until resistance stopped progress at Nertchinsk. Having stopped, Russia lay passive until it received another impulsion toward Cathay. That impulsion came from the United States. In 1854 Perry signed his convention with the Mikado, which was followed by a full treaty of commerce in 1858. In the summer of 1859 Moravieff explored the coast south of the Amur as far as Wei-hai-wei, visited Japan, and finally selected Vladivostok as the site of a provisional Russian capital upon the Pacific.

When, in 1689, Peter the Great began his reign, the two great economic systems of the modern world, though yet inchoate, were rapidly consolidating. The revolution of 1688 in Great Britain indicated that the concentration of commercial exchanges at London had already made the mercantile class the dominant influence in the kingdom, while the incorporation of the Bank of England in 1694 may be regarded as the first step taken by the nation in its career as a financial power of magnitude. In 1757 Clive conquered at Plassey, giving to the British the control of India and the plunder of Bengal. In 1759 Wolfe captured Quebec, and the "Industrial Revolution," which, by 1801, had won for the United Kingdom the monopoly of western manufacturing, opened with the invention of the flying shuttle in 1760, and the gradual substitution of coal for wood in smelting.

Thus the ocean routes between China, India, and America converged at the British Islands, which also, as a manufacturing centre, sold commodities east and west. No position could be stronger, provided the English could defend their connections and their bases, and provided they were not undersold by the transcontinental highways. A similar concentration took place in Russia. During Peter's reign the thoroughfares from Moscow to Peking, Samarkand, and Teheran were established. Peter policed the Volga, visited the Caspian, and entered into regular diplomatic correspondence with Peking, sending his embassies thither along the roads which have been followed ever since. A good account of Siberia at this period has been given by one of his ambassadors. In 1692 Peter despatched Evert Ysbrand Ides, a Danish merchant, with "a splendid embassy on some important affairs, to the Great Bogdaichan, or Sovereign of the famous Kingdom of Katai," and on March 14 Ides started from Moscow on a sled. He followed the course of the rivers, making a long detour northward to Vologda, then by the Suchona to the Kama, and so into Asia. The travelling was slow, but the expedition seems to have encountered few hardships, and it arrived safely at Irkutsk, which Ides thus described: "The suburbs are very large; all sorts of grain, salt, flesh, and fish are very cheap here; . . . beside great numbers of Russians have settled here, and taken up some hundreds of villages, all which with great industry and success promote agriculture." He reached

Lake Baikal on March 10, just a year after leaving Moscow.[1] Ides travelled to Peking by the Nertchinsk road. The country seems to have been safe.

To the south and west of Moscow, as the resistance was greater, the parts of the system united more slowly. The Baltic was closed by the Swedes and the Poles, while Turks and Tartars intervened between the states grouped along the Volga and the Kama and the Black Sea. Passing by, for the moment, Peter's great campaigns against the Swedes, and the foundation of St. Petersburg, the absorption of the Kirghiz opened the roads to Samarkand and India.

At the beginning of the eighteenth century the Kirghiz, divided amongst themselves and attacked by the Kalmucks and the Cossacks, asked to become Russian subjects. Peter declined, feeling, probably, too weak to extend his lines of communication with such powerful enemies on his western frontier. After the victory of Pultowa the Khan Abul-Khair again appealed to the Czar, who agreed to recognize his title to sovereignty provided he would protect Russian caravans travelling along the Syr-Daria and would respect the Russian territory. Following this treaty came the foundation of Orenburg in 1735, and thenceforward the Russians steadily absorbed under their administration the territory tributary to the main trade-routes of central Asia, until now their system approaches both Kashgar and Herat.

Nevertheless the fundamental difficulty remains. The traffic has never paid the cost of maintenance of these extended highways, for the bulk of the more

---

[1] *Three Year Travels from Moscow Overland to China*, written by his Excellency Evert Ysbrants Ides, London, 1705, page 35.

valuable merchandise passes now from the East to
the West by sea, as it did in the days of Dandolo or
of Elizabeth.   Still, consolidation continued, for consolidation was equivalent to economy.   As early as
1654 the Cossacks of the southern steppes coalesced
with the administration at Moscow, but a long
period of war intervened before the predatory population of the Crimea could be subdued.   At last the
Crimea became no better than an abode of bandits.
The Russian colonization spread steadily down the
highway of the Don, and in 1783 Catherine II.
annexed the peninsula, the Turks being too weak to
interfere.   Meanwhile, the partition of Poland had
begun ; but the fall of Sweden and Poland are bound
up with some of the most momentous incidents of
modern European history ; amongst others with the
rise of the German Empire.

Perhaps, relatively to the civilization in which it
flourished, the Hanseatic League was the most powerful and pervasive monopoly which ever existed ; nor,
so long as commerce followed the Elbe and the Rhine
from Venice, could its position be shaken.   The corporation, based on the guilds of the different towns,
was an association of capitalists spreading over
Germany, and controlling transportation between
domestic markets and foreign ports.   Therefore out-
lying countries drawing their supplies from the
North Sea and the Baltic were at the mercy of the
Hanse, which acquired a power over them always
considerable, and sometimes absolute.   In London
during some centuries the Merchants of the Steelyard were influential ; at Novgorod the Germans
were autocratic, and in Sweden they may be said to

have formed the ruling class.   Half the burgomasters
and the counsellors of the Swedish towns were nomi-
nated by the League.   Nothing escaped them ; they
dealt in all commodities, and speculated in most
industries.   In Russia they bought fur and wax, and
sold spices and wines.   In Sweden they sold everything which conduces to luxury and civilization, and
took in exchange dried fish and iron.   Under such
conditions the Swedes could accumulate little.   The
Hanse merchants, as creditors, kept manufacturing
to themselves.   For example, the Germans bought
the Swedish pig, took it to Dantzic, manufactured
it, carried it back to Stockholm or Bergen, and sold
it at their own price.

It is impossible to conjecture how long the League
would have retained its monopoly had trade followed
its old routes.   It fell, like Venice, with the discovery
of the ocean passage to India.   When undersold by
the shipping of the west, it lost vitality, and one
after another its vassals liberated themselves.   Gustavus Vasa emancipated Sweden.

Gustavus gained the throne partly through the
aid of Lübeck, therefore he did not begin reforms
before he knew that he could safely discard his ally.
Of much ability, Gustavus saw the advantage his
country would reap by the overthrow of the Hanse,
and by degrees projected measures of relief.   The
Hanse resisted, by plotting treason ; the king retali-
ated, hostilities ensued, Gustavus prevailed, and the
treaty of Hamburg, in 1533, reduced the corporation
to impotence.   Once free, Sweden soon earned wealth
and glory.   Gustavus, needing skilled labor to develop
the iron, prohibited the export of pig to Dantzic, thus

throwing the workmen, whom the Hanse had there collected, out of employment. Many of these emigrated to Scandinavia, and by 1611, when Gustavus Adolphus succeeded his father Charles IX., Sweden had gone far. Under Gustavus Adolphus the peninsula reached its full development. Gustavus followed the policy of his predecessors, and his kingdom became a leading industrial community.[1] The effect was immediate and unmistakable.

Drawing energy from her minerals, the nation fought the Thirty Years' War, and won for Gustavus Adolphus his victories. These victories shattered mediæval Germany, but no campaigns, however brilliant, would have built up the kingdom of Prussia, had the world in 1650 been centralized as in 1200.

The founding of Irkutsk was contemporaneous with the expansion of Brandenburg under the treaty of Westphalia, because it was through the opening up of Russia and Siberia that the region tributary to Berlin received the impulsion which caused it to consolidate. It was this core which in a little over two centuries developed into the modern German Empire.

The surplus production of eastern Europe and Asia, from Lake Baikal on the east to the Oxus on the south, sought more and more eagerly the paths of least resistance to Amsterdam and London. Some passed thither by Trebizond, and some by the ports of Livonia, but perhaps the more valuable portion went by river and by road to the German markets in the valley of the Elbe, and from thence to Hamburg.

Like all processes of nature, the construction of

[1] *Die Geschichte des Eisens*, Beck, II., 900, 1291.

modern Russia and Germany has been in accordance
with fixed laws. When the dominant market sought
the North Sea, and, in consequence, the lines of
communication in central Russia began to consolidate, the cost of administration increased, and it
became a question of life and death to the Muscovite
organism to obtain direct relations with its customers.
At Novgorod the Hanse occupied somewhat such
a position as the Arabs held at Cairo ; having a
monopoly, they raised the price of all their sales, and
depressed the price of all their purchases. Russia was
poor and suffered intensely. It tried war. On November 5, 1494, Ivan III. seized the warehouses at Novgorod, threw the merchants into prison, and carried
away their goods. But this did not end the difficulty.
Somewhat later the Baltic ports, but especially Reval,
Dorpat, and Narva, resorted to trade combinations to
enhance prices. As a result the Russians sent their
more valuable products direct to Poland, and from
Poland to Leipsic. The chief of these products was
fur. In 1549 the representative of Riga at Lübeck
stated that Novgorod's fur trade had been diverted
to Leipsic, and that it passed thither by way of Littau,
Cracow, and Posen.[1]

Another important export of Russia was leather,
made in the Ukraine. This leather, shipped by way of
Breslau, was exchanged for linen and manufactures,

[1] " In dieser Beziehung machten die Vertreter Rigas — 1549, 1554 —
geltend, der einstmals zu Nowgorod blühende Handel mit Pelzwerk
gehe jetzt durch die Hände der Littauer, Krakauer, Posener und an-
derer hauptsächlich auf Leipzig und werde schwerlich wieder nach
dem Contor gelenkt werden konnen," — *Berichte und Akten der Hans-
ischen Gesandtschaft nach Moskau im Jahre 1603*, Otto Blümcke, IV.

the whole trade centring in Germany. So large and so lucrative was the business that Russian leather, in Peter the Great's time, cost less in Breslau than in St. Petersburg.

It was this commerce which made the fortune of Leipsic. Ivan sacked Novgorod in 1494, and in 1497 and 1507 the Emperor Maximilian confirmed the charters which gave Leipsic her most important privileges, the town becoming forthwith the chief market of the world for furs. Both Leipsic and Berlin belong to the Elbe system of waterways, and thus enjoy cheap access to the sea. The roads from Moscow, Warsaw, St. Petersburg, and Breslau all converge at Berlin, where they unite in a single line to Hamburg. But Hamburg has always been an advantageous port for Russia, because, in the Middle Ages, by trans-shipping at Lübeck and Hamburg, merchants avoided the tolls as well as the dangers of the Sound; and, in later times, because by travelling overland to Berlin they escaped the exactions of the Livonian cities, and often the custom-houses. Smuggling on the Berlin route was practised on a large scale. In 1707, when Charles XII. was meditating an invasion of Russia, a panic seized on Moscow and the " great foreign merchants and capitalists hastened to go to Hamburg with their families and property, while the mechanics and artisans went into their service." [1] Such persons would certainly have travelled by the safest and best-established route.

Therefore Leipsic and Berlin prospered in the sixteenth and seventeenth centuries, because they became centres for the overland trade flowing from

[1] *Peter the Great*, Eugene Schuyler, 2, 76.

the East toward Amsterdam and London, and during the last century Berlin has been even more power-fully stimulated by the development of the Polish and Silesian minerals.

Prussia and Russia grew simultaneously, as parts of a single whole, and the Seven Years' War, in which Frederick extended his dominions south to the borders of Galicia, along the frontier of Poland, was only the supplement to the campaigns of Peter, in which he dismembered Sweden. At the close of the Thirty Years' War Sweden not only held most of the eastern coast of the Baltic, but Pomerania and other German provinces. Sweden then enjoyed preeminence. The Swedish soldiers were the most renowned, the Swedish statesmen the most respected, the Swedish industries the most active. Russia, on the contrary, still wallowed in barbarism. Yet the Swedes instinctively felt insecure and tried to destroy their enemy. Most nations have obeyed these intui-tions and have fought their bloodiest battles on some apparently trifling pretext, yet, as men have after-ward perceived, in anticipation of an approaching catastrophe. Few have resigned themselves to sink without a blow.

The mind of Charles XII. of Sweden is now usu-ally deemed to have been unbalanced, but his con-temporaries thought differently. Johnson said that at his name Europe grew pale. France and England both sought his alliance, but Charles cared not for them. His whole soul was fixed upon the east; his one idea to strike at Moscow. And men believed he would succeed. He himself, in 1707, expected within a year to dictate peace from the Kremlin. Nor did

his calculations seem unreasonable. According to
Napoleon, he commanded 80,000 superb troops, and in
his first campaign in 1708 he defeated the Russians on
the Beresina and at Smolensk. Master of Poland and
Riga, and only ten days' march from Moscow, Peter
lost courage, and sent Charles propositions of peace.
Charles rejected the overture, but, instead of advancing at once on Moscow, turned toward the south with
the expectation of forming a junction with the Cossacks under Mazeppa, and wintered in the Ukraine.
Napoleon has condemned his tactics, and on such a
matter Napoleon's opinion must be final, but probably nothing could have availed him. In these great
movements the genius of a general can seldom affect
the final result. The forces at work are too cogent.
In this war, as in 1812, the longer hostilities lasted,
the more the defence gained upon the attack. The
inference is obvious.

When Charles took the field in the spring of 1709,
he commanded only about 24,000 men, and with
these he invested Pultowa. Peter, on the other
hand, concentrated some 60,000 for the relief of the
place, and it is noteworthy that while the Swedes
lost in effectiveness as well as in number, because of
the hardships they endured, the Russians gained in
both. Charles, notwithstanding the disparity of
force, attacked. He met a repulse, and when the
enemy took the offensive his army broke, and was
either captured or destroyed. In his joy Peter ex-
claimed, likening Charles to Phaëthon, " The son of
the morning has fallen from heaven ; the foundations of St. Petersburg now stand firm."

Pultowa was decisive. Thereafter Germany and

Russia divided the heritage of Sweden.   It is impossible to follow the policy of Peter in detail, but his main conception has been well summed up by Rambaud in his *History of Russia:* "Peter always dreamed of making Russia the centre of communications between Asia and Europe.   He had conquered the shores of the Baltic, but he had, to indemnify himself for the loss of the Azov, to open at least one of the eastern seas.   Persia, mistress of the Caspian, was then a prey to anarchy, under an incapable prince whom rebels assailed on all sides.   Some Russian merchants had been plundered.   Peter seized the pretext to occupy Derbent, and took command himself of an expedition which descended the Volga from Nijni to Astrakhan.   After his departure operations continued, the Russians took Bakou."[1]   So, consistently, Peter's first work at St. Petersburg was to connect the Neva with the Volga, by the canal of Ladoga, and he planned also to unite the White Sea with the Gulf of Finland, and the Black with the Caspian by a canal between the Volga and the Don.

As an effect of more rapid communications Russian society received an energetic impulsion.   Success in competition depends on rapidity and economy of movement, and all barbaric civilization is costly because of defective administration, which engenders waste.   Peter's reforms tended to suppress waste and to augment speed.   His improvement of trade-routes illustrates the latter proposition; one or two examples will illustrate the former.

Every barbarous country pays its civil servants by fees charged to the individual who requires a service,

[1] *Histoire de la Russie,* Rambaud, 411

as elsewhere lawyers and doctors are paid. The conception of general taxation for fixed salaries is very advanced. Yet the exaction of fees by officials occasions loss and delay. The ancient Czars pronounced this formula when making an appointment, "Live off your place and satisfy yourself." Peter was stern toward peculation. He tortured and killed many officials who had peculated, banished others, beheaded several governors, and one great dignitary he compelled to produce his books, and convicted him, by his own accounts, of being robbed by his intendant and of himself robbing the state. Peter flogged him with his own hands, and sent him " to settle his own reckoning with his intendant." The military administration was wasteful, among other reasons, because the officers starved the recruits and stole the money allowed for food. The consequence was a large mortality. Peter offered the estate of any official convicted of such practices to whoever would give proof of guilt. He was soon overwhelmed with anonymous letters making all kinds of unsubstantiated charges, and this plan had to be abandoned. On the whole he accomplished little or nothing, for the salaries paid the civil servants were inadequate to their support. Peter also pursued the policy of his predecessors and encouraged the immigration of skilled labor, whether industrial or agricultural. The newcomers indeed could not mix with the natives, yet they may have increased intellectual flexibility in some degree.

Thus although in the eighteenth century the movement of Russia lagged behind the movement of the West, it had become rapid compared with the stagnation which prevailed when Jenkinson lived, and its effect may be measured on the steady lengthening out of Brandenburg, which was the continuation of its main trade-route.

At the accession of Ivan the Terrible Brandenburg was, what it had been since the thirteenth century, a somewhat compact block of territory lying across the Oder and the Elbe. When Ivan came to the throne in 1533, the overland trade, for the more costly goods, from Moscow to the Elbe was established, and it went on increasing and stimulating the region through which it passed. Ivan died in 1584, and already the old era approached its end. The Thirty Years' War which established a new equilibrium was at hand. The war broke out in 1618, and in 1620 Frederick William, the Great Elector, was born. This man laid the foundation of Prussian ascendency, and he did so logically by stretching out along his trade-routes toward Moscow on the one side, and toward the metals of the Rhine on the other. By the treaty of Westphalia, which closed the Thirty Years' War in 1648, Frederick obtained Lower Pomerania, which carried his territory nearly to the Vistula. Subsequently he conquered Upper Pomerania from the Swedes, but was forced to surrender it. Most noteworthy of all, in 1666, he obtained in the Rhine country the Duchy of Cleves and the counties of Mark and Ravensburg. Mark was then the very heart of the Rhenish iron industry, the three chief manufacturing towns being Lüdenscheid, Altena, and Iserlohn.[1]

Peter the Great's victory over Charles led to an

[1] *Die Geschichte des Eisens*, Beck, II., 1174.

expansion of Russia toward the west, and this expansion was followed by the Seven Years' War, in which Frederick seized Silesia, causing a corresponding Prussian expansion toward the east. A generation later the two great systems, steadily gravitating toward each other, divided Poland, and their frontiers met. In the attack on the overland system by Napoleon, Prussia, when conquered by France, freed herself through the defeat of Bonaparte in Russia.

Since then the same process has continued. A glance at a modern railway map will show the base on which the German Empire now rests. It is the old Brandenburg and Elbe system continued to the minerals of Westphalia. The lines of traffic run east and west from the Rhine to Moscow. They centre in Berlin, and have their outlet at Hamburg. The chief of these lines are those from Frankfort and Cologne to Berlin, and from Berlin to St. Petersburg, Warsaw, and Breslau. South Germany has never yet been thoroughly amalgamated with Prussia, because their trade-routes do not exactly converge. Now, as in the Middle Ages, the lines north and south naturally pass through Leipsic and Cologne rather than Berlin, with the exception of that to the Erzgebirge, which is in the Elbe valley.

After the wars of Peter and of Frederick the Great, Poland lay like a wedge between the two great wings of the overland system. Poland had been created by the same conditions which had created the Hanseatic League, and as long as commerce flowed from south to north, both organisms retained their vitality. In the Middle Ages, much of the Hungarian traffic passed from the Danube at Buda to the upper

Vistula at Cracow, and thence floated down to Dantzic and the Baltic.   Thus the Fuggers sent their
copper to Antwerp.   Accordingly Cracow developed
into the chief local market, and as such became the
capital of Poland.   In 1320 Ladislaus made it the
royal residence, in 1364 Casimir III. founded its
famous university, and during the sixteenth century
the city reached its highest prosperity contemporaneously with the prosperity of Augsburg and the
Fuggers.   In the seventeenth century the decline
began, just at the dawn of Berlin's fortune.   In
1609 the court moved down the Vistula to Warsaw,
which lies at the point where the river approaches
Moscow nearest, on the line between Moscow, Smolensk, Berlin, and Leipsic.   Cracow then decayed
fast, and in 1734 had fallen so low that it had ceased
to be used even as the royal burial-place.   The
migration of the capital of a country is demonstration of a displacement of trade-routes and of
energy.

Therefore the evidence shows that, by the time of
the death of Peter the Great, the direction of the
circulation of eastern and central Europe had changed
from the north and south arteries, to the east and
west, and with this change the cause which had created Poland vanished.   Accordingly the kingdom
dissolved, a portion of it gravitating toward the system of the Danube, and the remainder dividing
between the two powerful organisms which administered the transcontinental highways.   The first
partition of Poland occurred in 1775, the last in
1795.   Such an unification of interests by cheapen-
ing communications, sharpened competition at the

termini, and one of its effects was to make the position of France untenable.

During the third quarter of the eighteenth century France fell into isolation. Ejected from Canada and India, she could play no part in the maritime exchanges which centred in London ; while she lay beyond the zone of the Russian thoroughfares, which converged at Berlin and ended at Hamburg. From the close of the administration of Colbert France declined apace. Under her antique organization she competed at a loss, until a chronic deficit became insolvency. Then, nerving herself for a supreme effort, she simplified her methods of administration, and struck at her rivals.

CHAPTER V

WHEN the explorations of Vasco da Gama caused
the migration of the dominant market from Italy to
the Atlantic coast of Europe, a struggle began, between Spain, France, Holland, and England, for the
control of the ocean routes to India. Spain succumbed early, Holland had not the bulk to contend
successfully, and France and England were thus
left, toward the close of the eighteenth century, to
fight out the battle alone.

The disadvantages under which France labored
from her position at the extremity of a long peninsula,
isolated from her neighbors because of her converging waterways, and yet exposed to their attack, has
been described; but certain peculiarities of the Gallic
temperament also operated strongly against her.
Most of the modern Latin races seem to have inherited, in more or less degree, the rigidity of the Roman
mind. The Spaniards have always been tenacious
of their traditions, and the French have found social
innovation so difficult, that they have preferred to
try to crush competitors by arms, rather than to
undersell them by economics which would necessi-
tate changes in local customs. The Romans dis-
played the same instinct throughout their history.
Beck, in his *History of Iron*, has given an interesting
example of how injuriously conservatism affected

manufacturing: " This patriotic dogmatism, which is peculiar to the French, seriously influenced the development of their iron industry in the eighteenth century. . . . It stood in the way of a progressive development, since the hostility to England prevented the French from recognizing without prejudice the superiority of the English in the domain of forging, so that the greatest improvements, especially in the use of coal, gained entrance into France much more slowly than into Germany." [1]

When Spain sank, England did not rise very rapidly. Holland profited more immediately by the sack of Antwerp. From the opening of the seventeenth century the maritime provinces fattened upon the war with Spain; they captured the Moluccas, robbed American galleons, and even blockaded Lisbon and Cadiz. At length Spain could endure the drain no longer, and in 1609 Philip III. recognized the independence of the Dutch. Forthwith Amsterdam became the leading port of Europe, and the Bank of Amsterdam the most powerful financial corporation in the world. From 1610 onward Amsterdam throve, while France almost contemporaneously, under Richelieu, entered upon a period of centralization, which ended in 1653 with the collapse of the Fronde. Mazarin died in 1661. Louis XIV. then began his active life, and France soon saw her greatest epoch. Never before or since has France so nearly succeeded in establishing a supremacy over Europe, as in the third quarter of the seventeenth century. Louis XIV. was the first potentate of his age; his army the largest and the best organized, his

---

[1] *Die Geschichte des Eisens*, Ludwig Beck, III., 997, 998.

generals the most renowned; his navy, though not perhaps the most numerous, yielded to none in quality; his court was the most magnificent, and his capital the most materially and intellectually brilliant. All the world admired and imitated Paris. On the one hand, Molière, Racine, La Fontaine, Bossuet, Fénelon, and many others raised letters and science to an unrivalled eminence; on the other, Versailles ruled absolutely in fashion. As Macaulay has observed, the authority of France "was supreme in all matters of good breeding, from a duel to a minuet. She determined how a gentleman's coat must be cut, how long his peruke must be; whether his heels must be high or low, and whether the lace on his hat must be broad or narrow. In literature she gave law to the world. The fame of her great writers filled Europe."

Nevertheless, brilliant as had been her success elsewhere, in one department France betrayed weakness. The French people were innately conservative. While centuries of war, accentuated by foreign conquest, had finally consolidated the nation in a military mass which could be marshalled by a single will, in habits of life and methods of business the ancient provinces remained nearly as foreign to each other as they had been during the Middle Ages. They declined to amalgamate, and though the king occasionally exercised an arbitrary power in matters of police, in financial administration he was nearly helpless. The inferiority of France, relatively to her neighbors, lay chiefly in the cost of domestic communication, which, because of converging rivers, should have been cheap. Colbert proposed to abolish all internal

tariffs. Pierre Clément, Colbert's biographer, has thus
described the obstructions which then prevailed : —

" The provinces called the 'five great farms' as-
sented. Others who refused, because of their per-
sistence in isolating themselves, were designated
under the name of 'foreign provinces.' Lastly, they
gave the name of 'provinces reputed foreign' to
a final category. The districts comprised in this
category were, in reality, completely assimilated to
foreign countries, with which they traded freely without paying any duties. For the same reason, the
merchandise they sent into other portions of the
kingdom was considered as coming from abroad,
and that which they bought paid, on entering their
territory, the same duty as if brought from abroad." [1]

Trade languished, for the tariff of Languedoc had
no more relation to that of Provence than either had
to that of Spain ; and even the provincial tariffs were
trifling beside the rates and tolls of towns and bar-
onies. Thirty dues were collected between Lyons
and Arles, and manufacturers of Lyons complained
bitterly of the rigor of the taxes of Valence. A bale
of silk, they said, paid three times before it could be
used. Merchants protested that the city closed the
river. Nevertheless, in spite of conservatism, no
people has ever better loved lucre than the French,
and this yearning for wealth became incarnate in the
great minister of finance of Louis XIV.

Jean Baptiste Colbert, the son of a draper of
Rheims, was born in 1619, in humble circumstances.
Little is known of his youth, but at twenty he took
service as a clerk in the War Department, and in

1651 he passed into the employment of Mazarin. There he prospered, and in 1659 had risen high enough to dream of destroying Fouquet.

The farming of the direct taxes formed, perhaps, the most noxious part of a decaying system, and it was in the collection and disbursement of taxes that Fouquet ran riot. Louis himself afterward averred that the "way in which receipts and expenses were handled passed belief." Subject to little or no supervision, Fouquet appropriated vast sums. His famous palace of Vaux, Voltaire asserted, cost 18,000,000 livres, and all agreed that it outshone St.-Germain or Fontainebleau. France dreamed of becoming the centre of European industries, and Colbert conceived his mission to be the realization of this dream. To attain his end, he proposed to build up manufactures by bounties and grants of privileges; but he also comprehended that to make industries profitable he must reduce waste. Under Louis XIV. Fouquet embodied the principle of waste; therefore Colbert attacked Fouquet, and rose upon his ruin. When, however, Colbert had attained to power, he paused. He improved methods of accounting, but, raised to an eminence, he saw that existing customs went to the root of contemporary life, and that the reorganization of the administration meant the reorganization of society, or, in other words, a revolution. Yet he could not stand still and maintain himself.

International competition cannot be permanently sustained on a great scale by bounties; for bounties mean producing at a loss. Bounties may be useful as a weapon of attack, but they cannot, in the long run, bring in money from abroad; for they simply transfer the property of one citizen to another by means of a tax. One nation can gain from another only by cheaper production. If a certain process is dearer than another, the assumption of a portion of the cost by the state cannot make the transaction profitable to the community at large, though it may to the recipient of the grant. The Continental sugar bounties, for example, have doubtless been successful in enfeebling England by ruining her colonies, and they have also enriched the makers of beet sugar; but they have never, probably, been lucrative to France or Germany.

Like any other corporation, a nation can live beyond its means as long as its own savings last, or as long as it can borrow the savings of others; and now accumulations are so large that a country, like Russia, can maintain itself long on credit. In the seventeenth century accumulations were comparatively slender, and Colbert came quickly to the parting of the ways. He understood that to simplify the internal organization of the kingdom sufficiently to put it upon a footing of competitive equality with Holland or England would involve the reconstruction of society; yet to continue manufacturing on the existing basis, which entailed a loss, could only be made possible by means of loans, for the people were sinking under taxation. Colbert judged that he could not borrow safely upon the necessary scale; and thus the minister, very early in his career, found himself forced to make the choice which, under such conditions, must always, sooner or later, be made, between insolvency, revolution, and war. If left undisturbed, the mechanism which operates cheapest will in the end supplant all others; and this fundamental truth Colbert learned. In three years after he had entered upon his task he had broken down. In 1664 he formulated a scheme, part of which was a liberal tariff, and part the simplification of internal fiscal usages. He dared not press his reform, and, as waste continued, his whole policy fell, and with it fell his industrial system. The cost of production remained higher in France than in Holland, therefore commercial exchanges went against the kingdom; and in 1667, to correct exchanges and prevent a drain of specie, Colbert resorted to a prohibitive tariff, or, in the words of his biographer, tried the experiment of " selling without buying."

This course struck at the fountain of Dutch life. Holland being the distributing centre of Europe, her prosperity depended on keeping open the avenues of trade. If she allowed foreign countries to be closed against her, while her market remained free, she might be suffocated by the bounty-fed exports of France. Germany has recently suffocated the West Indies by identical methods. The Dutch understood the situation perfectly, and Van Beuningen, the ambassador of the Provinces in Paris, thus explained his views in a letter to John de Witt, " Since the French exclude all the manufactures of the United Provinces, means must be found, as complaints are useless, to prevent them from filling the country with theirs, and thus draw from us our quick capital."

As a financier Colbert constitutionally disliked war, more especially as war was not his trade, and, if successful, would redound more to his rival, Louvois's, glory than to his own. Without any question Colbert would have kept peace could he have done so and sustained the industrial system, with which his fortunes were bound up. For these reasons some of Colbert's partisans have maintained that he always deprecated the Dutch campaign. He certainly pondered the crisis long and anxiously, for it involved his tenure of office, as well as the destiny of France; but a perusal of his correspondence can leave no open mind in doubt in which direction he found the path of least resistance. The published documents abundantly justify Pierre Clément's conclusion, that "this time, at least, the only one perhaps, [Colbert and Louvois] worked with an equal ardor to attain a common end."[1] Colbert discussed the situation in all its bearings, and dilated upon his disappointments and mortifications. In 1669 he lamented the stagnation of French commerce. He estimated that, out of the 20,000 ships doing the traffic of the world, the Dutch owned 15,000 or 16,000, and the French 500 or 600 at most. The final blow, which is said to have almost broken his heart, fell in 1670, when, just as the French East India Company admitted itself to be practically insolvent, the Dutch Company divided forty per cent. From that moment Colbert recognized peaceful competition as impossible, and nerved himself for war. In May, 1672, Turenne crossed the frontier at the head of a great army, and the campaign opened which is the point of departure for all subsequent European history down to Waterloo.

Nor was the action of Colbert exceptional. On the

---

[1] *Histoire de Colbert*, Clément, I., 303.

contrary, he obeyed a natural law. Every animal, when cornered, will fight, and every nation always has fought and always will fight when war offers the path of least resistance. Competition is a choice of weapons. The French chose arms, and in this case they were justified by the apparent probabilities of a conflict.

Considered as a means of competition, war must be regarded as a speculation; a hazardous one, it is true, but one to be tried, where the chance of gain outweighs the risk of loss. To Colbert it seemed, in 1672, that he risked little, and might win much.

His deadliest enemy lay before him, rich and defenceless. There could be no doubt as to the value of the spoil, should Louis prevail. Amsterdam was opulent. As late as the time of Adam Smith, the Bank of Amsterdam held the position occupied by the Bank of England during the last century, while the commerce of the country exceeded that of all the other nations combined. Furthermore, if Holland was rich, she was peaceful. The navy still retained some degree of energy, but the army was both small and of poor quality. The urban population of the Provinces had not won credit in battle, even during the revolt against Spain, and in the years which had intervened since Alva's victories it was believed to have deteriorated. Lastly, the Dutch were divided; the Orange and De Witt factions hating each other as bitterly as they hated Louis.

Conversely, France stood as a military unit. The king's will met with no opposition. Louvois's administration far surpassed anything then existing. Throughout the army the officers were excellent, and

Turenne and Condé had no rivals as leaders in the field. The whole force of the community could be utilized, for the peasants could be drafted into the ranks, and the nobles served from choice. The odds were very great, and Colbert counted them as a man of business. Colbert understood perfectly that he was playing for high stakes, but he thought the dice were loaded, and, under the circumstances, felt justified in taking the risk. The country was in a dilemma. Much money had been invested in commerce and industry. These were undersold by the Dutch, and as matters stood the investment would be lost. Could Holland be crushed, competition would cease, and not only would the capital already embarked be safe, but it would be advantageous to employ more. Social reform had been tried and failed.

Against these manifold advantages was to be reckoned the outlay for hostilities; for Colbert, probably, never contemplated the possibility of ultimate defeat. The expense promised to be light. The soldiers all thought that a few weeks, or at most months, would put Holland in the hands of the French. At first, indeed, it seemed that no serious resistance would be attempted. The Dutch troops fled or surrendered; the towns opened their gates. In June the French threatened Amsterdam. Scandal even asserted that nothing saved the city but Louvois's jealousy, who feared that an immediate peace might exalt Colbert too far. Colbert, on his side, felt the victory won, and in those days of triumph laid bare the recesses of his heart. In a memorandum submitted to the king he explained the use to be made of victory. The paper may be read in *Colbert's*

Letters and Memoirs.[1]   Its ferocity is convincing.
In substance he proposed to confiscate the best of
the Dutch commerce, and to exclude the Dutch from
the Mediterranean.   Nevertheless, France was vanquished.   In July William of Orange became stadtholder, opened the dikes, and laid the country under
water.   Six years later Colbert purchased peace, not
only by the surrender of the tariff on which he had
staked his hopes, but by accepting a provision in the
treaty of Nimwegen, stipulating that in future freedom of commerce between the two countries should
not be abridged.

Thus Colbert failed in his speculation, and having failed, like any unsuccessful speculator, he fell.
Louvois succeeded him, as he had succeeded Fouquet;
but the preponderance of Louvois meant the triumph
of conservatism, and the postponement of social
changes in favor of war.   In 1672 France lacked
the flexibility to shed an obsolete system, and suffered
accordingly.   She succumbed because of administrative waste.   Had she been able in 1672 to effect some
portion of the simplification which occurred between
1793 and 1795, London might not have become the
imperial market during the nineteenth century.
Under Louis XIV. France broke down through
waste.   With cheap administration she might not
have needed war to enable her to compete; but if
war had come, her economic endurance would have
exceeded the endurance of Holland.   Holland absorbed, resistance by the rest of Europe would have
been difficult.   No Dutch stadtholder could have
been crowned in England, and no coalition would

[1] *Lettres et Memoires de Colbert,* Clément, II., 658.

have been formed such as that afterward cemented by William of Orange. William's league survived him, and lasted for twenty-five years. It proved profitable. It crushed France and humbled Louis, who, old and broken, sued for peace after the disasters of Blenheim and Malplaquet. Two years subsequent to the treaty of Utrecht Louis died, and under his successor the kingdom plunged onward toward its doom. At last the monarchy fell, not because it was cruel or oppressive, but because it represented, in the main, a mass of mediæval usages which had hardened into a shell, incompatible with the exigencies of modern life. Under it, a social movement of equal velocity to that which prevailed elsewhere could not be maintained. What Frenchmen craved in 1789 was not an ideal called "liberty," consisting of certain political conventions, but an administrative system which would put them on an economic equality with their neighbors. De Tocqueville perceived this forty-five years ago: "Something worthy of remark is that, among all the ideas and sentiments which have prepared the Revolution, the idea and the taste for public liberty, properly so called, presented themselves the last, as they were the first to disappear."[1]

One hundred and forty-three years separated the Dutch War from Waterloo, nearly half of which were filled with desperate fighting. On the whole, France steadily lost ground; her defective administration weighed too heavily. Evicted from Canada and India, she tended more and more toward commercial eccentricity, while England, by the development of her

[1] *L'Ancien Régime et la Révolution*, 7th ed., p. 233.

minerals, distanced her industrially. So far as peaceful competition went, France stood relatively less advantageously toward the United Kingdom, after the readjustment which ended in the empire, than she had toward Holland in 1667, even under the inequalities of the old monarchy. Napoleon judged the situation much like Colbert, only, being a soldier, he felt no repugnance to the remedy. He proposed to displace the seat of international exchanges by making London costly as a market, very much as Philip had made Antwerp costly in the sixteenth century. To accomplish this end, three methods of procedure lay open to him. They were of varying degrees of complexity; he tried them in order, the simplest first.

Napoleon saw that, if he could destroy the British navy, he might invade the islands directly, or isolate them by cutting their communications with America or India, or both. Failing in a naval battle, he might close the Continent to English trade, and by stopping sales cause insolvency. After insolvency he counted on surrender. Lastly, he nourished the idea of marching on India overland and conquering the British base. As a sea victory would be the most effective and cheapest, he risked Trafalgar. His defeat fell on October 21, 1805, and instantly he addressed himself to maturing new combinations. Perhaps no great captain ever conceived plans at once so stupendous, so logical, and so chimerical. Yet he acted with incomparable energy and fixity of purpose.

As he wrote to Joseph, "I have 150,000 men in Germany. I can with that subdue Vienna, Berlin, St. Petersburg." On September 26, 1806, the emperor set

forth on the Jena campaign.   On October 14 he fought
Jena, on October 27 his army entered Berlin, and on
November 21 he issued the celebrated Berlin decree.
By this decree he declared the British islands under
blockade, prohibited intercourse with them, condemned, as prize of war, merchandise coming from
them, and excluded neutral shipping, cleared from the
United Kingdom or her colonies, from the ports of his
dominions.   Napoleon issued this decree in anticipation of the Friedland campaign, for he understood
that, with Russia independent, it must be inoperative.
Merchandise landed on the coast of the Baltic would
always leak across the border into Germany by land.
Therefore Russia must be dominated.   On February
8, 1807, he fought the bloody battle of Eylau, and
failed, but on June 14 he triumphed at Friedland,
and Alexander capitulated.   By the secret treaty
signed at Tilsit, the Czar promised to "make common
cause with France" against England, should England,
after a specified time, decline Napoleon's terms of
peace.

Looking back at this great struggle for supremacy
from the distance of a century, it appears to have
proceeded from premise to conclusion with the pre-
cision of a mathematical demonstration.   Placed at
the extremity of the European peninsula, and practically isolated, France and England fought for the
ocean trade-routes east and west, because the ocean
routes were the cheapest.   England being in possession, and after Trafalgar and Copenhagen unassailable
by sea, Napoleon had to control the rival system, or
the overland routes to India, in order to cut the
communications of his rival.   He had no alternative.

To succeed, he could either occupy Moscow himself, or reduce the Czar to a point where he would serve as his agent.   Nor was this all.   Napoleon considered the problem in all its bearings, and worked it out in its minutest details.   India was his objective point, but he perceived that it would make no difference to Russia whether France or England held the peninsula ; competition between the land and water routes would continue, and Russia would be inimical to the victor.   In fine, he foresaw the inevitable jealousy which afterward disturbed the relations of Great Britain and Russia.

The emperor judged that cordial relations could not long continue between himself and Alexander, even should he confine his advance on Hindustan to the sea ; but he knew full well that if the French should occupy central Asia, they would stab Russian society in its vitals.   This measure Napoleon seriously contemplated.   In 1807 he sent General Gardane to Persia on a topographical mission to report on the military routes, and he even made a treaty with the Shah of Persia in which this paragraph occurred, " If his Majesty the Emperor of the French should decide to send an army by land to attack the English possessions in India, his Majesty the Emperor of Persia, as a good and faithful ally, will allow him passage through his territory." [1]

For these reasons Napoleon refused all material concessions to Russia, whether such concessions touched the partition of Turkey or the fate of the

[1] *Mission du Général Gardane en Perse sous le premier empire,* Alfred de Gardane; and see also, on this whole subject, *Napoléon et Alexandre I.,* Vandal, I., Chap. VI.

Duchy of Warsaw. At the same time he vigorously urged Alexander to renounce communication, direct or indirect, with Great Britain. No one knew better than Bonaparte the strain to which he exposed the Russian organism, nor did it displease him that it should be intense. If bankruptcy supervened and disintegration followed, France would be the gainer, for Napoleon assumed a rupture with Petersburg to be inevitable should England hold out, and the Muscovite empire retain its vitality. In either event, a wasting of the Russian energy would make his task easier, supposing him pushed to the last extremity; and he calculated on being ready to meet the emergency at the end of the two years which he allowed for the pacification of Spain.

The ordinarily patient Slavs, goaded beyond endurance, broke out into fierce denunciation of the Czar. The conversation in the society of St. Petersburg was regularly reported at Paris, and General Savary wrote bluntly what he thought: " The emperor and his minister, the Count Roumanzoff, are the only true friends of France in Russia; this is a truth which it would be dangerous to conceal. The nation would be ready to take up arms, and make new sacrifices for a war against us." In 1810 the break came. Alexander professed willingness to fulfil the letter of his agreement at Tilsit, and exclude British ships, but he declined to exclude American. The English, however, could sell to Americans, and Americans to Russians, and if exchanges could thus be effected between Great Britain and the continent, through the medium of neutrals, the attack on the maritime system collapsed. As

Napoleon said, in that war "there could be no neutrals." In September Champagny wrote to Caulaincourt that ships of all nationalities, chiefly American, sailed over the Baltic by hundreds and by thousands, "like the débris of a routed army." This great fleet Bonaparte commanded Alexander to confiscate, being resolved, in case of disobedience, to use force. He wrote: "My Brother: . . . Six hundred English ships wandering in the Baltic, and which have been excluded from Mecklenburg in Prussia, are bound for your Majesty's dominions. . . . It depends on your Majesty to have peace, or to prolong the war. Peace is and ought to be your desire. Your Majesty is certain that we shall obtain it if you confiscate these six hundred ships and their cargoes. Whatever papers they have . . . your Majesty may be sure that they are English." The result is thus described by Henry Adams in his *History of the United States:* —

"The Czar, pressed beyond endurance, at last turned upon Napoleon with an act of defiance that startled and delighted Russia. December 1 [1810], Roumanzoff communicated to Caulaincourt the Czar's refusal to seize, confiscate, or shut his ports against colonial produce. At about the same time the merchants of St. Petersburg framed a memorial to the imperial council, asking for a general prohibition of French luxuries as the only means of preventing the drain of specie and the further depreciation of the paper currency. On this memorial a hot debate occurred in the imperial council. Roumanzoff opposed the measure as tending to a quarrel with France; and when overruled, he insisted on entering

his formal protest on the journal. The Czar acqui-
esced in the majority's decision, and December 19,
the imperial ukase appeared, admitting American
produce on terms remarkably liberal, but striking a
violent blow at the industries of France." Napoleon
replied, "Your Majesty is wholly disposed, as soon
as circumstances permit it, to make an arrangement
with England, which is the same thing as to kindle
a war between the two empires." [1]

In 1812 Napoleon, driven onward by the inexorable
logic of competition, marched on Moscow to seize the
converging point of the roads between the interior
and the Baltic; and in his campaign met destruction.
It could not have been otherwise, because of the
geographical position of France. France, being
isolated and belonging to neither the maritime nor the
overland system, in order to obtain for herself the
wealth which falls to the dominant market, attacked
Great Britain. To prevail France had to cut her
adversaries' communications, and, failing to do so on
the sea, she attempted the task on land. This involved war with Russia and the whole overland
interest, and thus, with the world allied against her,
France fell.

Alexander the Great had no such difficulty to face.
His problem admitted of solution. In Alexander's
time the avenues east and west converged within the
narrow space between the Bosphorus and Suez.
Alexander held the Bosphorus. He had therefore
only to march to Suez to cut all connections. After
one decisive action, in which he forced the passes into
Cilicia, Alexander drove the enemy before him, and

[1] *History of the United States of America*, Henry Adams, V., 418.

so superior was his force that his operations amounted
to little more than clearing and garrisoning the roads.
He had no anxiety for his rear, and the war paid for
itself, as the traffic on the thoroughfares he seized
was the most valuable in the world.   Lastly, as trade-
routes converged, they could be consolidated under
one administration, at a reasonable cost, and a stable
equilibrium thus attained.   The Roman Empire was
the natural successor of the Alexandrine, and under
Rome peace prevailed for several centuries, substantially unbroken.   Napoleon failed because he attempted to consolidate various diverging systems.

On Napoleon's fall Great Britain was left in a commanding position.   Without a rival on the sea, she
decisively undersold her overland competitor, while
her minerals gave her an effective monopoly of
manufacturing.   For upward of a half a century she
enjoyed these unparalleled advantages, and it was
during this period that she amassed the wealth which
made her the banker of the world.   Instead of being
drained of her bullion, as ancient Italy had been,
England sold cottons to India, and instead of having
to buy grain from Sicily and Egypt, like Rome, her
own agriculture, down to 1845, nearly sufficed for her
wants.   No such favorable conditions had perhaps
ever existed, and an equilibrium so stable would have
apparently defied attack, had not the English themselves invented the locomotive.

Given effective land transportation, the continent
of North America seems devised by nature to be the
converging point of the cheapest routes between Asia
and Europe.   Lying midway between the two continents, which are divided from each other either by

vast expanses of water, or by almost impassable
deserts and mountains, the United States stretches
from the Atlantic to the Pacific, is penetrated by
navigable rivers and lakes, and is not broken by difficult mountain ranges. Even better, it possesses
almost all the more important minerals. Nevertheless,
until the railway had been perfected these advantages
were neutralized by the cost of carriage, and the
United States could never have competed with Great
Britain had waterways retained the preëminence they
held prior to 1850.

Even a generation ago competition remained much
upon the basis of the eighteenth century. Although
tending to shrink, the margin of profit stayed broad
enough to spare the individual trader, and distance
afforded Europe a defence against the attack of more
favored communities. America did not harass France
or Germany. On the contrary, America offered them
the best market for their surplus, the United States
buying manufactures with bullion, raw materials, or
food, and freight acting as a protective tariff in favor
of European farmers. The case of the United Kingdom will illustrate an universal condition.

As late as 1860 a marked disparity existed between
England and the United States. While England's
exports of manufactures then reached $613,000,000,
those of the Union only slightly exceeded $40,000,000 ;
and while in 1860 Great Britain had substantially
completed her railroad system, that of the United
States lay in embryo. Thirty thousand miles of road
were then in operation; 200,000 are now in use,
and even in 1900, 3500 more were added. The
United Kingdom, in 1899, possessed altogether 21,700

miles, and building has long gone on at the rate of a hundred miles or so a year. The burden of construction on the two communities can be measured. In 1860, with the facilities then existing, neither iron, nor coal, nor grain, nor meat could be exported from America in competition with the product of British mines or farms; while, on her side, Great Britain could sell her manufactures in the United States almost at her own price. Thirty years ago, land rates of transportation did not approximate sea rates; therefore, iron, for instance, could not be brought from the interior to the ports. England had in comparison no land carriage. Her resources lay on the coast. Furthermore, a chief source of British prosperity was agriculture. The manufacturing population grew apace; eating much, yet producing no food. Nevertheless they paid for food liberally, because the revenue from America provided ample wages. Thus passing from hand to hand, the landlords finally pocketed the larger share of American remittances, in the shape of rent. The gentry consequently throve, habitually saved a part of their incomes, and invested what they saved either in business paper or in foreign securities. Agriculture thus formed the corner-stone of the economic system of Europe during the decades which ended with the Franco-German War.

Bagehot wrote *Lombard Street* between 1870 and 1873, and in the introduction to that interesting essay he inserted a passage which has made luminous many subsequent phenomena. Commenting on the loanable funds always lying on deposit in London, Bagehot observed : —

"There are whole districts in England which cannot and do not employ their own money. No purely agricultural county does so. The savings of a county with good land but no manufactures and no trade much exceed what can be safely lent in the county. These savings are . . . sent to London. . . . The money thus sent up from the accumulating districts is employed in discounting the bills of the industrial districts. Deposits are made with the bankers . . . in Lombard Street by the bankers of such counties as Somersetshire and Hampshire, and those . . . bankers employ them in the discount of bills from Yorkshire and Lancashire."[1]

Almost as Bagehot wrote these words the economic equilibrium of the world began to shift. The movement started in central Europe. The consolidation of Germany between 1866 and 1870 overthrew France, and transferred to Berlin a large treasure, in the shape of a war indemnity. Besides entering on a period of mining and industrial expansion, the German Empire, by means of this treasure, restricted its coinage to gold. Silver, being discarded, depreciated until, in 1873, France also curtailed her silver coinage, and thus very soon silver bullion cut a poor figure as an asset. But to appreciate the catastrophe which followed it is necessary to go back to 1848, when the United States first succeeded in putting any considerable value of metal upon the international market, and observe the creation of her foreign debt.

Prior to 1848, not only had the United States been a poor country, but she had not prospered extraordinarily. She had contended with overwhelming

[1] *Lombard Street*, p. 12.

difficulties.   Her mass outweighed her energy and
her capital.   Confronted with immense distances,
and hindered from comprehensive methods of transportation by poverty, she could not compete with a
narrow and indented peninsula like Europe.   The
change wrought in these conditions by the influx of
gold was magical.

In the three years 1800–1802 the imports averaged, $93,000,000
In the three years 1848–1850 the imports averaged, 154,000,000
In the three years 1858–1860 the imports averaged, 316,000,000

That is to say, there was an increase of 66 per cent
in half a century, and of over 100 per cent in a
decade.

Exports during 1800–1802 averaged $78,000,000
Exports during 1848–1850 averaged 140,000,000
Exports during 1858–1860 averaged 299,000,000

A ratio of growth of 80 per cent in fifty years, as
against upwards of 100 per cent in ten.

Iron was equally remarkable.   In 1847 the exports
of iron and steel stood at $929,000; in 1858 they had
quintupled, reaching $4,884,000; while the authori-
ties hold that the modern era of iron-making opened
in 1855.   But, perhaps, the most impressive of these
phenomena was the accumulation of capital.   In
1848 the total deposits in the savings banks amounted
to $33,087,488, an average per capita of $1.52.   In
1860 they reached $149,277,504, an average per
capita of $4.75.   This corresponds pretty well with
the growth in purchasing power consequent on the
yield of the mines.   Between 1792 and 1847, the annual production of gold and silver had been less than

$500,000; in 1848 it passed $10,000,000, and in 1850 $50,000,000.

As America was organized in 1848, all bulky commodities lying in the interior, away from navigable waterways, were unavailable, but gold and silver, being portable, could be shipped abroad and sold. They were sold, and from their sale came both capital and credit. A satisfactory railroad system was thereafter attainable. The United States realized her opportunity and strained her means to the uttermost. The debt contracted between 1860 and 1893 cannot be computed, but its magnitude may be conceived from the fact that 35,000 miles of railway having been built up to 1865, 142,000 miles more were added between 1865 and 1893, that during the decade preceding 1893 construction had exceeded 6000 miles annually, and that in 1894 the total liabilities of the roads reached $11,000,000,000. And this huge debt constituted only a portion of the mortgage on the future, which the nation had contracted to obtain internal improvements and to defray the waste of war. Such figures convey little impression to the mind. Perhaps it may aid the imagination to say that Mr. Giffen estimated the cost to France of the war of 1870, including the indemnity and Alsace and Lorraine, at less than $3,500,000,000.

When America's creditors rejected her silver, in 1873, she had to settle in such commodities as they would take, and the chief of these were farm products. A general fall of prices set in, as marked in freight rates as in commodities. This shrinkage affected values abroad, and the worse the position of the creditor class became, the more peremptory grew their demands for payment.

The structure of society had not been simplified in Great Britain, during the French Revolution, as it had on the continent. Consequently, in 1870, much of the complexity of the Middle Ages survived, especially in regard to the tenure of land. In England land was expected to earn two profits, one for the cultivator, the other for the landlord; and though this had been possible when freights were high, it became impossible as they fell, accompanied as the fall in freights was by a decrease in the value of the crops themselves.

In 1873 it cost, on the average, about $0.21 to convey a bushel of wheat from New York to Liverpool, in 1880 only about $0.115; or, estimating the value of the bushel of wheat in London between 1870 and 1874 at $1.60, and allowing for the reduction in railway as well as in ocean rates, the farmer lost something at least equivalent to a protective tariff of 10 per cent. This difference seems toward 1880 to have about offset the rent. At a later date matters grew worse and farms went out of cultivation.

Then a very curious phenomenon occurred. In earlier days the manufactures of Great Britain had been sold in America; the proceeds had been remitted to Lancashire or Yorkshire, had for the most part been spent in wages, and by the wage-earner had been expended for food; the sale of food had paid the gentry's rent, and the gentry's accumulations had either returned to Lancashire as loans, or had been invested in American stocks. Such was the condition when Bagehot wrote *Lombard Street*. What happened in the next two decades a few figures will explain better than much argument. For example, the acreage under wheat in England, Scotland, and Wales fell from 3,490,000 acres in 1873 to 1,897,000 in 1893, while imports of wheat rose from 43,863,000 hundredweight in 1873 to 65,461,000 in 1893. Meanwhile, the population of the United Kingdom had only grown from 32,000,000 to 38,000,000. In other words, the imports of wheat had increased 50 per cent, the population 20 per cent; and this leaves out purchases of flour, which had swelled from 6,000,000 to 20,000,000 hundredweight.

The course of trade is obvious enough. The profits made on sales of merchandise abroad, and paid out in wages, no longer remained with English farmers as the price of food, thus forming a basis for English credit. After 1879, as soon as earned, these profits flowed back again whence they came, with the effect of gradually converting the landholding class from lenders into borrowers.

The landed class became borrowers largely because of the extravagant system of family settlements. The eldest son took the property, but he took it encumbered with settlements for the widow, the brothers and sisters. These settlements constituted a fixed charge on rent; and when rents disappeared, the owner had to make good the settlements, or pay the interest on his mortgages, which amounted to the same thing, out of sales of personal property. Hence, liquidation on a large scale became imperative; and frequently it proved impracticable to save the land. Nevertheless, though undersold in agriculture, Great Britain, with economy and an improved administration, might have prospered, if she could have maintained her advantage in transportation; but in this emergency British society proved inflexible.

Meanwhile America tottered on the brink of ruin.
Deprived at once of her silver, which then represented
a cash asset of upward of $35,000,000 annually, and
of much of the value of her other merchandise, the
United States had to meet the deficiency with gold.
In the single year 1893, the Union exported, on
balance, $87,000,000, a sum probably larger than
any community has been forced to part with under
similar conditions. Such a pressure could not continue. The crisis had to end in either insolvency or
relief, and relief came through an exertion of energy
and adaptability, perhaps without a parallel. The
United States escaped disaster because of intellectual
flexibility.

In three years America reorganized her whole
social system by a process of consolidation, the result
of which has been the so-called trust. But the trust,
in reality, is the highest type of administrative efficiency, and therefore of economy, which has, as yet,
been attained. By means of this consolidation the
American people were enabled to utilize their mines
to the full; the centres of mineral production and of
exchanges were forced westward, and the well-known
symptoms supervened. The peculiarity of the present movement is its rapidity and intensity, and this
appears to be due to the amount of energy developed
in the United States, in proportion to the energy
developed elsewhere. The shock of the impact of
the new power seems overwhelming.

From the age of Augustus downward Europe's
vulnerable point has been her minerals; but all
experience has demonstrated that the centre of
mineral production is likely, also, to be the seat of

empire. At all events, no region can long retain
an ascendency without an adequate supply of the
useful metals and coal. Also, in international competition, to be undersold is equivalent to being without mines, for unprofitable mines close, or else are
protected by a tariff which raises the cost of life
above the international standard. The condition of
the United Kingdom may, perhaps be taken as a
gauge of the condition of the chief industrial nations
of the continent.

As early as 1882, the iron mines of the United
Kingdom yielded their maximum, in round numbers,
18,000,000 tons of ore; in 1900, only 14,000,000.
In 1868, 9817 tons of copper were produced; in
1899, 637 tons. Two years later the turn came in
lead, the output in 1870 having reached 73,420 tons,
as against 23,552 in 1899; while tin, which stood at
10,900 tons in 1871, had dwindled to 4013 in the
same year. The quantity of coal raised, indeed,
increases, but prices have shown a tendency to
advance as the mines sink deeper, so that any considerable industrial expansion is likely to occasion
a rise in the cost of fuel. The end seems only a
question of time. England, France, Germany,
Belgium, and Austria, the core of Europe, are,
apparently, doomed not only to buy their raw material abroad, but to pay the cost of transport.

CHAPTER VI

In March, 1897, America completed her reorganization, for in that month the consolidation at Pittsburg undersold the world in steel, and forthwith the signs of distress multiplied. The Spanish Empire disintegrated, and Great Britain betrayed a lassitude which has attracted the attention of the entire world. One symptom has been the financial weakness discovered during the petty Boer War. To maintain their credit and their bank balance, the *Statist* computed that London financiers regularly employed, during the summer of 1901, 80,000,000 pounds sterling of French capital, and Lombard Street freely admitted that French bankers held the money market in their grasp. A notable feature of modern English civilization is the apparently meagre accumulation of popular savings. The loans needed for the Boer War were not excessive, yet they were negotiated with the utmost timidity, the government relying upon the aid of foreign bankers. In France, in the midst of defeat and revolution, the peasants sent carloads of five-franc pieces to Paris to pay the indemnity in 1870. In the United States a loan of $1,000,000,000 would, probably, be taken readily by popular subscription, and would hardly cause a very material fluctuation in the price of bonds if the operations were not hurried. Between 1900 and 1902 the mere rumor of a new issue of consols, however small the amount, regularly created weakness.   The actual depreciation approximated twenty per cent.

Meanwhile, the current of exchanges has run more and more heavily against the Kingdom, who, having for some years settled her balances in American securities, now apparently has recourse to the sale of such assets as her shipping to discharge upon the United States the burden of her floating debt.   Also, with the loss of her vessels a considerable income will probably vanish, although the earnings of her merchant marine have, perhaps, not been so great as supposed, at least from foreign nations.   British steamers habitually obtain outward cargoes of coal, and homeward cargoes of provisions or ore.   The *Economist* has calculated that thirty per cent of the coal nominally exported goes to coaling stations and is sold to English seamen.   Its price, therefore, becomes an item of freight to be defrayed by the purchaser of the goods transported, and if these happen to be ore or provisions, the English must meet it, and reckon it as dead loss.   The British iron mines are failing, the copper mines have failed, therefore ores have to be imported; the British railways, through conservatism, have been unable to reduce rates, so that the farmer of Devonshire cannot compete with the farmer of Ontario or Nebraska; therefore the British have to rely on Americans, Australians, Russians, and Germans for food, and have to pay for the transportation of what they buy. Meanwhile the English spend on the basis of their old profits now that their profits are gone, and hence comes that enormous and ever growing adverse trade balance, which seems already to have devoured

the savings which once represented gigantic investments, not only in the United States, but on the
continent of Europe. In the six months ending
July 1, 1902, the excess of net imports over net
exports reached £94,545,000, as against £89,753,000
in the first half of last year, and £77,859,000 in the
first half of 1900. In 1890 the adverse balance for
six months was £46,400,000, and at that time the
returns did not include the sale of new ships, which
in 1900 were valued at £3,940,000, and which would,
to a certain extent, diminish the deficit. Under such
conditions American capital would naturally flow
toward England, for the *Statist* has calculated that,
even on the basis of the year ending March 31, 1901,
and after every imaginable set-off had been allowed,
the nation was going behind at the rate of £40,000,000
per annum, or nearly $200,000,000.[1]

Germany has also been perturbed. Years ago
Germany was organized to meet English competition,
and while England regulated the pace, Germany paid
a dividend on her investments. When American
trusts entered the field this profit disappeared, and
Germans now comprehend that, however prices may
temporarily favor them by reason of activity in the
United States, to be permanently secure they must
adjust their whole system of agriculture, industry,
and transportation to a new standard. Conceding
this to be done, success still remains problematical,
for Germany can never match her bulk against the
bulk of the United States, or her mines against
American mines. She must always buy her raw
material. Also, Germany must face the destruction

[1] *The Statist*, April 13, 1901, p. 676.

of her beet sugar industry through the loss of the
American market by the inclusion of Cuba in the
American system.

Russia has, however, suffered most, for Russia is
the heart of the weaker of the two competing economic systems, and as such has probably contracted
the greatest debt, in proportion to its capital, of any
solvent community.   From the nature of the case,
Russia's trials are not new.   They began with the
rise of the Muscovite administration, and have continued ever since.   In 1588, just after the death of
Ivan the Terrible, Giles Fletcher visited Russia, and
thus described what he saw: "Besides the taxes,
customes, seazures, and other publique exactions done
upon them by the emperour, they are so racked and
pulled by the nobles, officers, and messengers sent
abroad by the emperour in his publique affairs, specially in the yammes (as they call them) and thorough faire townes, that you shall have many villages
and townes of halfe a mile and a mile long, stande all
unhabited; the people being fled all into other places,
by reason of the extreame usage and exactions done
upon them.   So that in the way towards Mosko,
betwixt Vologda and Yaruslaveley (which is two
nineties after their reckoning, little more than an
hundredth miles English) there are in sigt fiftie
darieunes or villages at the least, some halfe a mile,
some a mile long, that stand vacant and desolate
without any inhabitant."[1]

In Peter's reign affairs had not improved.   Between
1709 and 1725 the revenue of Russia rose from about

[1] *Of the Russe Commonwealth*, by Dr. Giles Fletcher, Hakluyt Soc.
Publications. 61.

3,000,000 to a little over 10,000,000 roubles, and, as Schuyler has pointed out, " this result could not have been reached without immense and oppressive taxation." "Strahlenberg tells us that to escape the oppression of the tax officials, who collected the taxes in the times of the year worst for agriculture, and seized the draft horses of the peasants, at least a hundred thousand men had fled to Poland, Lithuania, Turkey, and the Tartars. . . . Whole villages ran away to the frontiers or hid in the woods." [1]

Either of these paragraphs might be written of contemporary Russia, for in Russia poverty has long reached its limit, famine is chronic, and it is chronic because it is an effect of continuing causes. Russia's physical conformation is such that the traffic upon her highways has never paid for their maintenance and protection. For example, the revenue of Eastern Siberia has of late years yielded about 6,000,000 roubles, while the government spent 20,000,000 annually in the territory, and such deficits have been continuous for three centuries. The arrears have been made good from the food of the people, and the result has been hunger.

Nor is this expenditure economically made, for the conditions under which Russia exists preclude economy. By reason of her mass, her climate, and the mountains and deserts of central Asia, the circulation throughout the Russian organism is relatively defective. But a defective social circulation is tantamount to intellectual stagnation, and intellectual stagnation is synonymous with primitive methods or

[1] *Peter the Great*, Schuyler, II., 369.

waste. For example, the communal occupancy of land lingers in Russia, and yet communal tenure represents a stage of civilization at least three hundred years younger than the American. Also it is wasteful, because under it the farmer can have no incentive to improve his property, since another must enjoy the fruit of his labor. Consequently Russian methods of farming alter little, machinery is not extensively used, and the English papers intimate that Russian competition with American grain tends to diminish. Industry exhibits like phenomena. Being intellectually sluggish, the Russians are uninventive and unadaptable, and, since the reign of Ivan the Terrible, they have sought to make good their deficiency by the importation of foreigners to manage their factories. Nothing could be more extravagant. One illustration will suffice; they have of late essayed to build up iron and steel interests in the south. To tempt foreigners to immigrate they have imposed a high tariff, and as there is no private demand for steel, the government has bought the finished product at exorbitant prices. The money for these purchases has been borrowed. As the works are owned by foreigners, the earnings are remitted abroad, and then fresh loans have to be negotiated, or the furnaces would close. Sooner or later a pinch was inevitable, and for several years Russia has been struggling with a crisis, which is only alleviated when the Minister of Finance can obtain an advance from France, which enables him to invest in steel. Thus there is acute misery, and misery spreads nihilism and agrarian discontent. The emigration to Siberia is largely caused by an effort to escape from torment

at home. For the same cause Fletcher found the
villages deserted in the sixteenth century, and the
peasants fled to Poland under Peter the Great. Between 1879 and 1885 emigration averaged about
10,000 annually. In 1892 a bad famine began, aggra-
vated by the rise in taxes occasioned by the cost of
internal improvements. In 1892 itself 90,000 farmers found their position untenable, and in 1894 the
number is said to have risen to 600,000, though so
enormous a total suggests an error. Famine in
Russia does not imply an absence of food; it indicates a fall in the well-being of the people. When
crops fail, and poverty reaches a certain point, men
starve because they cannot buy, no matter how
cheap food may be. During these famine years
travellers have found villages whose whole population was rotting from hunger typhus, in which the
national rye bread sold for a cent and a half a
pound.[1]

Peter the Great, having convicted one Alexis
Nesteroff, an Ober-Fiscal, of peculation, condemned
him to be broken alive on the wheel. Afterward,
in his indignation, he dictated a decree punishing
with death all officials who received gifts. General
Yaguzhínsky, who acted as secretary, and who
chanced to be honest, demurred. Peter insisted;
then said Yaguzhínsky, " Does your Majesty wish to
remain alone in the empire? we all steal, some more,
some less but more cleverly." What Yaguzhínsky
meant to point out was that the custom of paying the
civil service by fees prevailed, and that to reform it
Peter would have to change his people. And yet

[1] *Through Famine-stricken Russia*, Steveni, 120.

the fee system entails incalculable waste, and is incompatible with efficiency.   The history of the Siberian Railway displays a gangrene which eats into the marrow of the nation.

The length of the entire Siberian line, including branches, fell short of 6000 miles.   The road runs for the most part through an easy country, except perhaps for the 669 miles from Lake Baikal to Stretensk; the land cost nothing; work can be carried on from several points at once.   In 1891 a French company offered to complete the task within six years, at an average cost of about $30,000 the mile.[1] No one knows precisely what the outlay on the road has been, but figures have been published relating to some sections.   The western division from Tchelabinsk to the Obi was estimated by the French engineers at 20,000 roubles the verst; it had already cost, in 1897, 53,000 roubles, and it will have to be substantially reconstructed before it will bear heavy traffic.[2]   In reality, the main division from Cheliabinsk to Stretensk on the Amur, where steam navigation to the Pacific begins, is less than 3000 miles, and M. de Witte solemnly assured the world that this vital section should be in thorough order by 1898, or 1899 at the latest.   In August, 1898, the first train reached Irkutsk, and the same year the portion from Vladivostok to the Amur was opened.   Yet so defective was the road-bed and material in the spring of 1900, that, when the Chinese outbreak occurred, not only did the main artery prove unfit for ordinary travel, but incapable of transporting enough

[1] 40,000 roubles the verst.
[2] *Où la Dictature de M. Witte conduit la Russie*, E. de Cyon, 63.

troops to guard the lines in Manchuria. As for the garrisons of Port Arthur and similar positions, they appear rather to have been sent by Suez than by Vladivostok. Incompetence could go no farther. Such is the fruit of nine years of toil, at an outlay estimated at more than double the price asked by Frenchmen, and with a product so inferior that experts are agreed the road falls very far below even the European standard, a standard incapable of comparison with the American.

In the United States, between 1880 and 1890, the average construction exceeded 6000 miles of road annually, all built by private enterprise; and in 1887 more than 12,000 miles of track were laid. Had the United States been under a stimulus of apprehension such as the Russians felt in regard to their eastern frontier because of the activity of Japan, the building of a line equal to that to the Amur could scarcely have occupied three years at the most.

Measuring thus Russian with American energy, the former could hardly hold a higher ratio than as one to four or five in relation to the latter. Before the Siberian Railway had been tested by actual experience, many maintained that it would ultimately " constitute a new commercial route for rapid travel and for exchange of the products of East and West,"[1] and this theory was industriously propagated by the French press.[2] Now, less confidence is expressed. The Siberian road will probably be used for passengers, but as a channel for freight it stands already condemned. All the conditions are unfavorable.

[1] *Russia and the Pacific*, Vladimir, 306.
[2] See, for example, *L'Illustration*, January 23, 1897, p. 55.

Siberia stretches over a narrow belt of several thousand miles of arable land, bounded by ice on the
north, and mountains and deserts on the south.
Thus masses of material can hardly be collected by
feeders, as in America, and it is by handling masses
that rates are reduced. Should the rates be fixed
artificially low by the government, the old sore is
opened. The peasantry must pay the deficit.

Under such limitations even an American management could not cope with the Suez Canal; but,
in the future, the Russian civil service will be in
competition with the Panama route. The probability is, therefore, that the trade of northeastern Asia
will eventually flow in larger volume toward the
West, and that all avenues to the East will decline
in relative importance. The Russian Empire in
Asia is an economic system based on overland
thoroughfares leading to Europe, and the experience
of mankind hitherto has been that, when traffic re-
verses its direction, empires dissolve. Japan represents the Western influence, therefore the kernel of
the catastrophe impending in the Orient is the struggle for survival between Russia and Japan.

Modern Japan, like modern America, is the effect
of the migration westward of the seat of energy and
the centre of mineral production. That movement
began with the Mexican War, which preceded the
annexation of California and the discovery of gold.
According to the official statement of the government
of the United States, these two events led to the
despatch of Commodore Perry to Asia to establish relations with the Mikado. "The treaty which closed
the war of the United States with Mexico transferred

to the former the territory of California. . . . If the shortest route between eastern Asia and western Europe be (in this age of steam) across our continent, then was it obvious enough that our continent must, in some degree at least, become a highway for the world. And when, soon after our acquisition of California, it was discovered that the harvest there was *gold*, nothing was more natural than that such discovery should give additional interest to the obvious reflections suggested by our geographical position. Direct trade from our western coast with Asia became, therefore, a familiar thought; the agency of steam was, of course, involved, and fuel for its production was indispensable. Hence arose inquiries for that great mineral agent of civilization, *coal*. Where was it to be obtained on the long route from California to Asia? Another inquiry presented itself; with what far distant Eastern nations should we trade? China was in some measure opened to us; but there was, beside, a *terra incognita* in Japan which, while it stimulated curiosity, held out also temptations which invited commercial enterprise." [1]

Perry sailed from Norfolk on November 24, 1852, and his squadron entered Yeddo Bay on July 8, 1853. Terror reigned on shore. The people of Yeddo prepared for defence. In 1623 the last Englishman withdrew from Hirado, and from that time until Perry's advent the Dutch alone had succeeded in preserving a foothold in Japan. Even the Dutch were limited to sending and receiving a single ship annually, and the notion that Americans would suc-

---

[1] *Narrative of the Expedition of an American Squadron to the China Seas and Japan*, 75.

ceed where others had failed roused general derision. Nevertheless, Perry opened communications with the Shogun.

During the Middle Ages the military class had risen to supreme power in Japan, and their representative, the Shogun, or commander-in-chief, had assumed the executive functions. Therefore, when Perry insisted on obtaining an answer to President Fillmore's letter to the emperor, the responsibility devolved upon the Shogun. Perry did not press the government unduly, but sailed for China, giving notice that he would return in the spring to negotiate a treaty. As soon as he had gone, the Shogun took the advice of the Daimios. The Daimios almost unanimously opposed foreign influence, but on the other hand, being soldiers, they understood that the country could not resist an attack. Accordingly the Shogun and his party determined to compromise. They would yield enough to keep the peace, and in the time thus gained they would arm. Punctual to his promise, Perry reappeared at Yeddo on February 13, 1854, and on March 31 signed a convention which, though not a complete surrender by Japan, opened the door to all that followed.

Forthwith a powerful fermentation set in, schools of languages were frequented, foundries organized, and an immense activity prevailed at the treaty ports. Yokohama in 1890 numbered 122,000 inhabitants, in 1884 70,000, in 1856 it was a mere hamlet. There was no stemming the impulsion. Nevertheless, the entrance of the empire into the vortex of Western competition caused an economic disturbance, which brought on a revolution. In 1868 the Shogun fell,

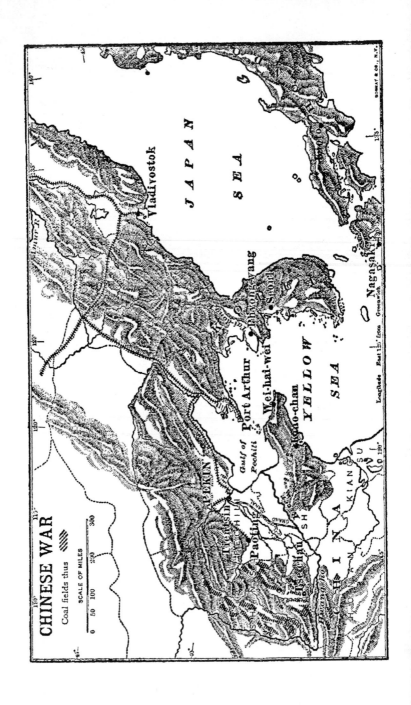

CHINESE WAR

Coal fields thus

SCALE OF MILES
0 50 100   200   300

Amur R.

JAPAN

SEA

Vladivostok

PEKIN

Tientsin
KECHIU
Pao-ting

Gulf of
Pechili

Port Arthur

Wei-hai-wei

Ping-yang
Seoul

Koto-cham

YELLOW

SEA

CHINA

KIANGSU

Nagasaki

Longitude East 135° from Greenwich

and three years later the Daimios surrendered their fiefs. Perhaps no community ever assimilated a new civilization so rapidly as did the Japanese during the decades which followed, and from this intellectual flexibility came success.   Yet, as usually happens upon a profound disturbance of the social equilibrium, the immediate effect was war.

Nothing would here be gained by attempting to detail the long and complex series of events which nominally led to the invasion of Korea in 1894, for the fundamental cause was simple.   It was, in fine, the attack of the economic system, in process of formation, upon the systems of the past.

Competing nations seek, along the paths of least resistance, the means which give them an advantage in the struggle for survival, and among these means the minerals, perhaps, rank first.   Tientsin, on the Peiho, is the port of Peking; and somewhat more than three hundred miles southwest of Tientsin, in the valley of the Hwangho, lies Tsechau, in the province of Shansi, which Richthofen considered as the centre of the richest beds of coal and iron now known to exist, and undeveloped, in the world.   The position of these beds is good.   Although the Hwangho is hardly navigable, and although it is uncertain whether it could be made available at reasonable cost, Tsechau is only about two hundred miles distant from the junction of the Grand Canal with the river, and Tientsin has grown up at the confluence of the Grand Canal and the Peiho. Clearly Shansi and Honan are not only accessible, but cheap transportation could be established between Tsechau and the coast.

In addition, an efficient administration could probably introduce an industrial system modelled upon the American, and could control Chinese labor. Therefore, granting Richthofen's estimate of the wealth of Shansi and Honan to be correct, there is reason to infer that the conqueror of these provinces could, were he capable, presently undersell all competitors in steel. Bearing these facts in mind, the recent disturbances in the East assume the appearance of an orderly sequence of cause and effect.

The greatest prize of modern times is northern China, and the Japanese advanced by Korea because Korea offered the path of least resistance to their goal. In 1894 the Japanese did not command the sea, on the contrary, the Chinese fleet was numerically their equal ; therefore a short passage for transports to the continent was essential to success, and the coast of Korea is only a few hours' sail from the island of Hondo. Accordingly, the Japanese marched through Korea, and seized Port Arthur, at the extremity of the Liaotung peninsula, which commands on the north the entrance to the Gulf of Petchili. Port Arthur having been occupied, the next move was upon Wei-hai-wei, in Shantung, opposite Port Arthur, on the south side of the strait, between Korea Bay and the Gulf of Petchili. That position secured, the Japanese could advance upon the interior at their convenience, for they had annihilated the Chinese fleet and army. The Hwangho and the Peiho empty into the Gulf, and a short and easy campaign would, probably, have made them masters of Peking, Tsechau, and the whole mineral region of Shansi.

The danger to Japan lay not in the enemy, but in

foreign intervention, and intervention came precisely because of the energy she had developed. The overland system perceived that its integrity was menaced, for, should northern China be turned into an active industrial region whose commerce would flow westward, the Russian Empire in Asia could hardly endure. At best, Siberia is long and attenuated, movement therein is imperfect and its cost heavy; but Siberia would readily split in twain were the cohesive force of a single line of ill-built railway, four thousand miles long to Moscow, pitted against the attraction of the markets of America and Japan, acting through a manufacturing community upon the border.

Aware of the danger, the Japanese did not press their victory, but granted China easy terms, the chief of which were an indemnity and the cession of Port Arthur. Even this was too much. Russia, with her appendage France, and Germany, or the overland system, forced Japan to retire from the mainland. Thus the war of 1894 left behind it an unstable equilibrium, with society moving with portentous velocity. The treaty of peace was signed on May 8, 1895, and within two years a heavier shock than the war came from the West. In March, 1897, Pittsburg achieved supremacy in steel, and in an instant Europe felt herself poised above an abyss. As though moved by a common impulse, Russia, Germany, and England precipitated themselves upon the shore of the Yellow Sea, grasping at the positions which had been conquered by Japan, and for the same reason. These positions commanded Shansi. In November, 1897, the emperor of Germany gorged Kaiochau, a month later the Czar grasped Port Arthur, and in the following April the British laid hands on Wei-hai-wei. Nevertheless, the movement came too late, the hour for partition had passed. On February 15, 1898, a torpedo sank the *Maine* in Havana harbor, and on May 1 Dewey destroyed the Spanish fleet in Manila Bay. The United States had expanded into Asia.

Although written documents are lacking, the circumstantial evidence points to the conclusion that, from near the time of the triumph of Pittsburg, an understanding existed between Berlin and Petersburg touching the division of China. Beginning with the German onslaught at Kaiochau, a series of measures were adopted which were either irrational or were intended to provoke an outbreak which would justify reprisals. In fact, the Chinese were so drastically used that not only did rebellion come, but it came prematurely. Even when so much is conceded, the problem remains unsolved how two cabinets could have refused to contemplate the inevitable effects of their work, when every week brought abundant warning that the people had been goaded too far. Regarding the result of the policy, the facts speak for themselves. Certainly the Chinese now, as in the past, hate all foreigners, but among the foreigners they hate the Germans most, and accordingly the first victim in Peking was the Baron von Ketteler, the German minister. On the whole, it seems fair to assume that, when the weakness of China had been demonstrated by the campaigns of 1894, Germany and Russia determined to thrust Japan aside, and divide the spoil themselves. A pretext alone was lacking. The fall in American steel supplied the needed stimulus, and, feeling strong enough to deal with England, they saw already the northern provinces at their mercy. They failed in their enterprise because they comprehended neither the effect of their own harshness nor the energy of the United States.

On June 20, when the legations were beset, every cabinet in Europe collapsed. Not one had a policy or an army ready. The Russians, with their new railway on their hands, could not concentrate men enough in Manchuria to disperse wandering bands of marauders and protect their works. So far as appears, their main line was nearly useless for practical purposes. The Germans, with an enormous army and with a murder to avenge, could not land a gun at Tientsin before Peking had been occupied, and when their force arrived it came ill-provided. The English, having met with a repulse in an expedition undertaken by one of their admirals, remained vacillating and helpless, waiting upon the Germans.

On the other hand, at Washington and Tokio statesmen developed clear views, and found the means of enforcing them. The two governments determined, cost what it might, that the integrity of China should be preserved.

The President of the United States took the lead and led to the end. On July 3, 1900, the State Department issued the note which has since become famous and which laid down the principle that peace continued unbroken between the United States and China, because, China being in insurrection, the Chinese government was unable to perform its obligations. Instead of declaring war, therefore, the

o

President announced his intention of landing an army as an ally, and reducing Peking to obedience. Although insurrection still raged in the Philippines, a column was rapidly concentrated at Tientsin under a soldier certain not to hesitate.

His orders were to march though he marched alone, but there was no danger of absolute isolation, for the Japanese were ready. The European officers were inclined to hesitate, but as none of the powers could contemplate being left behind, they had no option but to move with the Americans. Thus the United States and Japan succeeded in controlling the international policy. Peking was relieved, the legations saved, partition averted, and finally evacuation effected. The New Empire had stretched its arm over northern China.

The equilibrium of the East is now unstable. Two economic systems confront each other, competing for the same prize. Each knows that defeat may be fatal; neither has achieved a decided success.

In 1894 Japan, being the more agile, took the initiative. She fought a brilliant war, but, in the hour of victory, was menaced by an alliance of the whole opposing system, with which she could not cope. The United States had not then become the seat of energy, and had not entered on the field.

Six years later Germany and Russia made their onset; but they were far too slow. Before they could make ready the United States and Japan had anticipated them, and, with the United States and Japan in possession, partition was impossible. Then all fell back. Russia, in a relatively torpid condition, lies extended in a narrow belt along the endless trade-route which stretches from the Gulf of Finland to the Pacific. Her outlets are through Vladivostok and Port Arthur. Between these two ports Korea enters like a wedge. Should Japan seize the peninsula, she would threaten the flanks of both lines of communication, and the Russian position would become precarious.

Nor can the Japanese well afford to remain passive. Were they to abide within their islands while their competitors opened the richest mineral beds of the world at their doors, their very existence as an independent people would be endangered. The Japanese have developed a higher order of energy than the Russians, and such a supposition is hardly to be entertained. Yet the only path by which Japan can expand is through Korea; if she occupy Korea she will flank the Russian trade-routes; and when she flanks the Russian trade-routes the Russian Empire will totter.

Such conditions have heretofore led to well-defined results; and if the future is to be judged by the past, a collision is impending. Should it take place, it would tend toward a fundamental social and political readjustment.

Save as an amusement for the antiquary, history and economics which deal with the past without reference to the present have no significance. Research for its own sake is futile. The only practical value which these studies can have is the light they throw upon the present and the future.

The theory advanced in this volume may be condensed somewhat as follows: For the purpose of obtaining a working hypothesis, it is assumed that

men are evolved from their environment like other
animals, and that their intellectual, moral, and social
qualities may be investigated as developments from
the struggle for life.   If so, these qualities are to be
accounted for as means of offence, or defence, as aids
in satisfying their needs, or as survivals from the past
which have not been discarded.   In the effort to
live each animal will use the means best fitted to
its nature, but as external conditions are in eternal
movement, man's destiny must largely depend on his
flexibility.

Food is the first necessity, but as most regions produce food more or less abundantly, the pinch lies not
so much in the existence of food itself, as in its distribution.   To satisfy their hunger men must not only
be able to defend their own, but, in case of dearth,
to rob their neighbors where they cannot buy, for
the weaker must perish.   Men who cannot fight well
enough for these purposes, tend to fall into servitude
where their labor is valuable, and where it is worth-
less to be exterminated.

Life may be destroyed as effectually by peaceful
competition as by war.   A nation which is undersold may perish by famine as completely as if slaughtered by a conqueror.   Therefore, men thrown into
acute competition with rivals must have the ingenuity
to secure an equality of equipment, else they will
suffer; it may be by hunger, it may be by the sword,
but in either case the purpose of nature will be attained.   Nature abhors the weak.

For these reasons, men have striven to equip themselves well for the combat, and since the end of the
Stone Age no nation, in the more active quarters of

the globe, has been able to do so without a supply of relatively cheap metal. Thus the position of the mines has influenced the direction of travel. To supply themselves with what they lack men must trade or rob; and on the whole trading has been the cheaper. But to buy and sell there must be a market, which can only be reached by travel, and in travelling, as in all functions of life, men follow the paths of least resistance. It is because a highway offers slight resistance that it is a highway. Furthermore, the object of the inhabitants of each market must be to make their highways as little resistant as possible, that they may attract custom, and thus is generated an administration which supervises repairs and police.

Because wayfarers meet at cross-roads, markets grow at cross-roads. When the territory tributary to a market is considerable, and the administrative machinery is somewhat ramified, we call the organism a state ; when it is vast we call it an empire. Therefore the state or the empire is an outgrowth of trade, and usually spreads along the lines of converging trade-routes.

As important markets always lie at the meeting of several ways, and as the movement on trade-routes is variable, the prosperity of a market, or a nation, is uncertain. The travel on a trade-route is subject to contingencies, two of the chief being the discovery of an easier path, and the decay of the terminus. Perhaps the terminus most certain to lose its value is the mine. When different routes connect the same termini, the markets along these routes compete, and are sensitive to any diversion of trade. If the diversion be serious, and can be coped with by no cheaper means, war usually ensues, for war is one of the more drastic methods of economic competition. In the struggle for survival, it matters little how the adversary is overcome; the object is success. The problem presented is purely a choice of means. War, therefore, may be profitable by closing a rival route, or making it dangerous and costly, even if the enemy cannot be totally destroyed. When trade-routes shift, markets move and the seat of empire is displaced. This displacement we call a revolution. It is the most portentous of all catastrophes, usually involving long wars, and many thousands or millions of lives. Nevertheless, the dominant market of the world, or chief seat of empire, seldom abides very long in a single city; the causes which affect its supremacy are too complex.

For example, mines are at once the most ephemeral and the most valuable of possessions, and accordingly mines have always profoundly influenced the social equilibrium. As central Asia appears to have been the cradle of civilization, men exhausted the nearest mines first, and then prospected for more, the easiest path being by the Mediterranean and the ocean. The imperial market has, on the whole, only followed the avenue of least resistance westward toward the minerals.

The character of this oscillation to and fro of the seat of energy may be likened to a cyclone, where the highest velocity is attained within the central vortex, the tendency to calm being proportionate to the distance from the point of disturbance. As the vortex advances, agitation becomes violent in the communities lying in the path of the movement, while in its wake ebullition yields to lassitude, lassitude passes into torpor, and torpor not infrequently ends in death.

This theory can be applied to the history of the last fifty years and its soundness tested. A half-century ago the centre of mineral production lay, probably, in Great Britain. The most frequented trade-routes between the East and West converged at English ports, and Europe was the unquestioned seat of intellectual and physical activity, although the United States, lying in the path of the advance, was highly stimulated. Passing beyond the shore of the Pacific, quietude prevailed. Japan had slumbered for two centuries. On June 21, 1849, the first Californian gold reached Liverpool, and the United States entered upon her career as an international vendor of the metals. In 1897 she achieved supremacy in iron and steel. Meanwhile, if the theory advanced be sound, a certain series of phenomena should have occurred both in Europe and Asia. First, Europe should have declined in relative energy.

In 1850 Russia had reached her zenith. In 1849 she crushed Hungary, exiled Kossuth, and made Austria subservient to her. Within a little more than sixty years she had pushed her frontier 600 miles westward toward Berlin, and 450 miles toward Constantinople; she had so robbed Sweden that what she took exceeded what she left. She inspired general terror, and that terror took the form of a coalition for attack. The coalition succeeded; for, since the Crimean War, Russia has steadily declined in relative weight in Europe. On this point the

literature of fifty years ago is decisive. No one now
fears Russian aggression; no one dreams it possible
that Europe should become Cossack, as Napoleon
suggested at St. Helena. It will be much if
Russia succeeds in keeping the peace, in paying her
debts, and maintaining the integrity of her empire.
In the late Chinese rebellion, in spite of her railway,
and all the preparations of fifty years, she could not
concentrate an army corps upon her eastern frontier;
yet, in the Crimean War, perhaps her most brilliant
exploit was the rout of the allied squadrons in their
attack on the wretched and exposed hamlet of
Petropavlofsk, in Kamchatka.

In Germany a somewhat similar process has gone on,
only Germany has run a more brilliant course, as the
country is more compact. With the change in the
direction of her trade-routes, near three centuries ago,
Brandenburg received an impulsion. But Brandenburg is the nucleus of Prussia, which in turn is the
heart of Germany. The cause being permanent, the
effect was constant, and north Germany gathered
energy, compared to other countries, until the final
consolidation took place in 1870. That consolidation,
by accelerating domestic transportation and exchanges,
aided in the development of the German minerals,
and, through cheap minerals, stimulated industry.
The consequence was a steady relative advance, up
to a period subsequent to the French war. It is to
be noted that Russia and Germany, belonging to a
different economic system from America and England,
have, as yet, lost nothing through the displacement
of their trade-routes. On the contrary, they have
benefited by the tendency of England to fall into

commercial excentricity, for this has encouraged direct communications between the United States and Bremen and Hamburg.   As ocean routes have straightened, the German merchant marine has grown. Germany and Russia, therefore, have hitherto only been affected by a quickening of American competition, which has reduced the prices of grain, iron, steel, coal, and sugar, and has raised the standard of intelligence.

Yet, admittedly, Germany occupies a critical position, because of her lack of minerals and her difficulty in expansion.   Moreover, the absorption of the West Indies by the United States will, probably, ruin one of her chief investments.   In the future, also, there looms up the question of central Asiatic exchanges, and the permanence of the Russian Empire.   Nor is this all.   There are indications that Germany is not keeping fully abreast of the movement of the age. For example, the young Americans of 1850, who wished to be mining engineers, studied in Germany, because the Germans ranked first as miners.   Americans, educated in America, are now preferred in the international market.   The gold mines of the Transvaal are confided to American engineers.   There is no disputing such a test.   Notably also, doubts are growing as to the condition of the German army. The suspicion is abroad that, since 1870, it has not kept pace with modern methods, that conservatism has conquered the administration.   Certainly the expedition fitted out with such elaboration for China did little credit to the staff.   The position of Germany has hardly strengthened since the great quickening in America occurred.

It is, however, in the west of Europe, among the nations affiliated with the British system, that the more serious symptoms are to be anticipated. Of France it is needless to speak. France has long shown indications of decay, and of late she has almost retired from international competition. She still accumulates wealth, partly through the frugality of her people, partly because of certain monopolies which she enjoys, such as her vineyards, and partly because of artistic genius, which enables her to attract foreigners to Paris for education, for pleasure, or for the purchase of luxuries. Still, the France of 1900 has fallen far, in relative consequence, not only from the France of Colbert, or of Bonaparte, but from the France of the Crimea, of Solferino and Magenta.

Spain has disintegrated through diversion of the trade-routes of the West India Islands from Europe to the United States. When Europe bought the Cuban cane, Cuba was loyal to Spain. Now America buys, and Cuba turns to the Union.

Great Britain, however, is most suggestive, for the United Kingdom and the empire of Japan, both groups of islands lying on opposite sides of America, the one in the apparent path, the other in the wake, of the social cyclone, should be supplementary to each other.

In 1850 England held a position which has been rarely equalled. The centre of the maritime system, she was also the chief seat of production of the useful metals, the focus of industry, and the leading banker of the world. Her trade was the largest and the most active, her domestic transportation the most complete, rapid, and cheap, and her intellectual activity the greatest, of any community then existing. Her political institutions were generally taken as a model, her inventors, such as Watt and Stevenson, had, within living memory, revolutionized human relations, while Darwin was meditating his *Origin of Species*. The foundations of the Crystal Palace, in which the first international exhibition was held, were laid in Hyde Park, in September, 1850, and the Duke of Wellington did not die until 1852. Since Wellington, indeed, Great Britain has produced no famous commander, but in the Crimean War her soldiers still retained their ancient vigor in attack. The Charge of the Light Brigade will remain one of the heroic actions of the century. Meanwhile, in 1850, Japan, upon the opposite side of the globe, lay closed to foreign intercourse, a torpid, mediæval community.

At the breath of the advancing cyclone, Japan awoke, suddenly stimulated into feverish activity. Japan's movement is typical of the age of electricity and steam. In one short generation she reorganized her government, her education, her commercial and industrial methods, her navy, and her army. Her history is known to all Christendom, it need not be recapitulated, a single example will suffice; and, as a nation usually concentrates its energy in the highest degree on war, perhaps the institution most emblematic of modern Japan is her army.

Judged by any standard known to us, that army must rank high. The campaigns of 1894 and 1895 might serve as models. In a foreign, unknown, and difficult country, in midwinter, the troops kept the field; the commissariat and the medical departments proved effective; the transportation of 80,000 men

to Korea was managed rapidly and without loss, in
the face of a fleet of equal power; the men showed
endurance, patience, and courage; the officers, skill,
coolness, and impetuosity in attack, while the impact
of the navy was terrific.

Nor can it be urged that the Chinese were im-
potent. On the contrary, the Chinese were then
capable of a much sterner resistance than during
the rebellion of 1900, when their troops were little
better than a mob; and yet, in 1900, they were able
not only to repulse a British admiral, but to hold
Tientsin stubbornly against the allies. The Japanese shattered the Chinese military strength in 1894.

Among many brilliant operations, perhaps none
was more remarkable than the storming of Phyöngyang. Phyöngyang in Korea is a town of 20,000
inhabitants, to the west of the Taidong River, very
strong by nature, and very strongly fortified by the
Chinese. The banks of the river are steep, and the
stream winds round nearly three sides of the city.
The city was well walled, and surrounded by re-
doubts which had been skilfully built. The fortifica-
tions were mounted with field and mountain guns,
and the garrison armed with magazine Mauser rifles.
It was 13,000 strong. The Japanese had rather above
14,000 men available for the assault. After the victory
the Japanese officers admitted that they would have
awaited reënforcements had they appreciated the
power of the fortress.

The main attack was on the forts to the north, but
a feint to the south exemplifies Japanese fighting.
The demonstration began at 4.30 A.M. The forts
were held by the best Chinese troops, armed with

Mausers. There was no cover. Nevertheless the Japanese carried the outworks of two of the four forts, and planted their flag on the ramparts. The Chinese then retired to their inner lines and swept the enemy with a furious cross-fire, who, having exhausted their ammunition, had to search the bodies of their dead comrades for cartridges. Finally the Japanese assaulted again, but, being unable to climb the banks on account of their height, withdrew. Though only a diversion, the fighting had been sanguinary. All the officers were killed or wounded in the Second and Tenth companies of the Twenty-first Regiment, and the Fourth company was led by an ensign. The commanding general was wounded. The object of the battle had been only to divert attention from the main attack. On the north the assault on Peony Mountain was brilliantly successful, and the capture of the Gemmu Gate has become famous.

The details of the storming of Peony Mountain are too long and intricate to be described here. They should be studied with a map, but the capture of the Gemmu Gate was quick and simple, and has been thus related by an Englishman:—

The Gemmu Gate was the one nearest to Peony Mountain. Colonel Sato tried it, after the mountain fell, but the Chinese held the wall so well that the column recoiled before the fire. As the troops fell back, "Lieutenant Mimura, burning with shame at the repulse, shouted to his men, 'Who will come with me to open that gate?' and at once rushed toward the Gemmu Gate. Harada, one of the soldiers of Mimura, then said, 'Who will be the first on the wall?' and flew after his officer. They ran so quickly that only eleven other soldiers were able to join them under the wall after passing through a rain of lead.   Mimura and his small band of heroes found the gate too strong to be forced, so the lieutenant gave the order to scale the walls.   The Chinese were busy firing in front, keeping the Japanese troops back, and never imagined that a handful of men would have the boldness to climb the walls like monkeys under their very eyes.   Mimura and his men came upon them with such surprise that they were scattered in an instant.   The Japanese at once jumped down inside the walls and rushed to the gate, killing three of its defenders, and dispersing the rest, Mimura cutting right and left with his sword." [1]

Compare this energy with the lassitude shown by Great Britain in the Boer War.   The two salient characteristics of the English army were incompetence among the officers and feebleness among the men. Again and again detachments, as at Nicholson's Nec, surrendered under disgraceful circumstances to inferior forces of the enemy; while Gatacre's rout at Stormberg, Methuen's timidity at Kimberley, and Buller's panic at Colenso are too recent to be forgotten.   Japanese generals behaved not thus.   Japanese soldiers always display reckless courage and stubborn endurance.   Japan, though a poor country, with a fleet no stronger than that of her enemy, and transports bought for the occasion, landed between 80,000 and 100,000 men in a wild, difficult, and unknown region, in which she had no base.   Japan carried on her operations without foreign loans, and yet trade flourished.   In regard to soldiers, she had her whole male population at her call.

[1] *The China-Japan War*, Vladimir, 157.

The United Kingdom, the supposed seat of energy, of capital, and of empire, engaged in a petty broil with 50,000 farmers, with undisputed control of the sea, and a fortified base adjoining the enemy's frontier, not only failed to concentrate her forces in the field as rapidly and effectively as the Japanese, but with prostrated trade had to rely on France and the United States for financial support, and upon her colonies for men. She could not fill her ranks from her own citizens. Mark also the content of the British public with their military performance. Throughout the war they made no serious effort to improve, and since the peace they exult as in an heroic victory. He who reads the letters of Symmachus may observe the same complacency on the eve of the sack of Rome. Inertia pervades all English society. The system of education is admittedly defective because controlled by the clergy, who are a conservative class, and yet the hold of the clergy upon the schools is unshaken. The relative decline in the purchasing power of England may be gauged by a single example. A generation ago the United Kingdom bought two-thirds of the total American cotton crop. She now buys less than a quarter.

In industry the same phenomenon appears. As lately as 1866 she manufactured 48.7 per cent of the pig iron of the world. In 1901 only 19.2. Gold mining is, perhaps, the occupation which most excites the British imagination, and yet the British cannot work their own property. "The great mining magnates of South Africa, having the whole world before them to choose from, have preferred American mining engineers, and as the mining industry in South

Africa has proved to be so marvellous a success, it is hardly necessary to add that the result has justified the selection." [1]

Such instances might be multiplied, but these suffice. Each man can ponder the history of the last fifty years, and judge for himself whether the facts show that Great Britain apparently lies in the wake, and Japan in the path, of the advancing social cyclone.

The world seems agreed that the United States is likely to achieve, if indeed she has not already achieved, an economic supremacy. The vortex of the cyclone is near New York. No such activity prevails elsewhere; nowhere are undertakings so gigantic, nowhere is administration so perfect; nowhere are such masses of capital centralized in single hands. And as the United States becomes an imperial market, she stretches out along the trade-routes which lead from foreign countries to her heart, as every empire has stretched out from the days of Sargon to our own. The West Indies drift toward us, the Republic of Mexico hardly longer has an independent life, and the city of Mexico is an American town. With the completion of the Panama Canal all Central America will become a part of our system. We have expanded into Asia, we have attracted the fragments of the Spanish dominions, and reaching out into China we have checked the advance of Russia and Germany, in territory which, until yesterday, had been supposed to be beyond our sphere. We are penetrating into Europe, and Great Britain especially is gradually assuming the position of a dependency, which must rely on us as the base

[1] *The Statist*, July 12, 1902, pages 67, 68.

from which she draws her food in peace, and without which she could not stand in war.

Supposing the movement of the next fifty years only to equal that of the last, instead of undergoing a prodigious acceleration, the United States will outweigh any single empire, if not all empires combined. The whole world will pay her tribute. Commerce will flow to her both from east and west, and the order which has existed from the dawn of time will be reversed.

But if commerce, instead of flowing from east to west, as heretofore, changes its direction, trade-routes must be displaced, and the political organisms which rest upon those routes must lose their foundation. Russia, for example, could hardly continue to exist in her present form if the commerce of Siberia were to flow toward America instead of toward the Baltic. Yet if Russia should disintegrate she would disintegrate because of causes so widespread and deep-working that they would affect Great Britain with equal energy; for the inference to be drawn from human experience is that the rise of a new dominant market indicates the recentralization of trade-routes, and with trade-routes, of empires. Such changes, should they occur, would clearly alter the whole complexion of civilization. Speculation concerning their character, or the time of their advent, would be futile, as history offers no precedent by which we can measure the effects to be anticipated from an alteration so radical as the reversal of the direction of the channel of trade. It may, however, be permissible to draw certain inferences regarding the present.

Society is now moving with intense velocity, and masses are gathering bulk with proportionate rapidity. There is some reason also to surmise that the equilibrium is correspondingly delicate and unstable. If so apparently slight a cause as a fall in prices for a decade has sufficed to propel the seat of empire across the Atlantic, an equally slight derangement of the administrative functions of the United States might force it to cross the Pacific. The metallic resources of China are not inferior to ours, and distance offers daily less impediment to the migration of capital. Prudence, therefore, would dictate the adoption of measures to minimize the likelihood of sudden shocks. As Nature increases the velocity of movement, she augments her demands on human adaptability. She allowed our ancestors a century to become habituated to innovations which we must accept forthwith. Those who fail to keep the pace are discarded. Conversely, those who, other things being equal, first reach an adjustment, retain or improve a relative advantage. Under such circumstances but one precaution can be taken against the chances of the future. That intellectual quality can be strengthened on which falls the severest strain, so that our descendants may be prepared to meet any eventuality. The young can be trained to adaptability. The methods are perfectly understood; the difficulty lies in application. Success in the future promises, largely, to turn on the power of rapid generalization, for administration is only the practical side of generalization. It is the faculty of reducing details to an intelligent order. The masses generated in modern life exercise this faculty in its highest form.

On its theoretical side generalization necessitates the maintenance of an open mind. It is inconsistent with subserviency to *a priori* dogmas. Nothing is permitted to stand as fixed, and the individual is trained to hold the judgment in suspense, subject to new evidence. Such a temper of the mind tends to reduce the friction of adjustment.

If the New Empire should develop, it must be an enormous complex mass, to be administered only by means of a cheap, elastic, and simple machinery; an old and clumsy mechanism must, sooner or later, collapse, and in sinking may involve a civilization. If these deductions are sound, there is but one great boon which the passing generation can confer upon its successors: it can aid them to ameliorate that servitude to tradition which has so often retarded submission to the inevitable until too late.

APPENDIX

CHAPTER I

SECTION I

B.C.

Egyptian magnificence began with Sneferu, who conquered the Maghara copper mines about . . . 4000

Cheops, his successor, built the Great Pyramid about . 3950

Nubia conquered by Una under VI. dynasty, about . 3450

Period of decay and movement of the capital south, VII. to X. dynasty, probably caused by an invasion of a Mesopotamian conqueror, possibly a successor of Sargon.[1]

Rise of Mesopotamia, the distributing point between the East and Egypt. Sargon's empire included the copper mines of Cyprus, probably those of Sinai, and later, perhaps, northern Egypt 3850

Contemporaneous with Sargon probable advent of Phœnicians in Syria and the development through them of the basin of the Mediterranean, Crete's greatest prosperity, toward 2400

Utica, Cadiz, and Carthage probably began to flourish about this period.

Babylonian supremacy opened with Hammurabi about 2250

Following upon the development of the basin of the Mediterranean, and the extension of the market westward, the trade-route moved north from Babylon to the shorter line of travel from Bactra to the sea *via* Nineveh.

RISE OF ASSYRIA

Salmanassar founded Calach at the junction of the Great Zab and Tigris, twenty miles from Nineveh, about 1300

---

[1] *History of Egypt*, Petrie, I., 120.

The Assyrians fought steadily and successfully to keep
open the direct trade-route from Bactra to the Mediterranean coast, but failed to force the passes through
Armenia to the gold fields of Lydia and the Euxine.
The Assyrian Empire appears to have collapsed when
unable to check Grecian colonization in the Euxine,
which opened a cheaper route westward.

Tiglat-Pileser III. defeated at Van, which stopped
Assyrian advance   735

The eighth century was the period of the strongest
Greek expansion eastward.

SECTION II

Greek expansion eastward and attack on Mesopotamian
system. Siege of Troy about   1200
Athenians colonized Miletus toward   1050

Greek exploration of and trading to the Euxine probably began forthwith, but permanent colonies were hardly
established much before the eighth century.[1]

The Greeks established their commercial system between the Caucasus and the Rhone, centring at Athens,
Corinth, and Syracuse, between   800–600

They probably founded Panticapæum, Phasis, Trapesus,
Sinope, Lampsacus from 800–700 ; Syracuse (734), Magna
Græcia, and last Marseilles, about   600

Nineveh could not withstand this competition, which
diverted her trade; by 650 she was in full decline, and
fell in   606
Babylon captured by Cyrus the Persian . . .   538

SECTION III

AGE OF GREEK SPLENDOR

Mines of Laurium in operation in . . .   6th cent.
Temples of Corinth and Ægina built perhaps in .   7th cent.

About this time commercial competition between the
Mesopotamian and Greek economic systems acquired

[1] *Die Hellenen im Skythenlande*, Neumann, 344–349.

B.C.

the intensity of war. In the sixth century Lydia was
the centre of metallic production, which reached its
height under Crœsus 560–546
    The Persians under Cyrus attacked and absorbed Lydia,
and captured Crœsus 546
    The wealth thus absorbed by Cyrus enabled Darius to
consolidate the whole Mesopotamian system in Asia.
    Babylon taken 538–518
    Northern India absorbed 512
    The Persians then expanded into Europe. War with
Greece began by conquest of Imbros and Lemnos.
    Capture of Chalcedon and Byzantium 505
    Capture of Miletus 494
    Marathon 490
    Xerxes obeyed the impulsion which had moved Darius
and Cyrus. The whole Mesopotamian system from the
Indus to Spain, expanding westward, cast itself upon
Greece. Double victory of the Greeks, over the Cartha-
ginians in Sicily at Himera, and over the Persians at
Salamis 480
    Platæa 479
    After the defeat of the Persians, Athens under Pericles
reached her highest prosperity, and the silver mines of
Laurium their greatest productiveness.

Golden Age of Athens

    Until the competition between Athens and Corinth pre-
cipitated the Peloponnesian War. This war began when
Athens aided Corcyra against Corinth in . . . 433
    Destruction of Athenian military strength at Syracuse 413
    Destruction of Athenian naval strength at Ægospot-
amos 405
    Decline of Persia so that Xenophon marched without
resistance through the empire to Trapezus in . . . 401
    Relative decline of the productiveness of Laurium and
of the energy of Athens throughout the 3d and 4th cent.[1]

[1] *Les Mines du Laurion dans l'Antiquité*, Ardaillon, 150 *et seq.*

B.C.

SECTION IV

MACEDON

It was with the treasures of Mt. Pangeus and of those
conquered in Mesopotamia that Alexander unified his
currency and laid the basis of the consolidation on which
the Roman Empire rested.

SECTION V

ROME

The consolidation of the ancient world was made
possible by the mass of treasure collected at Rome by
pillage, which provided a material for exchanges with the
East for several centuries, and aided the development of
Italian energy by defraying the cost of administration.
As the mines of the basin of the Ægæum were gradually
exhausted during the third century, the centre of mineral
production and of energy was drawn westward by the pro-
fusion of the ores of Spain.   The Spanish mines have
always been famous, but it may serve to give some notion
of the wealth Rome drew from them to say that in thirty-
two years the Roman generals exported from the peninsula
767,695 pounds of silver and 10,918 pounds of gold, without counting fines levied on towns.   These were very

heavy; for example, Marcellus levied on the little town of Ocilis a contribution of $35,000, and it was thought that Ocilis had escaped cheaply. Marcellus is said to have extracted from the Celtiberians $700,000.

The flow of metal has always been from west to east, and this Spanish ore supplied Carthage, Sicily, and Magna Græcia. The abundance of the precious metals at Carthage seems almost incredible; but the splendor and copiousness of the coinage of Sicily and Magna Græcia are facts beyond dispute.

Before the Punic Wars no market of the ancient world equalled Carthage. Even after Zama (202 B.C.) Polybius called the city the richest in existence, yet it had then paid to Rome, in 241 B.C. 3200 talents (about $3,700,000), in 238 B.C. 1200 talents, in 202 B.C. 10,000 talents (about $11,600,000), and Scipio carried away 123,000 pounds of silver. The Temple of the Sun was sheathed with plates of gold worth 1000 talents, or about $1,200,000. The highest point ever reached in numismatic art was the Syracusan Persephone, by EYAINE, weight 660.9 grs., struck under Dionysius I. 406–367

Syracusan coinage, however, showed little decline until the Second Punic War. Two of the most exquisite pieces ever struck are of Hiero II. and his wife Philistis . 270–216

The coinage of all Magna Græcia was beautiful and copious.

The wealth of Tarentum was so great as to be proverbial, and Rome laid the basis of her fortune by the capture of the city 272

With the plunder of Tarentum Rome changed her coinage from copper to silver 269

With the wealth thus obtained Rome was enabled to conduct the First Punic War, and build the fleet with which she routed Carthage.

First Punic War 264–241
Plunder of Agrigentum 262

Ships first built by Romans and great naval victory won by the consul Duilius over the Carthaginians at Mylæ 260

Between the sack of Tarentum (272) and the crossing of the Rubicon by Cæsar (49), Rome plundered the whole civilized world from the Euphrates to the Atlantic, and as far north as the English Channel. The treasure amassed at Rome in the time of Cæsar was enormous. In 47 gold stood to silver only as $1 : 8.9$, a cheaper rate than it ever held before or after. This amassing of metal at Rome gave Italy an immense purchasing power, provided her with an universal commodity of exchange, and caused all trade-routes to centre at Rome as the imperial market. With the formation of the Empire, however, plundering stopped, and Rome had neither manufactures, agriculture, nor commerce, apart from the traffic caused by her purchases whereby to balance her importations from abroad. The Romans, moreover, were wasteful and extravagant, and bought lavishly from the East of both luxuries and food. Rome therefore soon began to impair her capital. Under Augustus gold had risen in relation to silver to the ratio of $1 : 9.3$ . . . .

A.D.
1

Thenceforward the depletion of the supply of metal which formed the capital and the only exchangeable commodity of Rome may be followed by the debasement of the coinage. The silver denarius, worth about seventeen cents, retained its weight and purity from the First Punic War (264 B.C.) until Nero 54–68

Under Nero it fell from $\frac{1}{84}$ to $\frac{1}{96}$ of a pound of silver. Alloy $\frac{1}{10}$ copper. The alloy reached $\frac{1}{5}$ under Trajan . 98–117

The alloy reached $\frac{1}{2}$ under Septimius Severus . 193–211

The denarius had become wholly base metal and was repudiated under Elagabalus 218–222

The golden aureus passed through like phases. Under Augustus the aureus weighed $\frac{1}{40}$ of a pound, under Diocletian $\frac{1}{60}$ 284

A.D.

When Rome had thus been stripped of metal, she lost her purchasing power and ceased to be the dominant market. Trade no longer centred there, and under Diocletian the capital of the Empire receded to Nicomedia on the Propontis, where Diocletian conducted the administration until his abdication 305

With the exhaustion of the metals traffic ceased to pay for the police of the western highways, and the barbarians accordingly crossed the border unopposed . . . 376

Rome was sacked by Alaric, who led bands of mercenaries who had mutinied for pay 410

There being no cohesive energy left, the western consolidation dissolved into its elements 476

The utter exhaustion of Europe in the sixth century and later in regard to minerals can be measured by its coinage. This fell for several centuries into complete degradation.[1]

There was a corresponding decline in movement and energy. Charlemagne attempted a reform, but it proved ephemeral. This is shown by the depreciation of the Venetian denaro, subsequent to Charlemagne's death in . 814

The Venetian denaro was 0.900 pure silver and weighed 34 Venetian grains in 814

The denaro had fallen to 0.260 pure silver and weighed but 22 grains by [2] 970

With the discovery of the Rammelsberg mines about 920, silver became gradually more plentiful. The coins of Otho III. are especially numerous,—but a reform of the currency did not take place until the change of equilibrium between the old and new economic systems. A change marked by the sack of Constantinople . . . 1204

And the Mongol invasions. Battle of the Kalka . 1224

The doge, Henry Dandolo, who sacked Constantinople, coined the grosso, 0.965 fine silver and weighing $42\frac{1}{10}$ grains. The grosso was the first standard western coin . 1202

[1] See for full details *Catalogue des Monnaies Françaises de la Bibliothèque Nationale. Les monnaies Mérovingiennes*, Maurice Prou.
[2] *Le Monete di Venezia*, Papadopoli, 41, 52.

A.D.

Fifty years later gold appeared. Florence coined the golden florin, Venice the ducat, and St. Louis the crown, between 1252–1284

The first half of the thirteenth century was also the period of the great development of the Harz, the Bohemian, and the Tyrolese silver mines. Thirty thousand men were employed in the mines of the Tyrol alone.[1] This was the epoch also when Europe developed the highest energy she achieved before the discovery of America. It was the era of splendor of the Fairs of Champagne, of the Gothic architecture, and of Flanders.

CHAPTER II

SECTION I

In the tenth century the old economic system, of which Constantinople and Bagdad were the *foci*, culminated.

Contemporaneously, western Europe fell to the lowest point of its decline during the Dark Ages.

I

Constantinople reached her greatest splendor during the Macedonian dynasty 867–1057

According to Gibbon, Constantinople actually culminated under Nicephorus Phocas and John Zimisces 963–976

Splendor of Kieff, from Saint Vladimir to Iaroslaf the Great 972–1054

Splendor of Bagdad, from Haroun-al-Rashid to Al Rhadi 786–940

SECTION II

I

Toward the end of the first half of the tenth century the discovery and working of the German silver mines,

---

[1] *Die Geschichte des Eisens*, Ludwig Beck, I., 759.

under Henry the Fowler and Otho the Great, provided the West with a commodity for exchange with the East. Simultaneously, the full introduction of the mariner's compass led to direct shipments by the ocean from China, the Spice Islands, and India to Egypt. Thus Mesopotamia and central Asia, Constantinople, Bagdad, Bactra, Samarkand, and their like were thrown into excentricity, and Alexandria, Venice, Genoa, and the Fairs of Champagne became dominant markets.

Western society in chaos when Henry the Fowler succeeded his father as Duke of Saxony . . . 912

Henry fortified the Harz containing the Rammelsberg silver mines (Goslar, Quedlinburg, 929, Nordhausen) 919–929

Established the Margravate of Brandenburg, invaded Bohemia, and began to fortify the line of the Elbe 926–930

Won great victory over the Huns at Merseburg . . 934

Otho the Great 936

Drove Huns from Germany 955

Otho master of Italy and crowned Emperor by Pope John XII. 962

II

Rapid Rise of the Cities of the New Economic System

Bruges walled 960

Augsburg dated its prosperity from the battle of Lechfeld, near Augsburg, when Otho I. defeated the Huns in . 955

Afterward building considerable additions to the town.

Venice became mistress of the Adriatic in . . . 1000

Cologne established a counting-house in London, which was the origin of the Steelyard, about . . . 1000

Copious finds of German coins of the reigns of the three Othos, especially of Otho III., in the island of Gothland, demonstrate the prosperity of Novgorod, Wisby, and the cities of the Hanse, as well as the growing abundance of silver in Germany toward the year 1000

Henry III. held Diet in Nuremberg 1050

St. Quentin chartered 1080

A.D.

Council of Clermont preached First Crusade . . 1095
First mention of Fairs of Champagne . . . 1114
Lübeck founded 1143
Vienna became a capital 1156
Crusade against northern Russia followed by founding
of Riga and formation of Teutonic Order . . . 1198
Dantzic became capital of the Duchy of Pomerellen . 1200
Bloom of the Fairs of Champagne . . . 1200–1300

III

EGYPT

Splendor of Egypt began with the building of Cairo
by the Caliph Maiz ed Din 969
University of El Azhar founded 988
Cairo walled 1176
Culmination of Egyptian power and splendor under
Saladin 1174–1193
Mosque of the Sultan Hassan 1356

IV

Decline and fall of the old economic system caused
by the establishment of a cheap ocean trade-route from
China direct to the Red Sea.
Decay of Constantinople indicated by revolution in
which Alexius Comnenus pillaged the city . . . 1081
Sack of Kieff by Andrew, Prince of Suzdal . . 1169
Sack and ruin of Constantinople by crusaders . . 1204
Jenghiz Khan marched from Kashgar on the valley
of the Syr-Daria 1218
Mongols ravaged central Asia. Otrar, Bokhara, Samar-
kand sacked 1219
Khiva sacked 1220
Merv, Herat, Bamian sacked 1221
Mongols invaded Russia. Battle of the Kalka . . 1224
Vladimir sacked 1237
Moscow 1237

CHAPTER III

SECTION I

MIGRATION OF THE SEAT OF EMPIRE FROM THE MEDITERRANEAN TO THE ATLANTIC

Flanders and the Fairs of Champagne decayed because
of the movement of the trade-route from Venice, from
the Rhone and Seine, to the ocean. This displacement
was the effect of the effort of France to consolidate under
one administration the valleys of the Rhone, Seine, Loire,
Garonne, and Scheldt. The wars which ensued, coupled
with the introduction of the mariner's compass, caused
sea freights to undersell land freights.

Ghent, Bruges, and Ypres reached the summit of their
fortune contemporaneously with the splendor of the Fairs
of Champagne and the high fortune of Venice. Trade-
route, Cairo, Alexandria, Champagne, Bruges, London, 1200–1296

Philip the Fair invaded Flanders 1297

Battle of Courtrai . . . . . July 11, 1302

Establishment of packet service between Venice and
Flanders 1317

Petition of merchants to avert ruin of Fairs of Champagne 1322

Hundred Years' War, caused by resistance to the extension of the administrative system of France over the
valleys of the Scheldt and the Garonne. The English
title to Guienne came through Queen Eleanor . . 1152

Alliance, in consequence, between the Flemish and English. Van Artevelde and Edward III. acted in unison.

A.D.

Battle of Sluys, in which Edward III. destroyed French
navy off Zealand 1340
   Battle of Crecy . . . . . . Aug. 25, 1346
   Capture of Calais by Edward III. 1347
   Removal of English wool staple from Bruges to Calais 1348
   Bordeaux became the capital of Edward the Black
Prince 1363

Beginning of Permanent Decline of Flanders

   Close of the Hundred Years' War. Charles VII. regained Paris from the English 1436
   Migration of foreign merchants from Bruges to Antwerp, rise of Brabant and Antwerp on return of peace . 1442
   Extinction of Fairs of Champagne 1443

SECTION II

Antwerp owed its supremacy to its geographical position. Situated just above the point where the Scheldt
divides into two branches, separated by the island of
Beveland, the East Scheldt leads to the Rhine, the West
Scheldt is the direct route to London. Toward France
the Scheldt now connects with the Oise by canals; formerly it connected by an easy portage. Antwerp thus
stood directly between the French and German economic
systems, being a market for both, as well as for England.
In 1500, when Antwerp achieved supremacy, Charles V.
was born, who represented the German interest all his
life. On his accession, competition at once acquired the
intensity of war. The debt Charles contracted in war
was due to German bankers, and was inherited by Spain.
Spain, being poor, became insolvent and tried to levy on
Brabant; Brabant revolted, Alva laid the country waste,
Antwerp was sacked and ruined, and England established
a system of piracy, by which she destroyed, first, the
resources of Spain, and, second, her navy, in . . 1588

A.D.

Thereupon, Holland and England seized the ocean
trade-routes east and west; and modern development
began with the germination of the British economic system. The first phenomenon was the incorporation of the
English and Dutch East India Companies.

Birth of Charles V., Emperor of Germany . . . 1500
Wealth and power of south Germany at its maximum
consequent on successful mining 1500–1550
Charles became King of Spain 1516

CONTEST BEGUN WITH FRANCE FOR POSSESSION OF THE DOMINANT MARKET

Fuggers bought imperial crown for Charles V. . 1517–1519
Culmination of the wealth and power of the south
German bankers, especially of the Fuggers . . 1525–1560
Continuous wars between Charles V. and Francis I.
The first sign of revolt in the Netherlands was the out-
break in Ghent, consequent on overtaxation . . 1539–1540
Uneasiness of Fuggers and German bankers at the
growth of debt and at Spanish methods of finance 1550–1553
Desperate condition of the Spanish and German
finances and abdication of Charles 1555
First Spanish insolvency 1557
Discontent in Netherlands at pressure of debt . . 1559

SECTION III

Outbreak of the beggars in Brabant 1566
Alva governor at Brussels. Sent to extort a revenue, 1567–1573
Devastation of the Low Countries to raise a revenue by
confiscations.

———

Migration of centre of economic system consequent
thereon.

Q

A.D.

ENGLISH HOSTILITY TO SPAIN

Elizabeth seized Spanish treasure 1568
English piratical warfare on Spanish trade-routes was
waged for a generation 1560–1588
Drake's Panama expedition 1572
Mutiny of the Spanish army in the Netherlands because
of the lack of pay; poverty of the government caused by
the cutting of communications by the Dutch and English.
Antwerp sacked 1576
Spain, on the brink of disintegration, attacked England.
Defeat of the Armada 1588
Rise of Holland and England following the conquest
of the trade-routes from the Spanish.
English East India Company founded . . . 1599
Dutch East India Company founded . . . 1595–1602

CHAPTER IV

SECTION I

Russia became organized along the east and west trade-routes of the Kama and the Volga contemporaneously with the supremacy of Antwerp.

Charles VII. regained Paris toward close of One Hundred Years' War 1436
Migration of merchants from Bruges to Antwerp. . 1442
Collapse of Fairs of Champagne 1443
Return of Vasco da Gama from India . . . 1499
Great fall in price of spice at Lisbon and rise at
Venice 1502–1503
Supremacy of Antwerp and corresponding depression
of Venice subsequent to League of Cambrai . . . 1508
Eastern trade of Venice ruined by occupation by the
Portuguese of island of Sokotra in the Gulf of Aden 1506–1509

A.D.

RISE OF MOSCOW

Ivan III. took title of Autocrat of Russia . . . 1462
Ivan III. threw off Tartar yoke 1480
Ivan III. seized the Novgorod counting-house and
ejected Hanse merchants 1494
Ivan III. died, having extended Muscovite influence to
Perm 1505
Organization of modern Russia under Ivan the Ter-
rible 1533–1584
Ivan the Terrible took Astrakhan 1554
Opened relations with England through Chancellor 1553–1554
Russia Company chartered 1555
Jenkinson's voyages and growth of English-Russian
trade 1557–1572
Russian overland trade to Leipsic and Berlin acquired
importance 1494–1550

SIBERIAN TRADE-ROUTE

First Russian attack upon the valley of the Obi . . 1499
Yermak began his invasion of Siberia . . Sept. 1, 1581
Tobolsk founded 1587
Irkutsk founded 1651
Nertchinsk founded 1654

At Nertchinsk the road turned south to Peking through
Chinese territory, which could not be conquered. The
Pacific being closed until the opening of Japan by the
United States, Nertchinsk formed the natural terminus
of the overland Russian route. Therefore, by the treaty
of Nertchinsk, signed . . . . . Aug. 27, 1689
Russia abandoned the valley of the Amur, and stopped
her expansion eastward for nearly two hundred years.

Meanwhile the Moscow-Peking trade probably was as
valuable an asset as Russia possessed. Route, Moscow,
Perm, Tobolsk, Irkutsk, Nertchinsk. In Peter the Great's
time return caravans from Moscow were "worth from
300,000 to 400,000 roubles, and in spite of the great distance the freight did not amount to more than five per
cent. of the whole capital." [1]

[1] *Peter the Great*, Schuyler, II., 380.

SECTION II

CONTEMPORANEOUS REORGANIZATION OF GERMANY

The migration of the main trade-route from the Mediterranean to the Atlantic toward 1500 caused the dominant market to seat itself on the shore of the North Sea, and also caused a rise in energy of the movement on the east and west lines of transit in central and eastern Europe and a proportionate decline in the north and south.

The Hanseatic League, which controlled the north and south lines of Germany and Poland and governed Sweden, lost power.   Sweden correspondingly gained.

Gustavus Vasa came to the throne   1523

Defeated Hanseatic League and emancipated Sweden
by treaty of Hamburg   1533

Strong development of Swedish iron industry from
treaty of Hamburg to death of Gustavus Adolphus   1533–1633

This rise in energy of Sweden decided the result of the Thirty Years' War, which ended with the consolidation of the nucleus of the modern kingdom of Prussia.

Thirty Years' War began   1618

Gustavus Adolphus invaded Germany.   .   .   .   1630

Victory of Lutzen, death of Gustavus   1632

Torstenson, Swedish general, defeated Austrians and
occupied Bohemia   1644

Peace of Westphalia, by which Frederick William, the Great Elector of Brandenburg, gained Farther Pomerania and other advantages, laying foundations of Prussia   .   1648

Frederick William acquired Duchy of Cleves and County
of Mark in the iron region of Westphalia   .   .   .   1666

Prussia became a kingdom   1701

Seven Years' War and conquest of Silesia by Frederick
the Great   1763

SIMULTANEOUS EXPANSION WEST OF RUSSIA

Peter the Great conquered the Neva from Sweden and
founded St. Petersburg   1703

Gained victory of Pultowa and conquered the Baltic
Provinces   1709

SECTION III

Therefore from the outbreak of the Thirty Years' War
in 1618 to the end of the Seven Years' War in 1763 a
steady consolidation of Russia and Prussia had gone on,
by which Poland had been hemmed in between the east
and west divisions of the overland economic system.

POLAND

Poland originally developed along the trade-route north
from the valley of the Danube to the Baltic. The early
road to Constantinople from the west lay through Vienna,
Gran, Belgrad, and Adrianople. This was the crusading
route until the thirteenth century. Trade crossing north
from the Danube to the valley of the Vistula, and so to
the Baltic, centred at Cracow, on the upper Vistula, as
the local market, and accordingly Cracow became a
capital. The kings of Poland were buried in Cracow
Cathedral from   1163–1733
   Cracow flourished under Casimir III. .   .   .   1333–1370
   University established   1364
   Member of Hanseatic League   1430
Highest prosperity and fame reached under Sigis-
mund I.   1506–1548
   Copernicus buried at Cracow   1543
This period of prosperity is coincident with the highest
prosperity of Augsburg and the Fuggers.

The Fuggers reached their prime with Anthony Fugger

1525–1560

The development of the Hungarian and Bohemian
minerals caused both phenomena. The Fuggers acquired
large copper properties in Neusohl near Gran ; in connection with powerful Hungarian families, they formed a syndicate for controlling the market, and shipped copper by
Cracow and the Vistula to Dantzic and Antwerp, instead

A.D.

of, as before, to Venice.   Cracow and Antwerp became
great metal markets from　.　.　.　.　.　.　1494

Change of the Axis of European Movement in Sixteenth Century

The change in the axis of European movement from
north and south to east and west during the sixteenth
century is clearly indicated by the following series of
events : —

Destruction of the Hanseatic House at Novgorod　.　1494
Rise of Leipsic Fairs indicated by grants of privileges
by Maximilian　.　.　.　.　.　.　.　1497-1507
Defeat of Hanse by Sweden and treaty of Hamburg　.　1533
Diversion of fur trade to Leipsic admitted by Hanse　1549-1554
Abdication of Charles V.　.　.　.　.　.　.　1555
Abdication of Charles immediately followed by Spanish
bankruptcy, and by the first shock to Fuggers' credit　1557-1562
The power of the current east and west is shown by
the union of Lithuania and Poland and establishment of
joint diets at Warsaw　.　.　.　.　.　.　.　1569
Thenceforward south Germany rapidly declined.
The Nuremberg Welsers left business about　.　.　1566
The Augsberg Welsers were sinking by　.　.　.　1590
The capital of Poland moved north from Cracow to
Warsaw in　.　.　.　.　.　.　.　.　.　1609
The Fuggers weakened steadily under the burden of
the debt of upwards of 5,000,000 ducats owing them by
Spain after　.　.　.　.　.　.　.　.　.　1610
Correspondingly London, Amsterdam, Berlin, Warsaw,
and St. Petersburg rose.

SECTION IV

Disintegration of Poland

Incorporation of Lithuania with Poland.   Process began
by accession to the throne of Poland of Alexander, Duke
of Lithuania, in　.　.　.　.　.　.　.　.　1501
Consolidation completed and diets of Poland and
Lithuania held at Warsaw　.　.　.　.　.　.　1569

A.D.

Sigismund moved the royal residence to Warsaw   .   1609
This movement was coincident with Thirty Years' War
and the consolidation of North Germany.

Thirty Years' War begun by Count von Thurn in
Bohemia   1618
Continued consolidation of North Germany produced
the Seven Years' War   1756–1763
Efforts of France, Russia, and Austria having failed
to check the consolidation of North Germany in the Seven
Years' War, the process continued by the absorption of
Poland. Partitions   1775–1795
As finally settled in 1815, the upper Vistula, with
Cracow, adhered to the Danubian system ; the central
Vistula, with Warsaw, to the Russian ; the lower Vistula,
with Dantzic, to the German.

Complete economic isolation of France, caused by the
junction of Prussia and Russia and the dismemberment
of Poland. Outbreak of Revolution   1789
Period of destruction of mediæval social system .   1789–1795
Bonaparte First Consul   1799
Napoleonic wars began with Marengo   .   .   June 14, 1800

CHAPTER V

SECTION I

France from her geographical position is isolated. She
forms no part of the overland system, and her long wars
with Holland and England, from 1672 to 1815, were all
caused by her attempt to conquer the ocean trade-routes
between China, India, and America.

After the sack of Antwerp Amsterdam became the chief
market of northern Europe, about   1610
The profits of her trade may be computed by the profits
of the Dutch East India Company.

The average dividends of the Dutch East India Company were 25 to 30 per cent between   .   .   .   1606–1661
Par value of shares was 3000 florins ; market value,
18,000 florins.

A.D.

The Dutch East India Company owned 150 merchant ships, 40 to 50 war-ships, had an army of 10,000 men, and divided 40 per cent in   1670

Contemporaneously in 1671 the French company showed a deficit of 6,000,000 livres.

On the death of Mazarin, Colbert became minister of finance and addressed himself to building up French industries   1661

Colbert attempted economic reforms in   .   .   .   1664

And failed   1664–1667

Abandoning his attempt to reform internal tariffs, he resorted to a prohibitive tariff against Holland   .   .   1667

This proved ineffective, while the great prosperity of Dutch shipping and the wealth of the Dutch East India Company inclined Colbert to war   1671

According to Colbert at this time, "of 20,000 ships doing the commerce of the world, the Dutch owned 15,000 or 16,000, the French 500 or 600 at most."

Colbert had the alternative presented to him of abandoning his industrial system, and with it his office, or of crushing the Dutch. He chose war.

Dutch war   1672–1678

Defeat of France and treaty of Nimwegen .   .   .   1678

Revolution in England   1688

Coalition against France formed by William III., which lasted substantially till treaty of Utrecht .   .   .   1689–1713

SECTION II

The French wars proving unsuccessful, competition continued unchecked, and, being undersold, the French industries fell into decline. The period of splendor of the reign of Louis XIV. ended with the Revolution of 1688 in England.

Complete industrial prostration in France from   .   1700–1715

After a short industrial revival during the middle of the eighteenth century, the introduction of coal in smelting in England, which gave England the supremacy in steel, put France at a further disadvantage after   .   .   .   1770

A.D.

The progress of France toward insolvency ended in
the Revolution in 1789
The Terror   1793
Bonaparte pacified the sections at Saint Roch   . Oct. 5, 1795
Napoleon Consul   1799
Peace of Amiens   1802
But the equilibrium proved to be unstable.
The impossibility of successful competition by France
led to attack on English trade-routes. War renewed   . 1803
As a means to victory the French made their army
absolute.
Napoleon Emperor   .   .   .   .   .   May 18, 1804

SECTION III

WARS FOR CONTROL OF OCEAN TRADE-ROUTES

Trafalgar   .   .   .   .   Oct. 21, 1805
Jena .   .   .   .   Oct. 14, 1806
Berlin Decree   .   .   .   .   .   .   Nov. 21, 1806
Eylau   .   .   .   .   Feb. 8, 1807
Friedland .   .   .   .   June 14, 1807
Russia capitulated to Napoleon — convention of Tilsit
signed .   .   .   .   July 7, 1807
Napoleon began the encouragement of the beet sugar
industry as a war measure to destroy the English colonies[1]   1808
Intolerable distress of Russia from loss of outlets of
trade   1808–1810
Ukase admitting American ships into Russian ports,
Dec. 19, 1810
Napoleon adopted policy of state encouragement for
sugar   1811
War with Russia   .   .   .   .   .   June 22, 1812
Napoleon crossed the Niemen   .   .   .   June 24, 1812
Retreat from Moscow began   .   .   .   Oct. 18, 1812
Waterloo .   .   .   .   June 18, 1815
English economic supremacy   1815–1873

[1] The sugar question is not treated in this volume. For its history
see *America's Economic Supremacy*, 54 *et seq.*

A.D.

Poverty of the United States until　.　.　.　.　1848

Discovery of gold in California　.　.　.　.　.　1847

Rapid development of the United States after the discovery of gold　.　.　.　.　.　.　.　1848–1860

Huge indebtedness of the United States, contracted for
internal improvements　.　.　.　.　.　.　1865–1894

Continuous attack of the Continent on the West Indian
sugar; control of the English market obtained by Continental sugar in　.　.　.　.　.　.　.　1871

Fall in the price of sugar ruined the West Indies　1868–1893

First insurrection in Cuba began　.　.　.　.　1868

Demonetization of silver by Germany　.　.　.　1873

Fall in prices from　.　.　.　.　.　.　1873 to 1896

English farming land began to lose its value from　.　1879

Panic of　.　.　.　.　.　.　.　.　.　1893

Unprecedented exportation of gold from the United
States　.　.　.　.　.　.　.　.　.　1893

Fall of 30 per cent in the price of sugar　.　.　1893–1895

Second Cuban insurrection.

Signs of exhaustion in English minerals became pronounced toward　.　.　.　.　.　.　.　1890

Readjustment of American social system toward European competition, by organization of so-called trusts,　1893–1897

CHAPTER VI

SECTION I

RISE OF JAPAN

Japan closed to foreigners　.　.　.　.　.　.　1623

Gold discovered in California　.　.　.　.　.　1847

California ceded by Mexico to United States　.　.　1848

Perry sailed from Norfolk for Japan　.　.　Nov. 24, 1852

Perry reached Yeddo　.　.　.　.　.　July 8, 1853

Perry signed first convention with Mikado　.　Mch. 31, 1854

Reorganization of Japan began with American commercial treaty　.　.　.　.　.　.　.　1858

Stimulated by the opening of Japan, Russia expanded
along the trade-route of the Amur. Muravioff negotiated
the treaty with China which made the left bank of the
Amur the Russian boundary, and opened the river to
Russian ships to its mouth   .   .   .   .   May 16, 1858
   Muravioff founded Vladivostok on the Pacific   .   .   1860
   Fall of the Shogun   1868
   War between Japan and China   1894–1895
   Interference of France, Germany, and Russia with
terms of peace; Japanese forced to give up Port Arthur   1895

SECTION II

AMERICAN SUPREMACY

   American supremacy in steel   .   .   .   .   Mar., 1897
   Germans seized Kaiochau .   .   .   .   .   Nov., 1897
   Russia occupied Port Arthur   .   .   .   .   Dec., 1897
   Hostilities between Spain and Cuba continued without
definite result, Spanish opinion becoming steadily in-
flamed against the United States, until the destruction
of the *Maine* in Havana harbor   .   .   .   Feb. 15, 1898
   The destruction of the *Maine* was thus a direct effect
of the attack by the Overland Economic System on the
English Economic System through the sugar bounties
which ruined the West Indies and caused the Cuban
insurrection.[1] The sugar bounties were a continuance
of Napoleon's Continental policy. The catastrophe of
the *Maine* made war between Spain and the United
States inevitable. The disintegration of the Spanish
Empire followed. Battle of Manila   .   .   . May 1, 1898
   Meanwhile the British acquired Wei-hai-wei   . April, 1898
   In consequence of the aggressions of Germany and
Russia insurrection broke out in China in   .   .   June, 1900
   Baron von Ketteler killed and legations attacked,

                                               June 20, 1900
   Circular note of the State Department   .   . July 3, 1900

[1] See *America's Economic Supremacy*, chapter III.

A.D.

The European commanders in a council of war decided
that 80,000 men would be needed before an advance
could be made on Peking.   Despatch to this effect sent to
Washington by Admiral Kempff   .   .   .   . July 8, 1900
Tientsin captured by the energy of the Japanese, who
blew open the south gate.   Allies entered the city   July 14, 1900
General Chaffee reached Tientsin   .   .   July 30, 1900
Conference of generals held on General Chaffee's arrival
decided on an immediate advance .   .   .   Aug. 1, 1900
Advance begun, the column about 19,000 strong, Aug. 4, 1900
Peking occupied .   .   .   .   .   .   Aug. 14, 1900
Field Marshal von Waldersee, in command of the
German contingent, reached Peking   .   .   Oct. 17, 1900

INDEX

R

Rammelsberg: 49, 50.

Rhine: trade-route of, 59; tolls on, 68.

Riga: founded, 65.

Romans. incapacity of, 40; defeat of, in Germany, 43, mental inflexibility of, 44.

Russia geography of, 47; Constantinople dominant market of, 63, Kieff and Vladimir capitals of, 64, Hanse holds monopoly in, 67, Mongols invade, 82; rivers of, 116; disintegration of, in 13th century, 117; Ivan occupied Narva, 128; trade-routes under Peter, 133, 134, consolidation of, under Peter, 135, Swedish war, 142; administration of, under Peter, 144; breach with France, 165; poverty of, 180, 181, bad administration in, 181 *et seq.,* suffering in, 183; civil service of, 183; Siberian Railroad, 184, hostility to Japan, 186, interferes in Chinese war, 191; seizes Port Arthur, 192; designs on Shansi, 192; weakness of, 193; antagonism to Japan, 195; culmination of, 199. See *Trade-routes.*

Russia Company: 122; counting-houses of, 125, 126.

Russians: backwardness of, 128; not mechanical, 129.

S

Saladin: 73.

Salamis: 34.

Samarkand: description of, 29, taken by Jenghiz Khan, 79; see *Trade-routes.*

Sarai: built, 118.

Sardis routes to, 15.

Sargon: empire of, 7; capital of, 12.

Scheldt: trade-route, 94, and note.

Scutari: Mongols reach, 83.

Septimer Pass: 59.

Shansi: mines of, 189.

Siberia: conquest of, 131–133; trade-routes of, 131, 133, rivers of, 132, Siberian Railroad, 184, 185.

Silver: increase in value of, 87; yield of American, 92, demonetization of, 170, see *Minerals.*

Sinai: see *Maghara.*

Sindbad: voyages of, 70.

Sneferu: 4; pyramid of, 6.

Sokotra: Portuguese occupy, 91.

Spain: mines of, 41; rise of, 90, poverty of, 99; character of people of, 104; decentralization of, 106, 107; losses by piracy, 108, recognizes independence of Holland, 150; war of United States with, 192.

Steelyard: 53, 54.

St. Petersburg: founded, 143.

St. Quentin: position of, 94.

Suzdal: 62.

Sweden: war with Hanse, 137; iron industry of, 137, 138; energy of, 138; greatness of, 141; war with Russia, 141, 142.

T

Tabriz · 27, 28.

Teutonic Order. foundation of, 65; acquires Dantzic, 65.

Tiglat-Pileser I., III.: campaigns of, 17, 19.

Tin see *Minerals.*

Trade-routes: basis of states, 2, 3; competitive, 2; the Ur, 7; Pattala, 8; Lake Balkash, 9; Samarkand, 9; Terek Pass, 9; Syr-Daria, 9; Kashgar, 9; Bactra, 10; northern Indian, 10; three leading ancient, 11; Tyre and Sidon, 11; Crete, Carthage, Cadiz, 11, Phœnician, 14; Lydian, 15; Lake Van, 17, Betlis, 17, Tabriz, 18, Greek, 22, 23; Black Sea, 26; Athens and Corinth, 35; mediæval European, 45, 46, 47, converge at Augsburg, 52; Semmering and Brenner, 58; Rhine and Elbe, 59; Kieff-Novgorod, 60; Lubeck and Hamburg, 62; northern movement of, in Russia, 63; Volga, 64; Hanseatic, 66; to Champagne, 68, sea, to Venice and Flanders, 69, ocean, to